FALLING
forward

The Pursuit of Sexual Purity

FOREWORD BY ANDREW COMISKEY

FALLING
forward

The Pursuit of Sexual Purity

By

CRAIG LOCKWOOD

DESERT **Stream**
P R E S S

Falling Forward by Craig R. Lockwood

Copyright © 2000 by Craig R. Lockwood

All rights reserved

Published by Desert Stream Press
P.O. Box 17635
Anaheim, CA 92817-7635

Website: www.dspress.net

Publication Coordinators: Annette Comiskey and Mark Pertuit

Creative Direction: Bob Mack, Immanuel Communications

Cover Illustration: Mir Weber Mueller

Cover Design and Production: Alex Pasieka

Text Layout and Production: Melodie Jones

Unless otherwise noted, all Scripture quotations taken from the HOLY BIBLE, NEW INTERNATIONAL VERSION, Copyright © 1973, 1978, 1984, by International Bible Society. Used by permission.

Scripture taken from the NEW AMERICAN STANDARD BIBLE®, Copyright © 1960, 1962, 1963, 1968, 1971, 1972, 1973, 1975, 1977, 1995 by The Lockman Foundation.
Used by permission.

Scripture quotations taken from the NEW REVISED STANDARD VERSION BIBLE, Copyright © 1989, Division of Christian Education of the National Council of the Churches of Christ in the United States of America.

International Standard Book Number: 1-930159-05-6

Printed in the United States of America, 2000 – First Edition

Dedication

This Guidebook is dedicated to my children Emily and Stephen.

"There is a difference between
knowing the path and walking the path."

May you walk the path, and so know it!

Thank You

Acknowledgements

By Craig Lockwood

No man is formed in a vacuum and there is nothing new under the sun. I first want to acknowledge all the written entries that are not original to me - especially those that I do not remember and that I think are mine.

I want to thank Andy and Annette Comiskey for creating Living Waters, a rich and powerful program, out of which the salt group was birthed. Living Waters gave me a perspective that I could not have had on my own.

Thanks to all on the Desert Stream staff who helped put this guide book together. Your life together is an inspiration and model for Christian community. Special thanks to Mark Pertuit, who spent hours editing this work.

I would like to pay tribute to the many authors from whom I gleaned and paraphrased: Dan Allender, Patrick Carnes, Leanne Payne, Doctors Earl and Crow, and many others who provided ideas and insight, even though they are unnamed here.

Richard and Leanne Paddison were fellow pioneers in developing salt. They gave many steadfast, selfless years to those struggling with sexual addiction, and to their spouses. Thank you for keeping the program afloat in the difficult times.

With deep gratitude, I would like to thank the men and women who have taken this material to heart, fearlessly faced the truth about themselves, surrendered to God, and gone on to help others. You have given me courage.

I want to acknowledge God the Father, Jesus Christ his Son and the Holy Spirit. They are in and around all things. Nothing happens without them, not even the grace by which unregenerate addicts get sober.

Falling Forward Contents

Foreword

By Andrew Comiskey

In the early 1980's, I came across a newspaper article that suggested some sexual behavior could be addictive, like a drug. I thought about the men and women with whom I worked: Christians in bondage to repetitive patterns of sexual and relational sin, destructive habits often decades old. Like chemical addiction, these sins were conceived out of historic pain and wounding, and fueled in the present by pressures and loneliness.

In short, these "addicts" coped with pain and unmet need through the repetitive misuse of their sexuality. Even though they knew such behavior to be wrong, they couldn't break the cycle, at least not without a lot of help. The newspaper's suggestion rang true–some sexual sin is addictive!

But these individuals were Christians. They knew the truth that their addiction affected themselves and others more profoundly than a chemical; they knew Paul's distinction in 1 Cor 6:18 between sins committed outside the body, and sexual immorality, which violates one's essential humanity.

Thus the guilt and shame seemed greater for the Christian than for the average pagan. As did the temptation to hide–these Christians sinned in secret, rather than boldly. The result of such guilt and hiddenness was often a double life that swung between upright believer and raging addict.

We began to minister to sexual addicts–heterosexual and homosexual alike–in the context of Living Waters. We did so with varying degrees of success. Part of the struggle involved the addict's need for focused and persistent accountability, as well as the powerful denial and self-delusion of the addict. Helping him or her to recognize and break the cycle of sin required more than what the average Living Waters' small group could give.

But the power and pervasive nature of sexual addiction was growing in our midst. Due to videos, then internet pornography, men and women alike were discovering dangerous new fuel for their addictions. More and more were seeking help to break free of perverse relationships with their computers. Desks and offices had become sites of ongoing sexual failure.

Thank God for Craig Lockwood! Craig served as the overseeing pastor for the first Living Waters group I ran at the Vineyard Christian Fellowship of Anaheim 1991. His belief and advocacy in our work there laid the foundation for a deep and longstanding relationship between Desert Stream Ministries and that church.

During that first Living Waters group at Anaheim, Craig led a small group for men coming out of sexual addiction. He then adapted some of the aspects of the program for a group exclusively for sexual addicts. For several years, he pioneered the group and entitled it *salt* (sexual addicts learning trust).

Craig put together a series of fine teachings–biblical and psychological in scope–as well as a more directive and consistent approach to accountability in the small group itself. Over the course of its refinement, Falling Forward has proven to offer an honest, spiritually profound reckoning with one's addiction and its cure.

That cure involves the fullness of Christ and the authority of His church. As a pastor, Craig knows well the barriers to ruthless honesty in the church, but also its absolute necessity if one is to walk free from addiction. Through Falling Forward, Craig has made a clear and effective way in the church for the sexual addicts to come clean. Truly. Not magically, but through the hard work of facing one's life–its pain, failures, and losses–and to break through to the real goal of human sexuality.

That goal involves learning to trust real people, and to meaningfully connect with them. People, not erotic or romantic objects. Craig has captured that essential truth well–freedom from addiction results in freedom for love.

Without a resource like Falling Forward, the church will be hard-pressed to provide genuine, Christ-centered solutions for those who have struggled to overcome habitual sexual sin. Without Falling Forward's clear, empathetic expression of the truth, combined with a focused track for accountability, the church will fail to make good its claim that Jesus liberates the sexual sinner. We need as the church to pronounce hope for purity in today's sex-addicted world; at the same time, we had better get ready to provide the way out.

Falling Forward is a door of hope. I heartily recommend to you this profound and compassionate way forward for sexual addicts seeking freedom.

Introduction

By Craig Lockwood

I began writing the Falling Forward manual in 1993 in response to a group of men who wanted to process the healing truths offered by Desert Stream's, Living Waters Program. This group of men was unique in its makeup – all ten were sex addicts. Throughout the program we listened to powerful talks related to sexual brokenness and gathered together in a small group. Yet, we were seldom able to process anything beyond the cycles of sexual acting out. I could see that these men were stuck in their addiction and so, not ready for the depths of Living Waters.

As a pastor, that reality sent me searching for an answer to the question of what heals addiction. I soon discovered that the addictive cycle creates it's own pain, hardens the heart, and darkens the mind. It made sense that stopping the cycle of acting out is the first step in bringing healing to the sexual addict. Then he could go on to deal with the deeper issues of the heart. For that reason the first part of this book is devoted to understanding the addictive process and the addictive cycle. The first, essential step is to break the patterns of the addictive cycle. Starting with behavioral interventions is fine as long as you end up with a spiritual process that leads to true, depth sanctification. That is the ultimate goal of this book.

This manual is really not about sexual addiction per say, it is really about all addiction and even the process of overcoming sin, which Keith Miller calls the "Ultimate Deadly Addiction." But beyond that, it is about a process through which the reader discovers little by little who he really is and, little by little, walks into the light of, and the restorative relationship with, the triune God of Christianity.

Sexual addiction is a devastating, personal bondage that reaches into all levels of society and infiltrates family systems with merciless stealth. Yet, it is just a cover-up for people who are afraid to make themselves truly vulnerable to a monogamous intimate relationship with another person. In the beginning, if the addict knew how to become truly vulnerable, he would not do so because he might encounter a reality about himself that is too painful to face. Throughout his history the addict likely chose the safety of his addiction because it held an illusion of safety and control for potential pain in relationships. But the sexually addictive strategy is really the out of control manifestation of run away sensuality. So even though we define sexual addiction and the addictive cycle, and by God's mercy stop our sexual sin, there is a greater healing that is needed. Each addict needs the ability to face all the possibilities and potentials of connecting meaningfully to others.

If the reader is looking for healing, above all, he must learn to receive love. That process has many facets including learning to embrace personal weakness, facing painful feelings and relying on an external God to reflect an understanding of the value of his uniqueness that cannot be generated from within himself. In order to do that he must risk. He must learn to trust. This manual is about discovering how a lack of being loved has made us afraid to believe in real love even when it is right in front of us. Thus, each person must unlearn the skills of self-defense that work so automatically within them. This manual is about a journey to the cross of Christ. Every addict must walk the path of the death of self, but the cross is ultimately the place where we remember God has cancelled our unworthiness.

The *salt* material is most effective in the context of small groups. My world-view in writing this manual is a belief that the Kingdom of God is available now for those who are willing to receive it. That has several implications for the way I think groups work best. First of all, I believe that the God of Christianity is a God of healing. It is therefore good to pray for one another in the context of going through the material. God will gladly add his power to our surrender if we are truly open to it. Second, I believe that sin is synonymous with separation in relationship. Therefore, in addition to confessing sexual sin, the goal of confessions of group participants should lead to removing barriers to relationship with God and others, thus reestablishing the participants ability to connect in meaningful, intimate relationships. In considering this, I have seen the benefit of a closed group setting for the duration of working through the *salt* material. As participants break out of darkness and isolation an inevitable connection and building of trust happens with other group members. That learning of trust happens best in an atmosphere where the people encountered are present consistently and on the learning curve.

The *salt* program was originally written to address the needs of male sexual addicts in a church setting. It is not a substitute for the 12 step process, although many men have come to sobriety and healing through it alone. I see no problem, and in fact recommend, that men attend the two concurrently. Women who are sexual addicts may also benefit from the material. But those who do use the material must realize it is not specifically written for them. I am certain some of the specifics of how sexual addiction is expressed through the feminine gender are left out.

As in all growth processes, head knowledge alone is not enough to bring a lasting change in a person's life. The addict who really wants to change must be willing to press in to new life patterns even though it hurts. Sometimes that willingness revolves around the readiness to give up the security and comfort of the addiction. Before proceeding into the material, the reader may want to ask the very important question, "Am I really ready?"

Spiritual Aspects of Addiction

Chapter One

For although they knew God, they neither glorified him as God or gave thanks to him, but their thinking became futile and their foolish hearts were darkened… Therefore God gave them over in the sinful desire of their hearts to sexual impurity for the degrading of their bodies with one another. They exchanged the truth of God for a lie and worshiped and served created things rather than the Creator who is forever praised. (Romans 1:21, 24-25)

Foundational Assumptions

Upon becoming a Christian a person is reborn – Jesus comes by His Spirit to abide with and in the believer. Once He comes to be with us, He remains and never leaves. Deepening in our knowledge of Him, however, demands that we receive the mind of Christ, a process which is neither instantaneous nor automatic. It requires our ongoing participation. We need His perspective on our lives, on Him, and on His creation.

God has created us so that only one thing will satisfy us: Himself. In the case of every human being, the thirst we have is infinite, endless. We thirst for love, acceptance, emotional nourishment, meaning, conversation, relationship, security. In fact, as one writer has put it, every person could rightly be called a *living thirst*. You are a living thirst, just as I am. The writer of Proverbs states that "what a man desires is unfailing love" (Pr 19:22). Through the Bible, the Lord has revealed to us that He, who is Infinite Love, is the only One capable of satisfying the otherwise unquenchable thirst. Only in ongoing relationship with Him do we discover why we exist and who we are. Only as we grow in communion with Him do we become the well-developed persons He means us to be. We either find our fulfillment in the Eternal Father through Jesus, or we become enslaved to the pursuit of that fulfillment in things-not-God, whether drugs, activities, sex or whatever else. We know this from scripture and from experience. Consider the discourse between Jesus and the woman at the well:

The question is never: "Will God heal me?" Rather, it is, "Will I choose to accept the certain healing that He promises, or not?" God's promise to you is deliverance; Paul assures you, "For sin shall not be your master, because you are not under law, but under grace" (Romans 6:14). This is God's gift to us; our part is to open and enjoy the gift by making our lives a constant pursuit of His loving Face.

Jesus answered her, 'If you knew the gift of God and who it is that asks you for a drink, you would have asked him and he would have given you living water.' 'Sir,' the woman said, 'you have nothing to draw with and the well is deep. Where can you get this living water? Are you greater than our father Jacob, who gave us the well and drank from it himself, as did also his sons and his flocks and herds?' Jesus answered, 'Everyone who drinks this water will be thirsty again, but whoever drinks the water I give him will never thirst. Indeed, the water I give him will become a spring of water welling up to eternal life.' (John 4:10-14)

In His interaction with the woman at the well, Jesus reveals that only the gift of God, only living water, ends thirst in the human heart. He uses the woman's natural thirst as a reflection in which she can see and understand her more profound spiritual thirst.

Addiction is a State of Thirsting Again and Again for Something that is Not Living Water

Come, all you who thirsty, come to the waters; and you who have no money come, buy and eat! Come, buy wine and milk without money and without cost. Why spend money on what is not bread, and your labor on what does not satisfy? Listen, listen to me, and eat what is good, and your soul will delight in the richest of fare. Give ear and come to me; hear me, that your soul may live. I will make an everlasting covenant with you, my faithful love promised to David. (Isaiah 55:1-3)

It is a fact common to all of us that we spend our resources on things that will not end our hunger. That is, we are all deluded, wasting our time in search of resources which are useless and can only lead to great disappointment. The Scripture points to this in the rhetorical question: "Why spend money on what is not bread?" There are things that appear to be bread, on which we spend money, time, effort and energy, and which are not bread at all. Such things cannot fill us, and they waste our resources. These bread-substitutes include everything that is not God! Even though this is contrary to what seems to be so, the fact is that anything that is not God will fail to satisfy us.

God alone can bring an end to our restless searching to be filled. Coming to God to be filled makes one's soul rich. He must be the primary Source to which we turn to fill our hearts.

God has made us for *life*. Jesus tells us, "I am the way, and the truth, and the life" (John 14:6). Without Jesus, what we experience is mere existence, not *life* at all. Life has to do with existing with Jesus; life is only present where we undertake the journey of our lives in partnership and intimacy with Him. Anything else is more or less lifeless. It's the experience of *death*, of existence without life. So, to the extent that we experience day to day reality apart from finding Him as the Source of our meaning and pleasure, we are experiencing death. Death has to do with the experience of sin and its consequences.

Those who die without faith in Christ experience eternal death; however, death is not felt by the damned alone. There is plenty of death that even the saved soul experiences in this fallen world. When we habitually seek life in created things, rather than the Creator, we habitually experience death. And, even worse, we become enslaved to our paltry substitute, even though it causes us to experience death! We become utterly pathetic, enslaved to lesser things, and unable to seek the One Remedy, even though He's what we most desire!

God is the Only Source of Life

Jesus came in the flesh to overcome the power of death. He is a quickening Spirit.

So it is written: 'The first man Adam became a living being'; the last Adam, a life-giving spirit. (I Cor. 15:45)

People, things, and activities cannot ever be living water.

Jeremiah names the basic problem with man in his fallen state:

Has a nation ever changed its gods? (Yet they are not gods at all.) But my people have exchanged their Glory for worthless idols. Be appalled at this, O heavens, and shudder with great horror, declares the Lord. My people have committed two sins: They have forsaken me, the spring of living water, and dug their own cisterns, broken cisterns that cannot hold water. (Jeremiah 2:11-13)

Those of us who have become addicted have participated in the two sins mentioned here. In our minds we may proclaim Jesus to be Lord, but in our daily actions we have entrusted our lives, our damaged hearts and our bodily members to another god - that of a sexual mood-altering high. Though we know better, our behavior has clearly placed sexual satisfaction over and above God's will.

In addiction, the objects of our desires become gods to us and amount to broken cisterns. They masquerade as life givers by covering our deep need for God, but can neither supply nor substitute the living water that God wants us to have.

Addiction Began with the Fall

From the beginning Satan has used our thirst in his strategy to separate us from God. Referring to Eve in the garden, Genesis 3:6 states,

When the woman saw that the fruit of the tree was good for food and pleasing to the eye, and also desirable for gaining wisdom, she took some of it and ate it.

Eve was experiencing the thirst of the senses as well as a spiritual thirst to be "wiser" than she was. Rather than subordinate her thirst to the directions God had given her, she took the Enemy's advice. The serpent capitalized on this thirst and used it to gain dominion over her.

Sexual Addiction is a False Thirst

Sexual addiction is a false thirst. It is a displaced desire for God resulting in compulsive attachment to, and unmanageable involvement with sexual behavior involving people, things, or fantasy, and usually ending in orgasm. As Patrick Carnes succinctly puts it, sexual addiction is "a pathological relationship with a mood-altering experience." [1]

The spiritual nature of addiction has its roots in the fall, and its patterns are worked out daily in the emotional and physical realm. The patterns of sin and stages of addiction can be seen in the writings of James:

When tempted no one should say, "God is tempting me." For God cannot be tempted by evil, nor does he tempt anyone; but each one is tempted when, by his own evil desire, he is dragged away and enticed. Then, after desire has conceived, it gives birth to sin; and sin, when it is full grown, gives birth to death. (James 1:13-15)

As our understanding of addiction unfolds, we will see that it is not a condition that can be relegated to one dimension of a person's life. It touches the spiritual, emotional, and physical dimensions of a person. All sin has the tendency to grow into a compulsion. To indulge oneself in sin is to court a compulsion; God has told us what is sin, and to avoid such things, because He wants to spare us the misery that comes with compulsive behavior. Addiction is simply a larger, uglier and messier form of sin.

We can see the pattern of sin/addiction as a progression that starts with desire (which is displaced from God) for some other object. Entertaining the desire is the worship of the object of choice. Idolatry saps our desire for God. (Worship means we respond and interact towards the object as if it can give us life.) *"Where your treasure is, there will your heart be also"* (Mt 6:21). This is true of addiction and sin. As the object of our desire gains more and more place in our heart, we increasingly participate in death. "Addiction makes idolaters of us all, because it forces us to worship these objects of attachment, thereby preventing us from truly, freely loving God and one another." [2]

Addiction is Idolatry

The idols of the nations are silver and gold, made by the hands of men. They have mouths, but cannot speak, eyes, but cannot see; they have ears, but cannot hear, nor is there breath in their mouths. Those who make them will be like them, and so will all who trust in them. (Psalm 135:15-18)

It is important to notice the characteristics of objects of worship other than God. False gods are mute, blind, deaf, and have no breath of life. As we become compulsively attached to anything, we replace a life-giving God with dead objects and activities that only leave us emptier.

When we start yielding to the force of our sexual desires, it may seem exciting, fulfilling, and bear the illusion that we are finally freeing our true selves. As involvement with sexual sin continues, the ugly death crowned by guilt and despair is soon revealed. The deeper our addiction goes, the more entrenched and twisted our desires become.

Addiction is the enemy of freedom. True freedom can only come from a living, spontaneous, and creative God. As the scripture points out, all who trust in idols will become like them – dead.

Jesus – Our Only Hope

Gratefully, the Father sent Jesus to us in our idolatrous state. He did so in light of our desperate condition, not in spite of it. Jesus is the fullness of God, the only One able to break the power of our addictions. Paul writes of Christ saying,

He is the image of the invisible God, the firstborn over all creation...All things were created by him and for him...For God was pleased to have all his fullness dwell in him, and through him to reconcile to himself all things. (Colossians 1:15, 16, 19)

Jesus is the image of God – He came in the flesh and was Himself the visible face of God, showing forth the nature of the Father to the world. In Genesis, we are told that man and woman were created by God on the sixth day.

So God created man in his own image, in the image of God he created him; male and female he created them. (Genesis 1:27)

Whereas Jesus is the image of God, humanity has been made in the image of God, created by the Father with Jesus and for Jesus. So, although Jesus alone fully reflects the image of the Father, we are made in that image, and so we too have the God-given capacity to reflect the Father. We do this, above all, as we live in love through faith and hope in Him.

Because God is love, He wants us to rest securely in Him, knowing His tender concern for us, knowing that He wants to care for every aspect of our lives. Because of this the apostle John writes,

There is no fear in love. But perfect love drives out fear, because fear has to do with punishment.
The one who fears is not made perfect in love. (I John 4:18)

The fear, pain and anxiety that we experience are related to the Fall of mankind, when Adam and Eve and all their descendants were separated by God by sin. Having become separated from the knowledge of who He is, fear came into our hearts.

One aspect of separation from the life of God is feeling a lonely emptiness and a longing to be filled. In his restless activity the addict is merely trying to complete himself with things other than God. These "fixes" are temporary and do not satisfy long term. They may seem to work for a time to cover up the pain of emptiness but will eventually behave like a lion cub which turns wild, becomes cunning, and devours its owner in a destructive addictive cycle. This is why the scripture admonishes us not to be conformed to this world or anything in it.

Do not conform any longer to the pattern of this world, but be transformed by the renewing of your mind.
(Romans 12:2)

How are we renewing our minds and to what are we being conformed? Our goal as worshippers of God is conformity to the knowledge of Jesus Christ, the express image of God. Addiction, in part, is an identity crisis in which the deep pain of not being conformed to God's image is covered by the restless activity of trying to find our identity in other things.

We Are Made For Relationship with God And Others

An important part of bearing God's image is the freedom, not only to be in right relationship with God, but to learn how to love other people well. Sexual addiction robs us of that freedom. God is not content with our simply stopping certain behaviors. His goal for us in coming out of sexual addiction is to grow in whole and trusting relationship with others. He wants our sexuality to be a servant of creative, honoring relationships. He does not want us to use others in the service of our sexuality. The first and second greatest commandments are relational commands. Notice the response of Jesus in the following well known discourse:

'Teacher, which is the greatest commandment in the Law?' Jesus replied: 'Love the Lord your God with all your heart and with all your soul and with all your mind.' This is the first and greatest commandment. And the second is like it: 'Love your neighbor as yourself.' All the Law and the Prophets hang on these two commandments. (Matthew 22:36-40)

Jesus died on the cross for our sins that we might be washed of our sins *and their effects*. Now that we have the provision of the cleansing power of the blood of Christ, God is calling us back from the separation of the fall. In our relationship with the Father He asks us to obey so that our desires, every part of us, might be attached to God. If we learn to seek Him for our meaning and satiation, we can learn, with Paul, the secret of being content in every situation. Because we can appropriate the grace He offers freely and in abundance, we can do this (progressively) one choice at a time, one act of the will after another. In doing this we receive new identities, understand our value, and begin to love ourselves. From that place of strength, we are then empowered to love others with the same knowledge regarding their importance to God. This occurs as God and His word mirror to us who we are in Him. It is this revelation that equips us to truly love others.

We Learn to Love God and Others

Developmentally, we gain our ability to be in relationship with God and others through our families of origin. Parents are image bearers of God. Parents become for us lenses through which we "see" and understand God and other people. Parental influence colors the way we perceive ourselves and others. In other words, our self-image and beliefs about relational realities are formed in relationship to our parents and what they reflect to us about ourselves.

As previously stated, God created us thirsty to know Him and to be like Him, that is, to be absorbed in His love for us and to pass it on to everyone around us. Developmentally this 'becoming' is facilitated, to whatever extent, by our parents as they administer both the nurture (love and affirmation) and the admonition (word, truth, and discipline) of God (Eph 6:4). By the time we reach adulthood we have already internalized a consistent set of understandings about God, ourselves, and others that either enables or hinders us as we move into loving, intimate relationships, including those which are sexual in nature. To the extent that our understanding of God, self, and other are incorrect, we will understand people and their motives wrongly. We thus will relate wrongly, thinking that we understand, but in fact unable to truly see ourselves and others as we actually are.

The ability to love and be loved (to relate properly, in other words) is possible for a person only inasmuch as (s)he is able to trust God and others. This trust is a primary need in the heart of every individual. When it is not established, there is a deep despair, loneliness and fear of relationship that sets itself into the soul. In other words, broken, distorted and painful experiences of intimacy leave a bad taste in their wake; relationships and intimacy thus are reminiscent of the sour and bitter past experiences. Families which are broken in the ability to love thus yield children afraid to be vulnerable – afraid to trust. Sexual addicts, as a rule, are afraid to trust; this is one of the marks of a person with a sexual addiction. It is, in fact, a major cause of the addiction (as we'll later see). This is why, for the sexual addict, learning to trust and giving up control in relationships is a major issue. Until this is accomplished, they are at some level lonely all the time and hungry for true intimacy.

In sexual addiction, this hunger (which is really for God) is displaced by sexual activity. **Connection without relational risk is the driving force of sexual addiction. One attaches himself to sexual objects in a vain attempt to satisfy the gaping hole in his soul. Overcoming sexual addiction involves dealing with this misdirected quest for emotional intimacy.**

Similarly, resolving painful events from one's history in the family is a crucial part of breaking addictive attachments; it is also key to developing meaningful relationships. Facing the painful realities of one's past, so as to resolve them with the Lord, will produce freedom to move into a healthy relationship with God and others.

Conclusion

Before the Fall, Adam and Eve walked with God and one another. Each one was in right relationship with both the human other and the divine Other. Together, they walked, talked and worked, all with unselfconscious joy and contentment. Because of their unity, they enjoyed more than mere existence – they lived. Taking Satan's advice and guidance they disobeyed their God and separated themselves from the Source of Life. They fell from a state of original justice into sin and its horrific consequences, bringing all of humankind with them.

We continue to be the heirs of the sin and death that began with them. Even this, however, does not change the fact that each person is made in the image of God, created in such a way as to reflect the goodness of God Himself. The result is that we find within our selves things noble and ignoble, that which is beautiful and profane.

Our families of origin, where we grew up, have had much to do in shaping and forming us fallen ones. To the extent that our families were broken, the effects of the Fall are more evident in us. The more broken our families have been, the more broken we will be.

Our Maker regards us with enormous compassion and kindness. In the light of our great distress He came amongst us in the flesh and became our Remedy. Jesus alone is our hope for healing; without Him we can never return to anything remotely like the ways that Adam and Eve enjoyed life.

Paul writes in Romans 8:

*For if you live according to the sinful nature, you will die; but if **by the Spirit** you put to death the misdeeds of the body, you will live, because those who are led by the Spirit of God are sons of God... Now if we are children, then we are heirs – heirs of God and co-heirs with Christ, if indeed we share in his sufferings in order that we may also share in His glory.* (Romans 8: 13-14, 17, boldface is mine)

Paul is asserting here that, having received the Spirit of God, the believer is transformed into a new creation, a son/daughter of God. As His children, we are heirs to His royal inheritance, which is boundless and which includes a "share in His glory" (v. 17). Having been brought from death to life, our inheritance has everything to do with freedom. And, until we attain freedom completely, part of our inheritance is the certitude that liberty is on its way – God wants us to trust Him and to know that while we are weak and cannot heal ourselves, He is strong and will heal His children. Those of us who, despite our long history of sin, have dared to hope in His deliverance have found His promises to be true. God delights in lifting us out of the pit of sin we've so long been trapped in. He in turn causes us to deeply believe in His love for us and power to save.

The question is never: "Will God heal me?" Rather, it is, "Will I choose to accept the certain healing that He promises, or not?" God's promise to you is deliverance; Paul assures you, "For sin shall not be your master, because you are not under law, but under grace" (Romans 6:14). This is God's gift to us; our part is to open and enjoy the gift by making our lives a constant pursuit of His loving Face. If by His grace we will but die to the old, sinful ways (step by step, and with the support, prayer and friendship of the church's fellowship), there is certain resurrection life for every believer: freedom from the enslavement of sin, and freedom to choose and to rejoice in life.

For if, by the trespass of the one man [Adam], death reigned through that one man, how much more will those who receive God's abundant provision of grace and of the gift of righteousness reign in life through the one man, Jesus Christ. (Romans 5:17)

References

[1] Patrick Carnes, Ph.D., *Contrary to Love* (Minneapolis: CompCare Publishers, 1989) 4.

[2] Gerald G. May, M.D., *Addiction & Grace* (San Francisco: Harper & Row, 1988) 4.

Homework

Homework

1. What about your sexual addiction seems alive or life-giving?

2. In what ways has your addiction already produced death in you?
    How do you look like your idol?

3. Do you have a gracious (marked by grace) or licentious
    (marked by license) relationship with God? Explain.

Sexual Addiction is False Intimacy

Chapter Two

This road leads to the pain that the addict has been avoiding and that Jesus wants to take upon Himself. As painful memories, fears of rejection, and core sinful beliefs are processed, the addict will begin to gain understanding about what intimacy truly is. He will begin to discover that his need to receive and to give true love is becoming more powerful than his addiction.

When the woman saw that the fruit of the tree was good for food and pleasing to the eye, and also desirable for gaining wisdom, she took some and ate it. She also gave some to her husband, who was with her, and he ate it. Then the eyes of both of them were opened, and they realized they were naked; so they sewed fig leaves together and made coverings for themselves. (Genesis 3:6-7)

Male and Female – God's Intended Design

God created humankind in His own image. This truth has many facets. It is important to note that what God has revealed to us about His triune relationship also applied to the relationship between man and woman. Our God is a Trinity; while there is only one God, there are three Persons of the Trinity. Although Father, Son, and Holy Spirit are distinctly different, they are yet intimately connected as one Being in a holy communion without conflict, fear, or disunity. So it is with God's creation of man and woman.

After creating Adam, God stated, "It is not good for man to be alone" (Genesis 2:18). Unlike most of His creation, God did not form woman from nothing. Nor did He form her from the earth, as He had with Adam. Instead, woman was taken from man:

The Lord God caused the man to fall into a deep sleep; and while he was sleeping, He took one of the man's ribs and closed up the place with flesh. Then the Lord God made a woman from the rib He had taken out of the man, and He brought her to the man. The man said, 'This is now bone of my bones, and flesh of my flesh; she shall be called 'woman,' for she was taken out of man.' (Genesis 2:21-23)

Adam was different after woman was formed. He now had a companion who had been part of him, with whom he desired union. Both felt a yearning to become one being, as they had been before being separated out from one another. For Adam there was now an emptiness, a longing for completion that could only be satisfied by Eve. God intended them to be related in a communion and oneness that reflects the Trinitarian relationships – one in heart, yet separate in identity and essence. Now, as two persons, the couple more fully reflected the image of God. Now, as in the Godhead, there was community, and the bond between them was love.

Furthermore, the loving relationship between a man and a woman is meant to reflect Christ's loving relationship with the Church, His bride. In Ephesians 5:32, Paul points out that in becoming one, husband and wife are a reflection of the Church (the bride) and her husband Christ (the Bridegroom):

For this reason a man will...be united to his wife, and the two will become one flesh. This is a profound mystery – but I am talking about Christ and the Church. However, each one of you also must love his wife as he loves himself, and the wife must respect her husband. (Ephesians 5:31-33)

Paul points to the similarity between the relationship of Christ and the Church, and that of the married couple, and exhorts the couple to be fully devoted to one another in love, in the same way that Jesus and the Church are related to one another. God has made us so that we might be joined by a profound love with Him, our Bridegroom, and that such love might also mark the relationship that man and wife share.

Before the fall, Adam and Eve enjoyed an ideal intimacy. Their communion was not colored by fear of rejection, or by doubt about each one's ability to please the other. They united relationally and sexually with full pleasure and freedom because they walked in the light of God's perfect love. They did not experience envy, fear of rejection, insecurity, lust or the temptation to measure themselves by the other's response because their souls had not yet become infected by sin. They were naked and felt no shame. In addition, Adam and Eve's physical nakedness matched their hearts and minds, which were likewise unveiled towards each other. Their primary identity and security came from their constant communion with God; secure in God's love, they had no need to hide.

God's meant for man to be free to move in this perfect intimacy. Adam and Eve did not despise each others' differences; rather, they revealed them to one another. They were able to celebrate each others' uniqueness. Man and woman were designed to experience deep enjoyment in response to the gender difference that God imparted to man and woman. This pleasure is as emotional and spiritual as it is physical. For the sexual addict, there is much confusion and blindness on this point.

True Intimacy

The effect of the Fall on human relationships is nothing less than catastrophic. Fear, shame, fighting and blaming are regular occurrences in all human interaction. Men and women now hide their flaws from each other in order to navigate the perils of intimate relationship. For man, in varying degrees, sexual desire is no longer tempered and guided by God's love. Instead his sexuality is frequently self-gratifying.

True intimacy means to know another and to be known. It implies sanctuary and safety where each partner can expose the sensitive and private places of the heart. True intimacy can only be achieved with sensitivity and care for the other person.

One key component of true intimacy is self-disclosure. For the sexual addict this can be terrifying. Exposure means the possibility of becoming an open target for rejection and shame. It means the possibility of reliving old life patterns that might confirm his negative beliefs about himself. For vulnerability (and thus true intimacy) to exist in a relationship, each partner must reflect God's graciousness and compassion in dealing with our flaws and failings. Just as Jesus is a High Priest who is able to understand our weaknesses as we confess our shortcomings to Him, a truly intimate human relationship is a place where weakness and vulnerability will be honored and protected rather than mocked or despised.

Trust

Truly intimate relationships must involve trust. Trust is "firm reliance on the integrity, ability or character of a person" (American Heritage Dictionary). To trust someone, I need reason to believe that (s)he values the truth and is compassionate. It implies security and confidence in another. In relationships it means that if one exposes himself to another or becomes emotionally "naked," the other will not hurt him.

All sexual addicts experience self-doubt related to the fear of being wounded by a partner who finds them unacceptable. Healing happens as this fear and self-doubt are overcome in real relationships.

In healthy relationships the ability of each partner to risk intimacy involves clinging to God's truth about his or her value. God's love and acceptance for each individual acts as a cushion against human acts of rejection. Inability to risk with others in relationship is a major barrier to true intimacy for the sexual addict. Somewhere along the line he has lost his ability to trust. If he is to be healed, he must gradually come to rely on the Lord's ability to give value and worth to devastated parts of his heart. These areas of the heart have been hidden for years beneath the defense of his sexual acting out. Sexual acting-out has masked the true problem, a fear of intimacy. Since no man or woman is perfectly safe, trust in God's acceptance must become the primary place of nurture for the addict.

The only way the addict can begin to trust again is to progressively risk dependency and vulnerability in present-day relationships. As he begins to experience emotional intimacy as safe, his internal irrational beliefs and generalizations about what will happen when he shows weakness will begin to change. This assumes that his current risktaking relationships, such as the "Falling Forward" accountability group or a twelve step group, are at least somewhat safe. Beginning to risk non-sexualized intimacy with the opposite sex can be especially frightening for the addict. Even though it is fearful, healing cannot occur unless the person is willing to risk trusting God and people.

Sexual Addiction is False Intimacy

In order to avoid the pain of exposure in intimate relationships, a person can adopt two basic strategies at opposite ends of a spectrum. On one end is a strategy of sexual and emotional avoidance. When opting for this a person becomes emotionally distant and sexually inactive. Safety is achieved through sealing off the heart and distancing from any physical connection.

On the other end of the spectrum is sexual obsession. This is where we find the sexual addict. His unspoken strategy is to substitute sex for love. The intoxication of the sexual activity with its momentary high covers up any relational pain that might occur. The addict's heart is left unavailable for committed relationship; instead he experiences a pseudoconnection by means of physical contact. The intense physiological feelings of sexual arousal combined with imaginary or real physical closeness has become a substitute for true intimacy. For the sexual addict, false intimacy is a way of connecting while still being able to avoiding the possibility of real relational pain.

Glamorizing his circumstances through fantasy is a regular part of the addict's sexual experience. The illusion that the addict provides for himself may be grossly exaggerated or subtle. For example, a man who thinks about a voluptuous actress while making love to his wife is avoiding reality by falsifying his relationship, since he is behaving as though he were having sex with someone other than his wife. He can give the actress in his imagination the emotional attributes that he wants and use her image to stimulate himself sexually. Thus, he can avoid emotional intimacy with his wife and the need to work through any real life relational issues that are hindering his sexual excitement or freedom to enjoy her emotionally. Instead of being an extension of love and caring, the marriage bed has become self-centered. It meets his needs non-intimately , and therefore leaves him feeling alone. As the pattern continues, his emotional isolation increases. He uses the same strategy as the man who minimizes his emotional risk by picking up prostitutes who, of course, do not expect any commitment beyond the money he gives. Both situations avoid true intimacy.

The addict comes to believe that "if the situation I set up happens, I'll be somebody. I'll be fulfilled. I'm the one who can define what will bring me fulfillment or prevent pain." ...If I think I'm pulling the strings, then I can view life as predictable and safe. In effect, the sex addict creates an illusion that brings some fulfillment and definitely less relational pain – in the short run. [1]

Sexual Compulsivity – Illusion of Control

Modern media puts out streams of images exalting men and women for detached and shallow sexual encounters, while sporting romantic, heroic images of strength and power. We all know the scores of women who have fallen to the macho virility of James Bond. He is able to answer the phone during 'love making' and aloofly utter a sexual pun on his partner's heightened arousal. He is totally in control. The message is clear: *James Bond is a "real" man.*

Back to reality. In truth the sexual addict uses sexually compulsive behavior as a way of avoiding his unmet needs. In his past, there was far too little love and affirmation; the present search for connection with others serves to temporarily quench that intense thirst. The addict has an intense need for love, but since he fears intimacy, he has the conflict of desperately desiring something he simultaneously deeply fears. He holds an irrational belief that sexually compulsive rituals are acts of love. But at the same time, he must control the objects of his lust in order to keep his real needs from surfacing.

Sex As Power

In general, the addict's life is chaotic and unmanageable. He lives in a world over which he feels he has little or no control. Desperate for attention and encouragement, he is enslaved to the sexual practices that have given him a kind of power over his pain and real needs. This, in part, accounts for the sexual addiction:

> Sex is one area in which sex addicts believe they can reclaim some of their power. Surprisingly most of the addicts we've treated describe the sexual act itself as something controlled by the sex object – who ultimately can either satisfy or thwart their sexual desire. Yet such a belief adds to the power trip...each time addicts do achieve a sexual high, getting the sex object to do what they want, they believe they have wrestled away the sex object's control and scored another point in the ultimate power game. According to the sex addict's belief system, sex is not an experience to be shared, but rather a prize to be won. [2]

In order to fend off feelings of powerlessness the sex addict must avoid his internal vulnerabilities by using the weaknesses of his sex object. In this, the addict is anti-relational and uses his skills to manipulate his conquest, as if he were playing to win a game. He scores by capitalizing upon the lover's neediness.

> 'The trick is to get a woman to have sex, or want to have sex with me without her knowing how much I want it,' Todd claims. 'If I let her know how much I want her, she'll play games with me, she'll toy with me, she'll jerk me around.' [3]

It is important to note here that not all addicts are involved in sexual compulsivity with real people. Often they keep a safe distance and maintain a sense of power and control through involving themselves in fantasy or watching sex via pornographic media. Masturbation and orgasm then complete the cycle.

> But these relationships are really self-made, seemingly safe fantasies structured to be what the addict wants them to be. The addict believes in the illusion of control because he or she controls the illusion. "The centerfold will be everything I want her to him to be." "The people I'm having affairs with will be cooperative and make me feel great."

Fantasy seems to be much safer than risking emotions in unpredictable relationships and suffering the pain that real intimacy can cause. For a brief moment, the centerfold or prostitute is enthralled with the sex addict. Acceptance is unconditional. Rejection is not possible. Sex is a conquest − imaginary or real − and abates the terrifying sense of not belonging. For at least a brief moment, fantasies become more real than life. [4]

Christians who are addicted often hold back physical involvement because of the Scripture's explicit prohibition of sexual immorality. Yet in the dynamics of his inner life, the Christian addict may fantasize about power plays with sex partners which yield the same sense of control, affirmation, acceptance and safety that he needs to get his fix. Fantasy, as Jesus taught, is just as evil a form of sexual immorality as is the full physical type which is being imagined:

You have heard that it was said, 'Do not commit adultery.' But I tell you that anyone who looks at a woman lustfully has already committed adultery with her in her heart. (Matthew 5:27-28)

Sex as Adequacy

In addition to priding themselves on their ability to snare sex objects of their choice, sex addicts, like Todd, usually feel that sex is something they do particularly well...Like alcoholics who pride themselves on their ability to drink others under the table, sex addicts often believe their sexual performance is the one special talent they have. [5]

The thought process of the addict often goes something like this: "If I can attract a sexual partner, then I must be desirable." He thinks of his sexual performance, and the attractiveness of his body, as an indicator and a measure of his worth and adequacy. What he may not acknowledge is that often there may be an addict on the other side of the interaction that is just as desperate to prove that (s)he is lovable.

Sex as Love

Sex addicts put their total dependence on sex to meet all of their love needs because they do not know how to be truly intimate. For the exhibitionist, the exposure of his body is a safe and shallow substitute for the exposure and acceptance of his soul. The addict confuses physical exposure with true closeness. In the case of the voyeur, the excitement and danger of peeking at someone's nakedness may seem like a point of connection, and provide a safe way to feel intimate. In visiting a prostitute, the addict pays for sexual favors and hopes she will know just what to say to affirm the insecure child within whose need to be loved drives him to someone who 'understands.' Understands what? The successful, high paid prostitute understands her patron's need for affirmation of his sexual prowess in order to feel loved and accepted.

The driving force behind the sexual addict's compulsion is a desperate need for love. He tends to interpret any kind of sexuality or sexual interest from another as love. Bill, a forty two year old married man, explained with anguish:

I need sex at least once a day. But my wife won't give me that anymore. Today makes three days since the last time we were together. I'm really scared that my marriage is falling apart. I know that it doesn't make sense, but I don't feel loved by my wife if we aren't having sex.

Bill has substituted sex for love. His perspective of what is normal in relationships has been overwhelmed by his deep, unmet needs for affirmation. His constant cry for love has become a constant cry for sex.

Bill's wife lives in a totally different reality. Lately, every time Bill approaches her for sex she feels used. She longs for the intimacy of an emotional relationship. Bill protests when she says no, and she feels misunderstood. The pain of the growing isolation that arises out of Bill's inability to see the relationship from her perspective only serves to deepen the divide between them.

> Through sensuality, the addict routinely avoids being connected to his heart. Because his heart is full of painful emotions, he represses his heart through the addiction. Because the heart has been split-off, the pain is not present, but neither can the beauty of God's love or joy be present. As a consequence, he cannot contain the knowledge of God's love for him, and the kingdom of God cannot take hold of his heart.

God wants to do a cleansing work of restoration in the depths of each heart. Participating in the kingdom of God requires that we let God into the depths of our hearts. To do this, we must obey Him, which means that all of our lives must be submitted to Him, sexuality included. Our sexuality really does affect our spirituality. Paul writes:

Do you not know that your body is a temple of the Holy Spirit, who is in you, whom you have received from God? You are not your own; you were bought at a price. Therefore honor God with your body. (I Cor 6:19-20)

The sexual addict must turn to God as his source of acceptance, affirmation, and love. He must put aside the self-focused illusion of control which fuels sexual addiction. As the addict continues on in sexual sin, he ignores the Holy Spirit within him. He deadens his ability to hear the still small voice of God and grows increasingly distant from Him.

Only by relying upon God's power to restore the soul can the addict begin to enter into truly loving and intimate relationships. In so doing, he will begin to receive his kingdom inheritance.

Two Roads of Pain

With regard to compulsive sexual acts themselves, the addict has only two options open to him; both involve pain.

The first option is to continue on with sexual compulsion and the probability of escalation into more dangerous and more victimizing trespasses against others. This is painful because he increasingly separates his soul from God, the true Source of the love and value that he longs for. In addition, each illicit orgasm (the inevitable result of sexual compulsion) will continue to be followed by the despair related to being ensnared by sin.

The second option open to the addict has already been stated. It is, through His grace, to choose to stop his compulsive sexual behavior and to allow the Lord to uncover the underlying wounds and needs of his heart. This road leads to the pain that the addict has been avoiding and that Jesus wants to take upon Himself. As painful memories, fears of rejection, and core sinful beliefs are processed, the addict will begin to gain understanding about what intimacy truly is. He will begin to discover that his need to receive and to give true love is becoming more powerful than his addiction.

Notes
Personal

References

1 Dr. Harry W. Schaumburg, *False Intimacy* (Colorado: NavPress, 1992) 24.

2 Dr. Ralph Earle and Dr. Gregory Crow, *Lonely All The Time* (New York: Simon & Schuster Inc., 1989) 24.

3 Dr. Ralph Earle and Dr. Gregory Crow, *Lonely All The Time* (New York: Simon & Schuster, Inc., 1989) 25.

4 Dr. Harry W. Schaumburg, *False Intimacy* (Colorado: NavPress, 1992) 28.

5 Dr. Ralph Earle and Dr. Gregory Crow, *Lonely All The Time* (New York: Simon & Schuster Inc., 1989) 25.

Homework

1. Have you ever felt hurt or rejected after risking emotional vulnerability with others (think over both childhood and adulthood)? Please describe any significant events. What patterns do you see that carry over to your current relationships?

2. Make a statement that assesses your ability to trust in intimate relationships.

3. Describe any way in which you use sex for affirmation or control in real or imagined relationships. For example (check if applicable):

___ "I think I'm particularly gifted at lovemaking."

___ "In my fantasy my partners are awed by my sexuality, especially turned on by me, and beg for more, shower me with compliments, etc."

___ "I feel powerful, significant and in control when I am manipulating my objects of sex."

___ "In real life or fantasy, I depend on affirmation from others based on body shape, size, etc."

___ "At times in my sexual fantasies I change my body size or shape to be more attractive."

___ "In my fantasies I have unlimited sexual energy and staying power."

___ Others:

4. Have you discovered any way in which you substitute sex for love? Explain.

Action Item: Write down one relational step that you can begin implementing which will increase your non-sexual intimacy skills.

The Pain of Sexual Addiction

Addicts have learned somewhere in their past that intimate relationships lead to the pain of rejection and must be avoided to insure survival...In the place of true intimacy, sexual addicts have substituted the false intimacy of sexual contact. Acts that substitute sex for intimacy are crippled jabs at true relationship; they attempt to offset hidden relational shame through the temporary accolades of sexual performance, conquest, or exposure in the presence of another.

Chapter Three

Blessed is the man whose sin the Lord does not count against him and in whose spirit is no deceit. When I kept silent, my bones wasted away through my groaning all day long. For day and night your hand was heavy upon me; my strength was sapped as in the heat of summer. (Psalm 32:2-3)

Addiction Enslaves the Whole Person

Addiction has the potential to snuff out life in every dimension of one's being. We may have told ourselves that ours is a harmless, inconsequential habit. In actuality, addiction is slavery.

The Pain of the Addictive Cycle

The sexual addict experiences pain on two levels. The most fundamental pain he will face during his healing is that which is found at the depths of his heart. It is the pain of a broken identity. This results from wounding interactions with his family of origin, coupled with the ache of unmet needs for love. The addict's wounding is the root of his addiction. This pain will be discussed in other chapters.

The second type of pain, the subject of this chapter, is the pain the addict experiences from the addictive cycle itself. This pain eventually brings the addict to his knees and motivates him to turn his life over to God. In addressing and identifying this pain, the addict faces the crucial decision of whether or not he will surrender to God.

The addictive cycle begins with exciting and often euphoric feelings. Through his acting out, the addict hopes in vain to deaden or heal the deeper internal pain of wounds and unmet needs. As previously stated, pursuing this course is idolatry and effectively closes the addict's heart to life in God. The end result is spiritual, emotional, and mental pain.

Spiritual Pain

Addiction causes separation from the spiritual life and energy found only in God. Consider the following passage in which Paul exhorts us not to live a life after the same pattern as the Gentiles (those unschooled in the life-dynamics of God):

So I tell you this, and insist on it in the Lord, that you must no longer live as the Gentiles do, in the futility of their thinking. They are darkened in their understanding and separated from the life of God because of the ignorance that is in them due to the hardening of their hearts. Having lost all sensitivity, they have given themselves over to sensuality so as to indulge in every kind of impurity, with a continual lust for more. (Ephesians 4:17-19)

This scripture is a snapshot of addiction, a picture of a growing enslavement to an unrelenting hunger. It clearly lays out the heart's condition as a result of ongoing patterns of sensual sin–darkened, hardened, ignorant of, and separated from the life of God.

The sexual addict suffers spiritual pain because he is caught in the cycle of avoiding his pain through sin. The addictive strategy seems to work as a painkiller. Yet in order to continue on this course, the addict must disobey God and violate his own moral belief system. As he repeatedly takes the wrong path, the one dictated by his sexual hunger, he feels the existential anxiety of having abandoned his life's true compass. In his heart, he knows that he is wounding the One who died for him, and this pains him. Even so, he simultaneously enjoys his sexual exploits. Within his soul is a civil war, waged by two distinct sides with very different goals.

Each repetition of the cycle increases the weight of treason upon his heart. As the addiction progresses, the addict feels less connected to God. He begins to wonder why God won't rescue him. He feels the pain of hopelessness and begins to question his faith. The result is a deep despair that crowns him. Probably one of the greatest pains for the addict is being cut off from the Father, the true source of confidence, love, and peace. In addiction, despite the lies one prefers to believe, the sexual addict has forsaken God for another source.

"Do not love the world, nor the things in the world. If any one loves the world, the love of the Father is not in him. For all that is in the world, the lust of the flesh and the lust of the eyes and the boastful pride of life, is not from the Father, but is from the world." (1 John 2:15-16 NASB)

The addict chooses to sear his conscience and deaden the responsiveness of his heart as he pursues his addictive cycle. One choice at a time, the will is progressively weakened as lust increases its grip. The result is that he spirals into a pit of guilt, despair, and self-hatred. Because he is good at deceiving himself (from consistent practice), he can rationalize, deny, and avoid the truth for a long while. But eventually family, friends, community, or his own self-destructiveness will catch up with him.

A person in the tight grip of a sexual addiction experiences the preeminence of the flesh. Ephesians 4:19, quoted earlier, speaks of the loss of sensitivity in the addict. A loss of sensitivity always spells moral decay. This loss of sensitivity means that the addict's growing degradation goes unnoticed by him. The escalating nature of sexual addiction leads to increasingly dark concessions to depravity as the addict enters new arenas of experience in his quest for a sexual high.

The Pain of Lust

Lust is an overpowering drive to possess something that substitutes for God's love. The object of lust is often discarded, as though the object were worthless. I use the word object here because sexual attachments are not always to people. Sometimes the 'object' of attachment is inanimate, imaginary, celluloid, etc. Because each of us exists in a network of relationships, our fallen compulsions cannot be anything but destructive to those around us, even though they may not yet know what is occurring.

Because the addict is cut off from his own tenderness, he is out of touch with the sensitivities of the one he encounters sexually. Lust, rather than love, becomes the governing force, which uses selfish sexual stimulation for fuel as it consumes the uniqueness and personhood of others. Lust is a user. It reflects the ultimate heights of the fallen self. Our own "evil desire," a component of the flesh, rules our propensity to be addictive. To be caught in lust is painful for the addict because the accompanying hard-heartedness keeps him disconnected and trapped in a prison of loneliness.

In addiction, the man driven by lust experiences a loss of freedom that has to do with his ability to choose. In his heart he knows that he is called to love others, but instead he has become accustomed to using them for his own pleasure. Although a part of him is disgusted at the notion, his motto is essentially: "As long as I achieve my sexual high, I don't really care about other people involved." Thus he loses what is unique to him as a human being created in God's image – the ability to willfully and reasonably love. At some level he knows that he has taken his place with the animals, as one who operates by instinct and apart from a will enlightened by reason. His thoughts hail vanity and his understanding is paralyzed. Being trapped in the power of lust produces the pain of hypocrisy, wherein the addict knows what is wrong and yet flagrantly disregards the truth for selfish gain.

The Pain of False Intimacy

As reflected in the first and second commandments of God (Matt. 22:36-40), man is made for loving communion with his Creator and with his fellow man. This communion involves knowing another and being known in a deep way and with a tenderness of mutual respect. That is the opposite of a fleeting sexual contact, or fantasy. Intimate relationships involve trust, commitment, and a sharing of the soul at an emotional level. These can be frightening to the sexual addict. Addicts have learned somewhere in their past that intimate relationships lead to the pain of rejection and must be avoided to insure survival . Healing the wounds of rejection is therefore an essential task in the process of healing sexual addiction.

In the place of true intimacy, sexual addicts have substituted the false intimacy of sensual contact. Acts that substitute sex for intimacy are crippled jabs at true relationship; they attempt to offset hidden relational shame through the temporary accolades of sexual performance, conquest, or exposure in the presence of another. Through his contorted thinking about his sexual behavior the addict convinces himself that what's been done was in some way truly great. This is a vain attempt to flatter himself and compensate for what is missing on the inside. In the end, this attempt to fix himself can only result in despair. Only God's love can fill the aching cavity in his soul.

Sexual Addiction Results in Relational Pain

Often the addict's spouse or girlfriend intuits his emotional unavailability. She may experience their relationship as shallow, confusing or, "all about him." One spouse said, "I don't feel like we are making love. It's more like he's making love to himself."

Some wives feel increasingly like sexual objects as their husbands demand high-frequency sex, or request that they act out perverted fantasies without regard for their feelings or comfort zone. Others languish under the insecurity of not understanding why their spouses are seldom interested in sex. They don't have the perspective that comes from understanding that their spouse's extramarital sexual activities are substituting for real intimacy and thus draining off desire for the marriage bed.

For the addict's wife, persistent torment plagues her in the form of suspicions that something is wrong. They can't put their finger on what is happening to their most precious relationship. Some spouses carry a crazy-making sense of unreality in which they begin to question their discernment about themselves and their husbands. Unexplained tensions often erupt into angry accusations and quarrels which begin to characterize the marriage relationship. The addict's double life acts as a cancer in the marriage relationship.

The escalating nature of the addiction is too powerful to handle and, ultimately, the addict will be found out. The effect on the spouse is devastation. For her there is always a sense of deep loss and betrayal. When the reality of the deception surfaces, many spouses feel the terror of being uncovered, unprotected and made vulnerable to the death threat of sexually transmitted diseases. The discovery of the infidelity often begins the heartache of broken trust. One spouse said, "It's like being punched in the stomach and not knowing if your wind is going to return." The spouse experiences a sense of being used. She realizes that she is not cherished with the love he once vowed.

Sadly, the addict often fails to understand the devastation of his wife and is impatient with her anger and hurt. He wants her to hurry up and get over her reactions to his betrayal. This testifies all the more to his insensitivity and critical need to gain understanding on the nature of relationships.

Narcissism

When our idolatry takes the form of lusting for other people, it is often an expression of narcissism.

Explaining the nature of narcissism, Andrew Comiskey points out,

> Narcissism is a wrongful kind of self-love, a type that expresses itself in a preoccupation with one's own image. The narcissist's energies are invested in that image – building up the body (or toning it down), buying the right clothes, posturing in a way that will elicit a favorable response from others. The outer image so painstakingly crafted serves as a lure that can entice others, reel them in, and cause them to worship themselves. [1]

The fact that a person is so significantly self-absorbed seems to imply an unqualified love of themselves. In fact, it points to something quite opposed to love. Alexander Lowen explains:

> The Narcissist is actually very wounded within, and has so little self-acceptance that he or she cannot afford to let sexual encounters be anything more than superficial. They are happy to accept the shallow affirmation of another's attraction to themselves and their well kept image. They make no deep connections with anyone because it threatens the illusion they have of their sexual prowess and the needed defense of denial. [2]

Often the addict's fantasy life involves exaggerating his personal qualities so as to inflate his self-image and simultaneously dismiss realities about his relational deficits. The truth is that sexual addicts seldom if ever have true courage and strength when it comes to risking in relationships.

The ability to risk in relationship, in fact, is exactly what is crippled, by fear. Gordon Dalbey writes,

> Certainly, we men do not fantasize before Playboy centerfolds because we are so courageous before real-live, three dimensional women, but rather, because we fear them; we do not beat up women because we are so strong, but rather because we feel so powerless before them; we do not impregnate women and leave them to consider an abortion because we are so self-reliant, but rather, because we feel inadequate to be responsible fathers and husbands. [3]

Narcissism is particularly painful because the addict must expend a huge quantity of energy building up a *false image of himself*. He is continually attending to his distorted thinking so that this house of cards will not topple and leave him devastated. Facing his true condition is a constant threat, which continually breathes down his neck as he runs from one act of sex to another.

All addicts must face the painful truth that they do not know how to operate intimately in relationships and lack the courage to be truly vulnerable. They are lonely all the time. No amount of sexual activity can heal this underlying pain. The fruit of sexual binging is always rotten.

Guilt, Shame and Despair

It almost goes without saying that all of the above leaves the addict feeling real guilt, increasing shame, and a hopelessness that brings despair. This very real pain is the last part of the addictive cycle.

Addiction is Mental Bondage

> Psychologically, addiction uses up desire. It is like a psychic malignancy, sucking out life energy into specific obsessions and compulsions, leaving less and less energy available for other people and other pursuits. [4]

As Gerald May notes, in the quote above, addiction always includes the elements of obsession and compulsion.

An obsession – A mental preoccupation with the object of attachment (real or fantasized). Obsessive thoughts are common to all forms of addiction and often build in intensity as the addiction takes hold of the addict's inner life. At first the struggling addict's obsessive sexual thoughts are minor intrusions into daily living. But, in later stages, the addict often sees daily realities as irritants interrupting his euphoric fantasies. Reality distracts the scheming surrounding his addictive attachment. Obsessive thoughts may eventually begin to occupy so much time that the addict will experience noticeable loss of productivity at work and increasing isolation in relationships. As his mind becomes captured by the addictive process, his life becomes unmanageable. Dr.'s Earle and Crow note,

> A sex addict's fantasies can continue for hours on end, and he or she sees the realities of daily living as an intrusion. The fantasies take control and the addict's life revolves around the ability to get the next fix, the specific, ritualized sexual acts that he or she knows will produce a high. The high is all that really matters. [5]

A compulsion – "Just as an obsession is a persistent repetitive thought, a compulsion is a persistent repetitive behavior…The compulsion is a virtually irresistible urge to repeat a behavior over and over again, regardless of the immediate harm it can cause or its long range consequences." [6]

An addict's compulsions are closely related to his obsessive thought life. They override his logical thinking, moral judgment and even the strongest desire to not act out. Because compulsions have to do with physical acts, they are harder to deny than obsessions. As the addiction progresses the addict gives his body over to acts that prove destructive to others and himself.

Addiction Is Physiological Attachment

Physiologically, addiction has mainly to do with the brain. Although it is too complex to explore here, it is enough to say that the brain adapts chemically and physically to the environmental or chemical stimuli and activity of the body. After prolonged sexual stimulation (beyond what's healthy and good), the equivalent of synaptic trenches form in the brain that cry out for more. Having grown accustomed to so great a need for undo stimuli, the brain demands that its former steady flow be maintained. This is the basis for attachment, and is the physiological reason why addiction is so persistent and powerful. The brain actually adapts and hardens into set ways of handling environmental stimuli. New neuronal grooves are formed. This is the basis for forming helpful habits but also, for powerful addictive habits. (In working with healing sexual addiction it is often significant to pray for the brain as to its part in the addiction process. A deeper discussion of the physiological aspects of addiction can be found in Gerald May's book, *Addiction and Grace*.)

Beneath the Cycle, A Soul Needs Healing

Beneath the all-consuming activity of addiction is emotional pain that has almost always been fostered in the family of origin and has made the prospect of intimacy terrifying. The addict does not know how to trust, and has a belief system that ensures that urges him to not risk the vulnerability of a truly loving relationship. Compulsive activity is often a long-standing attempt to cover and avoid real loneliness and relational despair. It is a flight from intimacy.

Emotionally, addiction can be seen as a painkiller. The addict uses the compulsive activity as a way to suppress the spiritual and emotional pain that results from a lack of love. The addict uses his false euphoria as a substitute for the real peace and joy that comes from communion with God. In the absence of his object of attachment the user quickly begins to squirm.

When the cycle of addiction stops, the underlying pain will begin to rise to the surface of consciousness and be felt. In this space, where there is nothing to cover the pain, Jesus can begin to come into the heart and heal the true source of the addiction.

One of the goals for the addict is to invite God to crack the hardened heart and allow His life to restore its sensitivity. As this happens, "objects of lust" can be seen as the people that they are; dear to God, not sexual toys.

Considering the reality of his addiction and its destructiveness to his relationships, emotional life, and productivity can have a beneficial effect for the addict. Honestly and squarely facing the "fruit" of the addictive slavery can be a helpful element in recovery.

Notes

Personal

References

[1] Andrew Comiskey, *Pursuing Sexual Wholeness* (Florida: Creation House, 1989) 153.

[2] Alexander Lowen, *Narcissism: Denial of the True Self* (New York: MacMillian, 1983)

[3] Gordon Dalbey, *Healing the Masculine Soul* (Waco: Word Books, 1988) 21.

[4] Gerald May, *Addiction and Grace* (San Francisco: Harper & Row, 1991) 13.

[5] Dr. Ralph Earle and Dr. Gregory Crow, *Lonely All The Time* (New York: Simon & Schuster, 1989) 16.

[6] Dr. Ralph Earle and Dr. Gregory Crow, *Lonely All The Time* (New York: Simon & Schuster, 1989) 17.

Homework

Homework

1. Chronicle the escalation of your sexual addiction. Look for patterns – times when the addiction becomes increasingly entrenched and involving of your time and energy.

2. Think about and describe your mental sexual obsessions.

3. What specific sexual compulsions do you act out?

4. Describe your spiritual pain (hardness of heart, cut off from tenderness, etc.).

Action Item: Describe to your accountability group the most painful relational consequence resulting from your sexual acting out.

Intervention in the Addictive Cycle

Chapter Four

By pondering past failures, one can begin to see what his specific triggers are. In making a conscious effort to unveil them, triggers rise up out of the subconscious and come to the forefront of the mind. This gives the addict a chance to observe the moment that he has been triggered. Once the addict is aware that he has been triggered, he can then choose a positive action such as calling a friend for prayer, or practicing the presence of God, rather than acting out.

Flee the evil desires of youth, and pursue righteousness, faith, love and peace, along with those who call on the Lord out of a pure heart. (2 Timothy 2:22)

The Addictive Cycle Described

Although particulars of each individual's sexual addiction may differ, the activities of his cycle will follow a generalized pattern. The addiction cycle includes **preoccupation**, **ritualization**, **sexual compulsivity** and **despair**. [1]

Stage One: Preoccupation or "Sexual Pressure"

The addictive cycle begins at the point where the addict's thoughts become focused on his behavior of choice. During the preoccupation phase, the addict's mental energy is directed towards reaching a mood-altering high without actually acting-out sexually. He thinks about sex to produce a trance-like state of arousal designed to blot out the current pain of reality.

Sexualized mental obsessions are prominent during the preoccupation stage, choking out most external demands for attention. Thinking about sex and plotting how to reach orgasm can continue for minutes or hours before a transition to the next stage of the cycle occurs.

What follows is a quote from a man who describes his specific preoccupation:

> But, a couple of years back, I started looking around a lot, looking for a hitchhiker to pick up, someone I could come on to. You would not believe the time and energy I spent just looking. And when I wasn't looking, I was thinking about looking, and thinking about what I would do once I found what I was looking for. The fantasy was the thing. It only takes so much time to have sex...well, that was what got me to the point where I'd be at work, but my mind wouldn't be there at all. I'd count the minutes until I got off work so I could drive around, hoping some wild thing would happen. [2]

During the preoccupation phase, the addict experiences a heightening of energy due to the release of adrenaline in his body , as well as euphoric emotions associated with thoughts of giving into the sexual activity. As all of the aspects of his being become focused on sex, he experiences a powerful force or pressure which the Bible calls temptation (James 1:13-14). The name for this stage, preoccupation or "sexual pressure," has to do with a temptation that the addict has come to habitually entertain.

Stage Two: Ritualization or "Acting Out"

Addicts use rituals to enhance their mental preoccupation, excitement and euphoria. Rituals stoke the fires lit by erotic preoccupation. Rituals are regularly followed methods of preparing for sexual activity to take place. Rituals involve a specific context, especially cruising areas (singles' bars, adult bookstores, beaches, certain streets, public bathrooms, stairwells) in which the person focuses his sexual search and brings what began as a fantasy closer to happening. This heightens the sexual intensity of his experience, which is now steadily approaching orgasm.

The ritual in the example cited above (see Stage One) is driving around. This driving was used to extend the time of euphoria and obsession. The anticipation of encountering the desired sexual object builds momentum and excitement.

Other examples of rituals are:

The exhibitionist taking regular routes or settings.

The incestuous parent making elaborate plans to be alone with the child.

The female addict showing up at a local hotel during the cocktail hour.

The fetishist or cross-dresser shopping for clothes at garage sales.

The compulsive masturbator secretly frequenting seldom-used bathrooms on his college campus in order to find erotic graffiti.

In addition to these more obvious rituals, **negative rituals** are often a part of the addict's cycle. He may pick a fight with his spouse and binge in self-righteous anger. He may think, "She's not putting out, so I'm justified in finding it elsewhere." Regular self-defeating behavior may also be a part of the set-up. Living from crisis to crisis adds energy to rituals. After a tough day the addict might think, "I deserve it because I have had such a bad day," or "I need it to survive."

Once the addict has begun his ritual, the chances of stopping that cycle diminish greatly. He is giving into the pull of the compelling sex act. With the ritual engaged, the momentum is too great and the will too weak, resulting in the inevitable act that relieves the building sexual tension. Although the word "ritual" accurately describes the repetitive acts of getting ready for the sex act, these patterns change as the addict's need for a fix escalates and he moves to a new kind of sex act. A worsening addiction demands greater variety, which thus may change the forms of expression of the different stages. For the sake of simplicity we have called this leg of the cycle, "acting out." Even though the addict may not reach orgasm, or make a sexual contact, he was hoping to, and willing, if only the circumstances had been "right."

For example, Joe has a field job. Between appointments he begins to experience "sexual pressure" in the form of erotic thoughts and a strong desire to cruise for a prostitute. He is still at the point of temptation until he turns down a street known as a prostitute hang-out. On this particular day he does not make a connection. He goes on to his next appointment and then home to his wife. Even though he made no sexual contact, he still "acted out" that day because he was actively looking to engage in the sex act.

Stage Three: Sexual Compulsivity or "Sex Act"

Sexual compulsions have to do with the inability to control the particular sexual activity. Engaging compulsively in these acts is the addiction's cornerstone. The compulsive act, which normally ends in orgasm, is perhaps the starkest reminder of the degradation involved in addiction, as a person finds himself reduces to a terrible slavery, his will paralyzed. Examples of what we mean by the sex act include:

For the voyeur, it is the actual sighting

For the homosexual, the sex act with a member of the same sex

For the pedophile, sexual contact with a child

For the fetishist, masturbating in his girlfriend's underwear

The sex act is the breaking point in the sexual pressure that began the cycle. For a time there is a type of resolve for the addict. The physical pressure release also brings an abrupt end of denial and sanity-bending rationalizations that allowed the addict to get as far as he did. The fog of lies and illusions suddenly lifts. The "sex act" is the point at which sin becomes undeniable. It is hard evidence that the scriptures have been violated and the mood suddenly changes.

Guilt – Despair

Despair is the sharp emotional pain that follows the addict's realization that he has fallen again. Like a dog, he has returned to his vomit. Remorse stabs his heart as he is forced to look at the depravity of his heart. The addict feels hopelessly trapped because he is powerless in preventing his compulsions from overpowering his life time and time again. The addict also feels the guilt associated with sin. He has betrayed God, possibly his wife, and his own sense of integrity as a Christian man of character. Guilt and despair are the part of the cycle that had previously been eclipsed by the addict's denial and distorted thinking in the first part of the cycle. But when he comes to his senses, he promises himself he will never do it again. Now that he has come to the end of another cycle, he can't help but notice reality, in all its ugliness, staring him in the face. At a superficial level the addict hopes that this will be the last battle. Yet somewhere within his heart remains a deeper pocket of resignation to the nauseating (and yet exciting) roller-coaster ride of alternating euphoria and misery produced by the addiction.

Stage Four: The Resolution

With the end of the cycle the addict can go one of two ways. He can either get help or sink back into familiar patterns of denial that submerge his pain. The thought of sincerely getting help is very threatening because, 1) he might really have to give up his addiction and, 2) he would be forced to admit that he is out of control. Usually the fear of being known and the shame of shattering the public façade of the "good Christian" are too much for the addict so he resolves never to act out again, yet without breaking the stranglehold of secrecy. This promise to himself is a vow that seems sincere at the time, but is really an oath of self-sufficiency and a type of denial. "He flatters himself" into thinking he can handle the problem alone. The phrase, "This time I see I really am addicted. I don't need to tell anyone," becomes the doorway into another cycle.

Despair builds with each addictive cycle. Because the addict hides his secret life, he tries to go it alone but cannot withstand the painful isolation (though he doesn't admit this to himself). Even though he may feel like a fraud and a coward, these feelings are insufficient to motivate him to meaningful change. Eventually the need to medicate his guilt and remorse propels him into another cycle of seeking sexual euphoria. Self-hatred increases with each relapse, supercharging the unmanageability of his life.

The addictive cycle produces its own pain, which will continue to multiply until external intervention takes place. No addict can overcome the power of his addictive cycle on his own. Part of the sickness of addiction is the delusion whereby one believes oneself able to be set free without the assistance of other people. God does not give us grace to find freedom by ourselves. Rather, He is willing to let us stay miserable in our muck until we are ready to commit ourselves to the body of Christ, where the grace for freedom is made readily available through the fellowship.

Intervention in the Addictive Cycle

Initial intervention in the addictive cycle is not even a possibility until the addict reckons with the fact of a fallen world, and a culture fully infected with fallen values, attitudes, and norms. The addict must first acknowledge that the way of the world is the way of addiction, and be willing to reject the world's ways with its many enticements and snares. The sexual behavior of the world is orchestrated by *"the ruler of the kingdom of the air, the spirit who is now at work in those who are disobedient"* (Eph 2:2).

Satan desires each of us to discard the ways of God's Kingdom of love. Awareness that Satan is our personal enemy makes freedom more compelling. Freedom from the world's captivity and influence is possible when, within the fellowship of believers, a covenant is made to reject the values of its culture. Also, the addict must gain an understanding of what triggers our learned allegiance to those destructive values and ways.

The Importance of Covenant

The primary focus of the gospel is relationship with God and others. Receiving the grace of Jesus implies our surrender to God and commitment to relationship with Him. He commits Himself to us, promising to forgive our sins and bring restoration to our souls. Our promise to Him is to be what Paul calls a bondservant: one who forever makes himself a servant to the one who set him free. A covenant is an agreement between two parties to be committed to their relationship. Any successful relationship has covenant at its core and is committed to the principles of integrity that guarantee that relationship will be preserved.

Satan, the great deceiver, wants to break our covenant with God. He is not obvious in his endeavors but, instead, shows us evil from a perspective that makes it seem beautiful, so as to entice us from fellowship with God. Satan's elaborate trappings look innocent, beautiful, desirable, and pleasing to the senses. But in reality they are deadly to our spirit, with which we worship God.

Satan may appear to us as the great harlot of Revelation, dressed in the red and purple linens of Egypt, lips dripping with honey, offering us a bed sprinkled with sweet smelling spices, persuading us to drink her sensual pleasures to intoxication. She whispers in our ear that our master is gone on a long journey. "Don't worry," she says. As we partake in the temporary delights of her offerings, she gets drunk on the blood of another saint, and the life is sucked out of us. The scripture declares that,

A young man lacking sense passes through the street near her corner and he takes the way to her house. (Proverbs 7:7b-8 NASB)

Lacking the wisdom to avoid sexual immorality, the man is lured by this woman who is a personification of deception.

Suddenly he follows her, as an ox goes to the slaughter, or as one in fetters to the discipline of a fool, until an arrow pierces through his liver [the organ for cleansing poison]. (Proverbs 7:22-23 NASB)

Only a covenant with God can allow His grace to save us from involvement with this beautiful vampire. Only when we say with Job, "I have made a covenant with my eyes," and mirror his convictions, "How then could I gaze at a virgin?" can we begin to change. We also must become sober with regard to the consequences of our sin.

What is the portion of God from above or the heritage of the Almighty from on high? Is it not calamity to the unjust and disaster to those who work iniquity? Does He not see my ways and number all my steps?
(Job 31:2-4 NASB)

Although He is not vengeful, God will let us receive the consequence of our actions. If we sleep with the enemy, we will be enslaved by him. Therefore, we must flee from the world and seek Jesus, our Savior. Thus can we receive the power of the Holy Spirit to free us from our sin.

These truths are worthy of our meditation. It is essential that we have the correct perspective on our plight. Satan hides his deceptions behind a beautiful facade. (The deceitfulness of the harlot of deception can be found in Proverbs 5, 7, 9, and in Revelation 17.)

We must see beyond the physical pleasure derived from our addictions and recognize that we are forsaking our spiritual lives through fellowship with demons. When we act out, we break our end of the covenant with God.

Triggers and the Addictive Cycle

As we begin to have success in our fight against sexual addiction, we may find ourselves, at times, falling back into patterns of the addictive cycle without knowing how we got there. By the time we realize what is happening, it is often too late. Under the power of impending release, we sell our souls to the moment. Then, disgusted with ourselves, we ask Jesus to cleanse us from the vomit to which we have so unwillingly returned.

This can be avoided by discovering what has triggered our addictive response. A trigger is a catalytic event that breaks through to the addict's pain and sets into motion the addictive cycle. An example of a trigger is a man working in an office with a flirtatious woman who wears clothes that are seductive and revealing. For the male heterosexual addict, this situation could set off hours of preoccupation and fantasy that will eventually end in orgasm. In this case the trigger is the visual stimulus of the woman who becomes a sexualized object. If the addict does not know at the moment of impact that he has been triggered, he will advance into his cycle and its power will eventually become virtually irresistible.

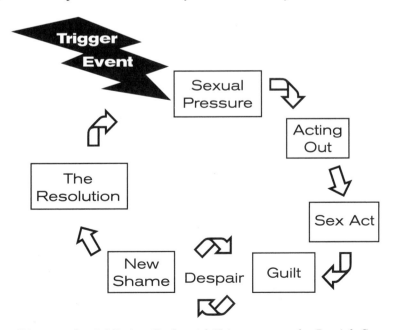

Diagram 1 : Addictive Cycle with Trigger event, by Patrick Carnes

The trigger is like the harlot of Proverbs 7:

Boisterous and rebellious…she lurks by every corner…she seizes him and kisses him, and says with brazen face…"I have come out to meet you, seek your presence earnestly, and I have found you."
(Proverbs 7:11-15 NASB)

Like this harlot, the temptations of the enemy strike us suddenly and without warning, unless we've grown savvy to Satan's ways. If the addict does not learn to recognize the enemy's deceptive strategies, then he will continue to fall under his spell. Learn to recognize your triggers!

Baseballs and Beach Balls

Identifying, naming, and taking action with respect to triggers is an important part of intervention in the addictive cycle. Most of the time what triggers the addict is outside of his conscious awareness. Often triggers are not as obvious as direct visual stimuli; they can be like fastballs that streak by almost without notice. In the case of sexual addiction, one strike usually ends the game.

By pondering past failures, one can begin to see what his specific triggers are. In making a conscious effort to unveil them, triggers rise up out of the subconscious and come to the forefront of the mind. This gives the addict a chance to observe the moment that he has been triggered. Once the addict is aware that he has been triggered, he can then choose a positive action such as calling a friend for prayer, or practicing the presence of God, rather than acting out. When a trigger can be recognized immediately, it is transformed from a fastball into a beach ball that is easy to swat from the ballpark of our covenant with God.

Common Triggers for the Sexual Addict

Triggers are often obvious. In the course of daily life, the senses are barraged with stimulating billboards, talk radio programming with the content of an audio peep show, loosely clad people on magazine covers in the local grocery store, pornography in a stand next to your local paper, and the like. However, not all triggers are plain sexual stimuli. More often, triggers of the addictive cycle have to do with seemingly unrelated environmental stresses. These break through the addict's defenses and access residual, unresolved pain. Some of this pain originates in early life experiences.

Rejection

Rejection is a common trigger, especially in marriage or dating relationships. True intimacy involves risk and the possibility of conflict. For instance, a fight with one's significant other will involve accusation, blame, and pain. At the time of the fight, the addict may only be aware of feeling angry. But, at a deeper level, the fight may be felt as an assault on his adequacy, which threatens to expose his deep fear of rejection. This assault on his broken self has accessed his painful belief system about his inferiority and worthlessness. Rather than face these feelings (partly because he wouldn't know how to deal with them), he may instead use his preferred coping method, which is turning to his addictive cycle.

Stress

Stress also acts as a trigger for the addict. It is possibly the most insidious trigger because it builds slowly and quietly. Stress applies pressure to the addict's internal world until he finally seeks relief from undue pain. A common stress pattern would involve feeling overwhelmed at work by an immense workload, then slipping into a sexual fantasy as an escape. The cycle is then underway. Stress is a common trap for the addict because addicts often do not care for themselves by getting sufficient rest. Fatigue lowers the addict's defenses, which gives unresolved pain an easier path to his conscious mind.

Abandonment

Abandonment, which is similar to rejection, can also be a trigger for sexual acting out. The loss of a loved one (such as a parent), or the removal of a favorite supervisor can connect with deep-seated childhood abandonment issues. Fleeing this intense pain, the addict may go spiraling back into his old patterns.

Present-Day Catalytic Environments

As a normal course of life, an addict may encounter work or family environments that mirror the catalytic environment of his youth. For example, the pain of having grown up in a family of origin that was very demanding and which offered little nurture may be re-encountered as an adult at a sales job with high-productivity requirements. The present-day environment may summon pain that came from earlier, similar experiences. Having to experience this environment on a daily basis may trigger old painful feelings of abandonment, a need to perform, and unacceptability, which may lead to the pain-killing cycles of sexual addiction.

Places that Trigger

Once the addict has addictive-ritual patterns in his life, certain places that symbolize sexuality can become triggers. These places may remind him of past sexual experiences, and may lure him down the path of addictive thought-patterns again. An example might be the freeway exit on the way home that leads to the adult bookstore. Or perhaps, for the habitual masturbator it is the shower stall. In advance stages of sexual addiction, almost anything can become sexualized and trigger a cycle.

Flee from Evil

For effective intervention, it will be important for the addict to intentionally avoid triggers. For example, the man who is triggered by a particular freeway exit might need to take a new route home that bypasses the triggering exit. By not passing the triggering freeway exit the addict makes a healthy choice and participates in breaking his cycle. By avoiding the trigger, he has chosen the right path, in contrast to the addictive path where his will has been in slavery. An important transition point is reached when the addict chooses, out of respect for himself, to avoid the triggering locale. Instead, he must flee from sin, shunning the temporary fix of his sexual cycle.

A prudent man sees evil and hides himself, the naive proceed and pay the penalty. (Proverbs 27:12)

According to the Scripture, we are responsible for our choices and must choose to avoid people, places and things that we know may lure us into greater evil. If we put ourselves in a circumstance where we may be overwhelmed with temptation, we are responsible for such bad choices. It is essential that each man take the time to discover how the "kisses" of the harlot (his triggers) are personalized for him, and flee from them as best he can. This always means finding accountable relationships and, when the occasion calls for it, picking up the phone to talk and receive prayer.

Once a person identifies his triggers, intervention is possible. He can decide to do something constructive, and to avoid getting too close to the slippery slope. The addict may then opt out of the cycle by seeking support. The following diagram illustrates the two options: continuing on into the cycle, or seeking support.

It is important to state here that identifying triggers is not the same as being healed. It is only the first behavioral step in stopping the addictive cycle.

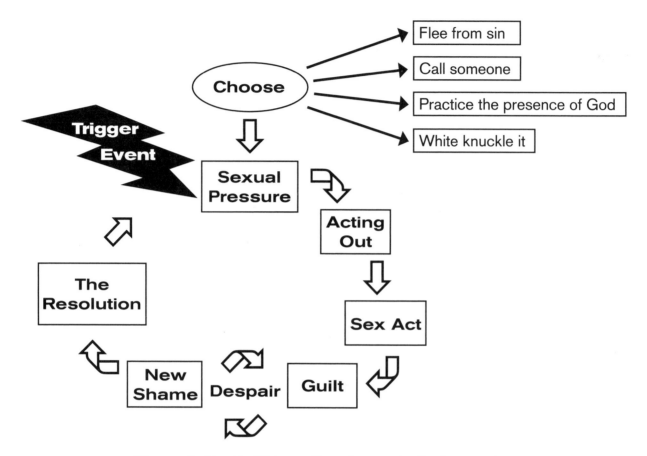

Diagram 2: Identified Trigger Gives Opportunity For Intervention

Notes
Personal

References

1 Patrick Carnes, Ph.D, *Contrary to Love* (Minneapolis: CompCare Publishers 1989) 68.

2 Dr. Ralph Earl and Dr. Gregroy Cow, *Lonely All The Time* (New York: Simon & Schuster Inc. 1989) 12.

Homework

Homework

1. List and describe any triggers that are connected to your sexual acting-out.

2. On a separate piece of paper, journal five sexual cycles that you can remember. Be specific in describing the four stages: preoccupation, ritualization, sexual compulsivity, despair. What triggered each cycle?

3. Describe any patterns that you see running through the cycles journaled above.

Action Item: Share what you have written in question three with your accountability group. Identify and become accountable to at least one way you can avoid a key trigger.

Planning Your Way of Escape

Chapter Five

We have escaped like a bird out of the fowler's snare; the snare has been broken and we have escaped. Our help is in the name of the Lord, the maker of heaven and earth. (Psalm 127:7-8)

The Importance of Breaking the Addictive Cycle

A commitment to live (permanently) within God's guidance must be made despite personal discomfort or inconvenience. Avoid looking for a quick fix! The truth is that things may feel worse (emotionally) before they get better. Don't project yourself far into future successes. They will come if you commit yourself to the day-at-a-time fight to living within God's plan for your life. Patiently accept healing as a process.

As stated in the previous chapter, the addictive cycle produces its own pain, namely the guilt, shame, and despair that results from repeated relapses. This pain actually increases the probability of falling into sexual sin again.

Underlying pain fuels addiction. If we deal with the root-level emotional hurts, the fruit that comes from our hearts will change. A renewed root will produce a renewed fruit. **However, in the first stages of healing, the task is to modify our behavior, which interrupts the driving power of the addictive cycle.**

You cannot fix an engine unless you first turn it off. In the same way, our hearts cannot be accessed for fixing unless we first shut off the mechanism of addiction. Before the heart can be healed, behavior must change. In Col. 1:21 Paul writes:

Once you were alienated from God and were enemies in your minds because of your evil behavior.

As a person gives himself over to a sinful action again and again, the mind weaves twisted thoughts to support and accommodate the duplicity of the behavior. In other words, behavior contrary to our moral and relational sensibilities breeds "futile" and "darkened" thinking. Whereas we might usually think of thoughts leading to behavior, our souls also function so that our behavior shapes our thought-life. To change behavior will make way for thoughts and feelings to be changed.

We have all experienced breaking our resolve and returning to our sin. We may use denial to avoid reality, thinking things such as, "God knows how great my need is," or "This really isn't so bad, " or "Just this one last time." But if we fail to turn firmly from our sin, we will always remain vulnerable to distorted thinking and relapses. Healing does not come to us as we passively wait for it. Rather, a person can choose to fight and win by God's empowerment or drown in his sin.

Change begins with actions. Changing behaviors eliminates the need for the distorted thinking formerly used to justify sin. Our thinking will become more truthful. This reduces the addictive cycle's power to drive behavior and allows us to get to the deeper issues which fuel the addictive machine. In our covenant with God, our part is to become obedient to His Word. His part is to supply supernatural power and grace to keep us from sin. Paul underscores this in his letter to the Philippians:

Continue to work out your salvation with fear and trembling [our part], for it is God who works in you to will and to act according to His good purpose. (Phil 2:12-13)

In other words, the way to take hold of the grace God offers to us is to choose to obey Him. By repenting of sin and deciding to obey we are, so to speak, turning the faucet, to which God responds by pouring forth living water. We are foolish to passively wait for living water without turning the faucets of our wills. To let Jesus work in us means we need to let Him deal with the self-will whereby we unseat God and take His throne by insisting on doing things our way. We need to actively choose to do things His way. Then, seeing that we are serious, He happily obliges us with abundant divine power.

Essential Tactics for Stopping Relapses

Living Inside God's Guidance

Relapse happens, in part, because of ignorance about what behaviors we have agreed upon in our covenant with God. If we do not know what God has said about sexual sin, and are not doing anything about our ignorance, then we have decided to live outside of His guidance. It is critical that we do not look to the norms of this world for our sexual guidance. The advice found in newsstand magazines does not have authority over Scripture. Each Christian needs to know what is truly "normal" from God's point of view. God means for us to engage with others sexually only within the bonds of heterosexual marriage. This precludes sexual fantasy or behavior outside of that context.

Living inside of God's guidance involves a commitment to staying in accountable relationships. Bringing things to the light through honest sharing is the best way to stay out of the "I can do it myself" trap. If a man is committed to the idea that his own strength is sufficient and that he does not need to be accountable to others, he will eventually slide back into his addiction . If left unchecked, the addictive death spiral will suck him back into a pattern of relapse.

After having been free awhile, a return to relapse will often spawn doubt in the addict's mind. He may begin to think that the gospel is not true and that God has forgotten him. In truth, he failed to attend to his triggers, rationalized his behavior and so made bad choices. Departing from accountability, he probably thought something like:

"This isn't so hard. I can do it my way"
or
"This homework is too much work. I can't see the value anyway"
or
"I'm back under control now. If it gets out of control again I'll come back"
or
"Attending this group is too time consuming. I have better things to do with my time"
or
"These guys are really perverted. I guess I really don't have a problem after all."

A commitment to live (permanently) within God's guidance must be made despite personal discomfort or inconvenience. Avoid looking for a quick fix! The truth is that things may feel worse (emotionally) before they get better. Don't project yourself far into future successes. They will come if you commit yourself to the day-at-a-time fight to living within God's plan for your life. Patiently accept healing as a process.

Develop a Low Risk Life-Style

The homework exercises for the last chapter were designed to help you begin to identify specific triggers and places that provoke the need to deaden pain through acting out. You can use this information to build a lower-risk lifestyle.

If you examine your life carefully and honestly you may discover that the environments you place yourself in support your addiction. In other words, the details of your life may actually be arranged to support and enable the sexual sin from which you supposedly want to escape. At one level you do want to escape. Yet, at another, your sneaky heart likes directing you towards situations that allow for "irresistible" temptation. Ask yourself if this is true. You will want to be brutally honest here because your mind will want to deny the truth. For example, you may rent videos from a store with a tempting X-rated section when there is another store that does not offer that trigger. Or you may have a habit of putting yourself under tremendous financial stress through leveraging every available dime. Thus, you are often in financial crisis with its increased stress.

Since we know that stress is one of the most common triggers, we can and should arrange our lifestyles to reduce stress and lower the risk of relapse. This might mean finding a different job, developing a realistic budget, and living within our financial means. Reducing financial stress might mean selling the car on which you make payments and buying a used car for cash. Does this seem too radical? You must ask yourself how serious you are about overcoming your addiction. You will need to be radical in many ways to beat your addiction. It is common for an addict to seek to stay sober in a very high-risk environment,where circumstances that he could change make it nearly impossible to stop acting out.

In developing a low risk lifestyle it will be imperative for the addict to reduce encountering his triggers as much as possible. If you claim to desire sobriety so badly and yet refuse to make simple, common-sense changes to avoid temptation, then you need to consider how serious you really are. As fallen human beings, we are able to be quite self-deceptive. If you refuse to reduce the likelihood of encountering triggers, you are deceived in thinking yourself sincere.

Developing a low risk environment may include activities like:

Getting rid of certain TV cable stations

Eliminating the VCR from your home

Finding a different route home

Confronting fellow workers about the pornography on their walls

Calling your wife with a specific time that you will arrive home from work

Finding a new, less stressful job

Developing a life-style in which you are less isolated socially

Getting your family into therapy to reduce the chaos

Quitting a job that is in the field; taking a position that is anchored to a desk

Logging onto an internet provider that automatically blocks access to pornographic sights

Cancelling your internet service altogether

A common pattern for an addict is to repeatedly enter into high-risk situations and attempt to prepare himself by merely working up his will power (as though he had reason to trust this method). He may passively let his circumstances control him. Thus, he becomes like a man who when his clothes are set ablaze fails to jump into a nearby pool of water. **We must begin to see that identifying our high-risk situations, and staying away from them, is essential and non-negotiable.**

No temptation seized you except what is common to man. And God is faithful; He will not let you be tempted beyond what you can bear. But when you are tempted, He will provide a way out so that you can stand up under it. (I Cor. 10:13)

We are wrong to believe that this passage applies when you are tempting yourself. God won't let you be overwhelmed by surprise attacks of temptation. He will let you make poor choices that cause you to overwhelm yourself. God's provision of escape is available to us to the extent that we take responsibility for our behavior. Even if we think we are victims of circumstance, our responsibility remains. In order to lower environmental risk, every struggler needs to identify and understand the following:

> What are your current stressors, repeating ritual events, dangerous environments, and sexualized stimuli?
>
> What specific phrases do you 'think' that empower you to act out: rationalizations, entitlements, rewards, excuses?
>
> What ineffective methods of escape have you tried before?
>
> What are your specific triggers?

Realize that sexual addiction is a spiritual battle for your soul

One of Satan's core strategies in addiction is misdirecting the hunger that is meant to be satiated by knowing Jesus. By luring us to feed off of false addictive food, he seeks separate us from God. Our battle with sexual addiction is therefore more than merely trying to control our behavior. It is a reminder that, just as we have a personal savior in Jesus, so do we have a personal enemy in Satan. If we allow it, our addiction will kill us spiritually. We are in a battle for our lives. Our remaining time on earth holds the promise of freedom in Christ, or the alienation of addiction. Sin, at its core, is separation from God. Ongoing sin is ongoing separation.

When our sexual activity moves us beyond God's moral boundaries it has become a destroying lust. Our battle with addiction is ultimately a spiritual war. We must, therefore, rely on spiritual means to win. Choosing life means entering into a real relationship with God through the Holy Spirit. It is only the power of the Holy Spirit working in us that causes us to bear fruit in the Kingdom. He is our Counselor in times of crisis, but we must choose to listen to His voice. He is the Spirit of truth, but we must be willing to come out of denial. He is our Teacher and will remind us of all that Jesus has said, but only if we are seeking God's truth (see John 14:16-17, 26). Real healing can only take place to the extent that we enter into an ever-deepening relationship with Jesus through the Holy Spirit.

Being sincere is not enough; we need the power of God. That power comes through developing a personal relationship with Him. Intervention in our addictive activities gives us the time and place to turn toward God.

Developing Your Plan of Escape

If we are going to avoid relapses, then we must plan our lives accordingly. This means developing a plan of escape in preparation for emergency situations.

Consider how airlines prepare their attendants for emergencies. First, they must think of all the possible emergencies that could happen. Next, they must develop policy and procedure for each emergency. Then, a crucial step is to train the attendants what to do in times of emergencies. This training involves memorizing emergency plans so as to perform them automatically and well. The procedures must become the flight attendants' reflex so they will not panic with the passengers when the emergency actually occurs. If they have been prepared, they can remain calm and many lives may be saved.

Our task in preparing for escape from potential relapses is analogous. In developing our plan, we must be thoroughly ready so that when the time comes, we know what to do and can avoid a "crash" if at all possible. Do not merely develop a plan of escape; rehearse it again and again until it becomes a part of you. This means that you need to have worked-out a plan long before an emergency occurs.

Crucial steps to forming a good plan:

Get involved and stay in accountable relationships

We must establish new rituals for ourselves. Rather than destructive rituals, the Scripture prescribes healthy ones such as confessing sin (James 5:16), walking in the light (I John 1:5-7), plowing up the fallow ground (Hosea 10:12), and carrying one another's burdens (Gal. 6:2). The body of Christ is intended to be a place where we can experience the transforming love of God. We need the priestly ministry of others in the body of Christ. God has chosen His body to help mediate the indwelling presence of Christ through the Holy Spirit and prayer. God will use other Christians to whom we open our hearts to bring His healing grace to us.

Identify your sobriety

Each man or woman must clearly and firmly establish his or her own sexual boundaries regarding his or her sexuality. If you don't know where to start, then start with something that you know. The scripture is very clear about adultery, joining yourself with prostitutes, incest, and the like. Those are firm boundaries. Some people may feel that they cannot eliminate masturbation at first, or that they are not sure the scripture calls for abstinence from this activity. The important thing is to establish firm boundaries as a starting place, and know what is off-limits. By doing this, you can eliminate any ambiguity in your mind during times of rationalization. Boundaries can always be moved towards more abstinence if necessary. Once you decide what your boundaries are, write them out. This list will serve as an objective witness.

Confess every fall

Part of developing this grace relationship with yourself is to confess every fall to another safe person. Some people, after going through a period of time without relapsing, will plummet into a pit of self-hatred and despair when they fall. This type of person tends to look at the failure, rather than the progress made so far. This is also the type of person who does not confess his or her sin, secretly thinking he can make it alone. Through regular confession one breaks the shame and fear of failure associated with perfectionism. He also avoids the trap of sinking back into the darkness of denial. Each time we fail to confess our sin, we imperceptibly wander a little farther back into the quicksand until we are stuck and in danger of death.

Nurture yourself

In all of this planning you must take an honest look at how you care for yourself. People who've struggled with self-destructive behaviors in the past (like those involved in addiction) have a greater need to care for themselves. This is not to be confused with selfishness. Caring for yourself is agreeing with God's love for you. Develop specific concrete steps to insure that you get the rest, nutrition, fun, protection, and affirmation that you need. Alcoholics Anonymous uses the acronym H.A.L.T. when speaking about situations we need to avoid in order to care for ourselves. The letters of H.A.L.T. stand for Hungry, Angry, Lonely, and Tired. If you do what you can to not become hungry, angry, tired and lonely, or if you seek to swiftly remedy these feelings when they come, you will be treating yourself well. You have needs. It is perfectly Christian and part of God's plan to make sure they are met. You cannot truly love others until you know how to love yourself.

Develop an Action Plan

What follow are important aspects of what you must do to avoid relapses:

Know your cycle

Dismantle your denial factors

- Be aware of your triggers, stressors, mental preoccupations, ritualistic actions and specific compulsions.

    Journal them in an ongoing way by using your Addiction Intervention Weekly Assignments worksheet. Be able to identify when you are in any part of your cycle. If you can separate yourself from your cycle by observing yourself, even when you are going through it, then you will be able to choose to take intervention steps.

    For example, let's assume one of your rituals is to pick a fight with your spouse so that you can binge in self-righteous anger. You can first become aware that any fight with your wife is a trigger. With some effort to walk in awareness of your cycle, you can anticipate its patterns. With the above example, practice will cause you to become aware that after any fight with your spouse you have been triggered and can choose to call someone for help.

- Know your deluded thinking

    Write down all the ways in which you rationalize, justify, and deny so that you can act out. Be very specific. For example, a habitual masturbator might say, "I'm not fantasizing, so this is not sin," or, "The scripture is really silent on masturbating, so there must be some grace for this." Memorize your list. When you begin to think one of these thoughts, a psychological red flag will go up and remind you that you're in a dangerous place.

Develop an action plan tailored to your needs

- Line out action steps for emergencies

    When you have been triggered you are in a cycle. After having taken careful note of the elements of your cycle, seeing any of those elements will offer you an opportunity to decide what to do about the danger you're in. It is important that you plan, what you will do to get out of a cycle once it's begun. Include the following four steps in your plan:

1. **Call someone**
    Get out of the darkness and run for the light! Get prayer! Begin to surrender any strategy, other than relying on God, to deal with the problem at hand.

2. **Begin meditating on the relevant aversion**
    Using an aversion technique simply means that you meditate on the possible negative outcome of acting out. This may be 1) imagining the possibility of contracting AIDS; 2) seeing your pastor witnessing outside of the adult bookstore as you exit; 3) concentrating on the fact that God is watching you and is actually living in you (your body is the temple of the Holy Spirit); 4) being honest about the fact that sexual sin is passed on generationally and that your sins are opening a spiritual door that allows Satan to influence your children.

    Aversion techniques are ways of applying the truth to combat denial-thoughts which empower us to act out. Meditating on the destructiveness of sin in our lives actually promotes the hatred of sin, which will help to keep us safe. (Please see attached appendix for suggestions on aversion meditation.)

3. **Plan activities to occupy unplanned down time**

   Being home alone with unplanned free time is very dangerous for some addicts who are trying to break their addictive cycle. Look ahead in your schedule regularly and fill empty spaces with some sort of planned activity - even if that activity is rest. An example of good self-care is to plan to be around friends or your spouse after you are aware you have been triggered.

4. **Practice the presence of God**

   We'll elaborate on this activity in a later chapter.

Schedule time to practice your plan

- **Practice your action steps**

  You will need to drill yourself. Take time to practice your planned steps before you are in a crisis. Take time to practice calling a friend. Pretend that you have just been triggered and activate aversion meditation. Call your spouse periodically as you are leaving work and tell her when you are going to be home, for example. Integrate all aspects of your plan until you know them like the back of your hand.

- **Use your action plan**

  Implement the use of your action plan as a regular part of your healing. If you fail, don't give up on yourself or on God. Start over. Ask yourself what part of the plan didn't work and modify your plan if needed.

Develop a grace relationship between yourself and God

This means that you stop hiding from the reality of your brokenness. In order to do that, you must be able to receive the grace of God to forgive your failures, cleanse you of wrong beliefs, release you of your idols, free you from vows of the heart, and more. God cannot free you unless you are willing to forgive yourself and face the powerful feelings of shame that drive your addiction. You must be willing to embrace your true and broken self and participate with the Holy Spirit in your redemption. Future chapters will elaborate on this.

You are a special person to God. You are unique. God loves you, and wants to fellowship with you.

Homework

Personal Action Plan for Cycle Management

This action plan is a way for you to take personal responsibility for intervention in your additive cycle. Use the worksheet below to form a concrete plan of action that you will commit to using during times of temptation. Review your completed plan with your accountability group for feedback and accountability.

Worksheet

1. I will increase my awareness of and commitment to sobriety by listing specific behaviors that I have participated in which are off limits to me:

   a.

   b.

   c.

   d.

   e.

   f.

   g.

2. Write out a statement that defines your sobriety. Be specific!

3. Identify your triggers. By giving specific definition to what catalyzes your cycle, you will know when to implement your action plan.

   I know there is a high probability that I am in a cycle when one of the following happens:

   a.

   b.

   c.

   d.

   e.

   f.

   g.

   h.

4. Write out, in sentence form, the thoughts that you think to convince yourself that acting out is alright. What truths do you know that can counter these thoughts? Truth empowers you to move away from your addiction. If you can't tell yourself the truth then you are not sure why you want to give up your addiction.

Denial Thoughts

Truth from the Word of God or other truth that will counter these thoughts

a.   a.

b.   b.

c.   c.

d.   d.

e.   e.

f.   f.

I plan to speak the truth to myself using these thoughts. (This activity is called "Internal Communications on your month at a glance accountability sheet.)

5. To what extent do you understand God's guidance regarding your sexual activity? Describe your efforts to discover and live within that guidance.
Are there any changes you plan to make?

Specific actions I can take when I become aware of:

1) being triggered,

2) being preoccupied with sexual thoughts,

3) breaking sobriety.

I commit to the following steps:

Call someone. Commit to contacting one of the following people:

_____ Ph.Wk: _____ Hm: _____

_____ Ph.Wk: _____ Hm: _____

_____ Ph.Wk: _____ Hm: _____

_____ Ph.Wk: _____ Hm: _____

Begin Aversion Meditation or meditation on other truths in the Bible.
The following passages have helped me:

Aversion:

_____

_____

_____

Other truth, including what I loose if I act out:

_____

_____

_____

_____

Plan to be around other people. Below are some people or places that will keep me out of isolation:

1. _____

2. _____

3. _____

4. _____

12-Step Groups I will attend:

Group Name	Day of Mt'g	Phone	Contact Person	Address Rm #
_____	_____	_____	_____	_____
_____	_____	_____	_____	_____
_____	_____	_____	_____	_____
_____	_____	_____	_____	_____
_____	_____	_____	_____	_____
_____	_____	_____	_____	_____

Confession of sin with prayer: Below are people to whom I can confess my sin and receive prayer:

_____

_____

_____

_____

Ask God to come into my cycle. Below are the actions I plan to take in accessing the presence of God:

_____

_____

_____

_____

What are the high-risk aspect of your lifestyle? Are there any environments, objects, or ways of living that empower your addiction? What could you change? Write out specific steps you can take to lower your risk.

1. _____

2. _____

3. _____

4. _____

I plan to avoid certain triggers in my life by taking these actions:

Trigger	Action to be Taken	Date/Deadline
_____	_____	_____
_____	_____	_____
_____	_____	_____
_____	_____	_____
_____	_____	_____
_____	_____	_____

I plan to discipline myself to use the following helps:

Month-At-A-Glance accountability sheet.

Weekly Intervention Worksheet

Doing my reading and homework each week

Action Plan. Write out your plan of escape in paragraph form. I plan to share this paragraph on (date) _____.

_____

_____

_____

_____

_____

I will practice my action plan in non-emergency phases so I can use it instinctively in times of emergency. (After practicing your plan record it below.)

Planned date _____   Actual date _____   ☐ Successful
                                                                  ☐ Unsuccessful

Planned date _____   Actual date _____   ☐ Successful
                                                                  ☐ Unsuccessful

Planned date _____   Actual date _____   ☐ Successful
                                                                  ☐ Unsuccessful

Planned date _____   Actual date _____   ☐ Successful
                                                                  ☐ Unsuccessful

Planned date _____   Actual date _____   ☐ Successful
                                                                  ☐ Unsuccessful

Action Item: Write out your action plan for cycle management and share it with your accountability group.

Surrendering to God

Surrender is a change of attitude, a change of heart. Surrender is a spiritual activity which goes beyond religion and releases our precious bastions of self-will into the hands of God. In giving ourselves over to God, we die to the idea that our life is our own. We reckon with the fact that we've been bought by the blood of Jesus, and that we are therefore to spend our lives for Him. This reality, when taken seriously, will radically alter our priorities. If we see Him truly, as little creatures looking up to our great Creator, the humble, natural response will be to give Him our full attention.

Chapter Six

You do not delight in sacrifice, or I would bring it; you do not take pleasure in burnt offerings. The sacrifices of God are a broken spirit; a broken and contrite heart, O God, you will not despise. (Psalm 51:16-17)

The Law of Sin and Death

Sin plagues all of mankind because it "dwells in our members" (Romans 7:20-23). Since Adam, we have all suffered with the constant pull of sin, toward death. Sin is more than the bad things that we do. As long as we live in this body and away from the Lord, we are destined to wrestle with our own "evil desire," and the resulting temptation of sin (James 1:14).

The pervasiveness of sin in our lives forces us to reckon with our inability to subdue our own rebelliousness. Paul confessed his own powerlessness over sin:

I do not understand my own actions. For I do not do what I want, but I do the very thing I hate...I can will what is right, but I cannot do it. For I do not do the good I want, but the evil I do not want is what I do. Now if I do what I do not want, it is no longer I that do it, but sin which dwells within me. (Romans 7:15, 18-20)

Everyone can relate to this passage. The only antidote to sin is being reborn through the "second Adam," Jesus. When a person is saved, freedom from sin and its effects are made available. Still, the person must be taught how to appropriate God's grace. The problem is that, even after salvation, we often use the same coping methods for overcoming the flesh that we used in our pre-Christian state; we continue to rely upon our own strength and efforts to control. Many or most of us have never been taught how to take hold of Christ's grace.

Our Illusion of Control

In essence, there are two ways to wrongly attempt to take control of our own lives: The first way we deceive ourselves into thinking we're in control is by rebelling against God's laws regarding sexual sin. The rebellious heart cries out, "I am tired of suppressing the real (sensual) me by following a bunch of rules that make me feel guilty and don't fit my inner life." Thus the sexual addict fools himself into thinking that he has the right to determine his life. As previously mentioned, he does this through rationalization, denial, and distorted thinking which justify acting out. He uses sex to gain affirmation and love. He lies to himself, saying that his chaotic, unmanageable life is enriched rather than degraded by many sexual encounters.

Really, though, he uses his immoral lifestyle to feel in control. He uses it for adequacy, closeness, and as a painkiller, always thinking that he is in control of his situation and objects of lust. The addict uses his sexual acting-out to keep his painful, twisted, and diseased inner feelings from surfacing.

This attempt at control merely fuels the addictive process. Eventually, because it is out of sync with God's created order, it stops working.

"It begins with an overpowering desire for a sexual high, relief, pleasure or escape.

It provides satisfaction.

It is sought repeatedly and compulsively.

It then takes on a life of its own.

It becomes excessive.

Satisfaction diminishes.

Distress is produced.

Emotional control decreases.

Ability to relate deteriorates.

Ability for daily living is disrupted.

Denial becomes necessary.

It takes priority over everything else.

It becomes the main coping mechanism.

The coping mechanism stops working.

The party is over." [1]

Before long, his attempt to manage his life through unmanageable means collapses, leaving only destruction.

The second way the addict may try to use his own strength to control his life is by forcefully suppressing the truth about the sexually addictive patterns of his heart. Through this "religious" process, he may try not to think about sex. Instead, he may white-knuckle his way through temptation, stay busy in his good Christian life, claim his healing, confess he is a new creature, try harder to snap out of it, condition himself with rubber bands, take cold showers. But merely draping a sheet of "holy facts" over the addiction only causes the sexual tension and pressure to build until another cycle erupts with more fury than before.

All people, not just addicts, are in the habit of using their own personal power and will to control their lives. This is the fallen way of man. It is the wisdom of the world. However, it is a solution doomed to failure. Pitting our own strength against the law of sin and death is like trying to extinguish fire with gasoline. In trying to use our own strength we become gods unto ourselves and actually decrease the Lord's access to our dilemma. Our ability to cope becomes our god, an attempt to fix our lives without the Creator. Paul made this point, regarding the futility of self-designed solutions when he spoke into the ascetic tendencies of the Colossians:

Since you died with Christ to the basic principles of this world, why, as though you still belonged to it, do you submit to its rules: Do not handle! Do not taste! Do not touch! These are destined to perish with use, because they are based on human commands and teachings. Such regulations indeed have an appearance of wisdom, with their self-imposed worship, their false humility and their harsh treatment of the body, but they lack any value in restraining sensual indulgence. (Col. 2:20-23)

Mobilizing our own efforts to control our lives through a set of rules may have the appearance of wisdom but, according to Paul, lacks any real value in restraining sensual indulgence. Why is this true? Because trying to follow the rules inevitably becomes its own sensual indulgence. This method does not rely on God and, therefore, lacks humility. By adopting self-designed solutions, the addict is in a subtle way saying, "I can be godlike. I can be infinite. I can trust in me!" Trying to handle lust himself, the addict becomes grandiose, and sees himself as stronger than he really is. Completely missing the value of acknowledging his weaknesses, he separates himself from God's power and desire to change his inner life.

God, however, has an effective prescription for our sexual addictions:

Sow with a view to righteousness, reap the fruit of unfailing love; break up your fallow ground, for it is time to seek the Lord until He comes to rain righteousness on you. (But you have planted wickedness, you have reaped evil, you have eaten the fruit of deception. Because you have trusted in your own strength). (Hosea 10:12-13)

A way to sow towards righteousness and to reap the experience of the kindness of God is to break up the fallow (hard) ground of our own methods of control. Instead, we seek the Lord for strength. Only then can He begin to rain righteousness upon us. It is at this point that the power of habitually acting out will be broken.

The Process of Turning Our Lives Over to God

Surrendering to God cannot be done alone, in a vacuum. We need the assistance of those who have walked this road before! We need others to call us out of our darkness, to challenge our denial, to help us see the devices by which we skirt the will of God, and to support us in prayer as we surrender. It is they who walk with us through our pain, help us see relationships clearly, and encourage us when our strength is flagging. We need the community and, in particular, a accountability group. Surrender can only happen in the context of community.

Surrender is an act of our will

The time has come to make a decision to turn our wills over to God. All journeys start with a first step. We must surrender decisively.

No one is exempt from surrendering to God. Paul had a "thorn in the flesh" which he begged God to take away (no doubt he had done everything in his power to control it, or make it go away). God's response to his petition was:

My grace is sufficient for you, for my power is made perfect in weakness. (II Corinthians 12:9)

We are called to walk in surrendered weakness so that God's power can reign over sin's death grip on our flesh. As we begin to walk in weakness, we may feel very vulnerable and out of control. It is at that point that God will show us His faithfulness. But we must be willing to stand in the fire, looking straight up to God to fill the emptiness and pain that will surface as we stop acting out. In prayer we ask Him to empower our wills so as to withstand the allure of idolatry.

Paul's response to his personal trial and to God's response was a notable one, and the only effective one:

Most gladly, therefore, I will rather boast about in my weaknesses, so that the power of Christ may dwell in me. Therefore, I am content with weaknesses. (II Corinthians 12:9-10a NASB)

He went on to say about Christ,

For indeed He was crucified because of weakness, yet He lives because of the power of God. For we also are weak in Him, yet we shall live with Him because of the power of God directed toward you. Test yourselves to see if you are in the faith; examine yourselves! Or do you not recognize this about yourselves, that Jesus Christ is in you – unless indeed you fail the test? (II Corinthians 13:4-5 NASB)

What is the test Paul is talking about? He asks us to test and see if God's power is operating through our weakness – are we surrendered to God? Surrender is a major principle of God's kingdom. If we do not accept this truth, we close the door of our lives to God and the healing He longs to bring.

To remain surrendered, we must not forget the futility and unmanageability of our own lives apart from God. Addicts know all too well the deep despair that marks the end of a sexual cycle. At that time it is easy to think: "This is too painful. I'm going to stop. I'll never do this again." But, as surely as they know despair, addicts all have experienced the power of denial. Addicts easily, automatically fool themselves so as to believe their lame pseudo-resolutions. In truth, our historical denial about our need to surrender to God has regularly and dangerously deceived us. This state of denial is reminiscent of the Lord's words to the church of Laodicea:

You say, 'I am rich; I have acquired wealth and do not need a thing.' But you do not realize that you are wretched, pitiful, poor, blind, and naked. I counsel you to buy from me gold refined in the fire, so you can become rich; and white clothes to wear, so you can cover your shameful nakedness; and salve to put on your eyes, so you can see. Those whom I love I rebuke and discipline. So be earnest, and repent.
(Revelation 3:17-19 RSV)

We need to repent of our pride in thinking we are not in need of Jesus. It is critical that we allow the Holy Spirit to give us the eye salve that we need to see our own devices. We must "hit bottom" and say, "I can't fix myself."

Facing the Fear of Powerlessness and Losing Control

At this point, you may be thinking, "I have tried this before and have always ended up back in my old cycle." Hidden in this objection is the fear of being out of control and vulnerable to the care of an unseen God. All of us must acknowledge that surrender to God is not only an act of the will, but that it is an issue of trust. Learning to trust God is analogous to a child learning to ride a bicycle with no hands. In the beginning, the release of the handlebars comes with the anxiety of wondering if the tires will stay straight. Little victories, in letting go and not crashing, allow for incrementally longer victories, until an expert, hands-free bike-rider is born. By learning to trust for short spans of time, trust grows and, with it, so does skill.

In the process of learning to surrender to God, our hands will inevitably return to the handlebars as we return to our own strength and methods for trying to cope with our sexual addiction. This reality is heralded by finding ourselves back in isolation. When this happens, we can know that we have not yet learned how to trust.

Our surrender to God is ultimately bound to our involvement with community. Submitting ourselves to the crucible of confession and the healing dynamic of the body life of the church provides the experience that builds trust in God. In our voluntary decision to embrace Christ-centered community, we walk out our surrender to God by learning to trust a source outside of ourselves. Trusting that God's strength will emerge out of our surrender is the bridge from the futility of self-effort to walking in the power of resurrection life. Only through the power of death and resurrection can our lives be transformed. We need to put our trust in God's ability to restore us, and in the fact that He knows best when He directs us to seek this healing within the body of Christ.

Meditating on His promises regarding restoration will bolster our trust:

I am confident of this very thing, that He who began a good work in you will perfect it until the day of Christ Jesus. (Philippians 1:6)

Be anxious for nothing, but in everything in prayer and supplication with thanksgiving let your requests be made known to God. And the peace of God which surpasses all comprehension, shall guard your hearts and your minds in Christ Jesus. (Philippians 4:6-7)

As we seek the wisdom of God, He will restore us to peace. Proverbs 2 is about the liberating power of wisdom for those who seek it from God. It gives this promise to those who cry out to God:

For wisdom will enter your heart, and knowledge will be pleasant to your soul; discretion will guard you, understanding will watch over you, to deliver you from the way of evil, from the man who speaks perverse things; to deliver you from the strange woman, from the adulterer who flatters with her words. (Proverbs 2:10-12)

James 1:5 promises that if we lack wisdom and ask for it, it is available to us. God will be sure to answer our request. It compels us to ask God for wisdom. This again points to the need to rely on someone outside of ourselves to be our Source for truth and stability, lest we remain self-focused, inward, and closed to wisdom. For the humble man, there is hope. He has a chance to be confronted in his distorted thinking and then restored to sanity. God resists the proud and gives grace to the humble. If we will humble ourselves before the mighty hand of God, He promises to heal us (James 4).

And if we fail to stay sober, we must keep on trusting in God – trusting that He is kind and loving and does not give up on us. He gives a fresh start daily through the blood of Jesus.

The Lord's loving kindness indeed never ceases, for His compassions never fail. They are new every morning; Great is Thy faithfulness. 'The Lord is my portion' says my soul, 'Therefore I have hope in Him.' (Lamentations 3:22-24)

Facing our powerlessness is a Christian step. We see it in the gospels, when Jesus walked down that sandy beach and said to Peter, "Follow me." Roughly translated this means: "Drop you nets, your business, family, everything and follow me." Peter was at that moment faced with the decision to give up all his security and to be out of control. He had to entrust himself completely to Jesus for his provisions. This is exactly what He asks us to do as we admit to Him our powerlessness over sexual sin. Jesus said, "He who has found his life shall lose it, and he who has lost his life for my sake shall find it." We must risk giving up our old ways to find new life in Jesus. Like Peter, Jesus is calling us to a spiritual journey.

As long as we cling to our solutions, they will continue to deceptively promise success, and yet bring failure. Our sexual addiction is more powerful than we are and will always win. Only when we let go does the freedom begin to come. We can only enter the Kingdom of God if we become like little children, dependent on the Spirit of God. In the following chapters we will cover further steps to surrendering our old broken selves and corresponding sexual patterns to God.

Facing the Fear of Loss

As we admit our powerlessness over our sin and begin to release ourselves to God, we may begin to feel what we have been trying to avoid: the feelings of loss associated with losing our primary relationship in life – our sexual addiction. The end of that relationship is a true death; there may be feelings of loss and anger. Admitting that we are powerless over our sexually addicted life is the first step in getting ready to face this loss. It is letting go of that source of nurture. Stating that our lives have become unmanageable is acknowledging that sexual addiction is not the source of nurture that we want.

Doing the next right thing

You might also be thinking, "What is the next thing I can do in surrendering to God?" My suggestion is, relax and begin to focus on God. You must learn to believe that God alone can empower you sufficiently. Thus, knowing your powers to be inadequate, you will by faith tap into God's power which will flow through you. Surrender to God is an active declaration of your inability to do life without His help.

> Addiction cannot be defeated by the human will acting on its own, nor by the human will opting out and turning everything over to divine will. Instead, the power of grace flows most fully when human will chooses to act in harmony with divine will. It is the difference between testing God by avoiding one's own responsibilities and trusting God as one acts responsibly. Responsible human freedom thus becomes authentic spiritual surrender, and authentic spiritual surrender is nothing other than responsible human freedom. Here, in the condition of humble dignity, the power of addiction can be overcome. [2]

When we surrender to God, we open our minds to letting Him tell us what to do next. The person who asks God to hear His voice, *with the intent to obey*, will grow in his ability to hear the Lord. Our goal is to gradually become more teachable, rather than always thinking we know what to do. The Alcoholics Anonymous Serenity Prayer is applicable here:

> God, grant me the serenity to accept the things that I can't change, courage to change the things that I can and the wisdom to know the difference.

Surrendering Our Agenda to God

One practical way to begin to turn our lives over to God is to begin to look at our agendas for life, including self-preservation and control. Each barrier to relationship with Him needs to be turned over to Him, one at a time, in prayer.

Looking at our prayer agenda

Often our prayer agenda is no more than a reflection of our need to control the outcome of our lives. We pray prayers according to our darkened understanding. If we pray at all, we are often guilty of trying to make God serve us according to our controlling way of doing things. James saw this when he wrote:

You ask and do not receive, because you ask with wrong motives, so that you may spend it upon your pleasures. (James 4:3)

An example of a self-centered prayer is: "Lord please increase my wife's sex drive," or, "Please change my wife so that she won't need so much romantic activity before sex." Both of these prayer examples reflect a selfish motive: that of not having to change how one thinks about or relates in his sexual relationship. Selfish prayer avoids letting God show us how we need to change.

By our loveless prayers, we restrict God. It is for this reason that we are not helped. God will not answer prayers that are not asked according to His will (I John 5:14). We need often to pray for wisdom from God.

Next time you are praying, listen to the words you pray. Does it sound like, "Your will be done. Your kingdom come," or, "I did it my way?" Our prayers should reflect surrender to God.

Evaluating our life's goals and lifestyles

There is a popular, modern-day view of God that is a stumbling block to our recovery. It asserts that He guarantees our time on earth to be happy, prosperous, and in line with the "American dream." Subtly, this reduces God to some sort of supernatural bellhop who is there to do our bidding, rather than the potter who is shaping us out of clay.

Some of our life goals may be keeping us from using our time wisely in the service of our recovery from sexual addiction. Healing must become a priority. It may be the case, though, that we seldom question our goals. We say, "God give me these abilities so that I can be successful according to my goals and desires," and lazily expect Him to do everything. It is vital that we first ask Him what our goals and priorities should be. He needs to be our primary priority, and our primary goal must be to know Him more.

In the same way that we need to let God speak to our life's goals, we also need to let Him show us how to change our lifestyles and patterns. Identifying high-risk areas of living will also involve letting go of the comfort associated with them. Readjusting to a new way of living will involve hard decisions and feelings of loss. In this process of dealing with sexual addiction, we may discover that pleasures we've taken for granted are in fact idols that need to be submitted to God. We must be willing to face loss so that we might gain Christ. *The actual surrender of relevant aspects of our lives is where the rubber meets the road.*

Surrendering to God means giving our lives over to Him, and efforting to learn His will. As we begin to obey His direction, our lives take on lasting change.

Throwing Out Our False Concepts of God

Listen to this scenario – a man named Fred is speaking about turning his life over to God:

> There is no way I am going to give God control of my life! He has brought everything crashing down around me, and I know that I probably deserve it. God is just a big cop in the sky waiting to whack me with his night stick when I get out of line.

It is likely that Fred is seeing God through the image of a harsh and punitive father. He is responding to a god who is not the God of the Bible at all. Fred's god is harsh, demanding and ready to punish him, rather than patient, forgiving and ready to heal him. Usually our distrust of God is rooted in misunderstanding. Sometimes we understand Him intellectually, but have not turned over the wounded places of our hearts.

> The fear may be that God, like some cosmic rapist, is going to come into the innermost parts of our lives and control our every move or thought, or stop us from doing or thinking anything that is fun; or send us off to dangerous or primitive mission fields, or force us to sell our homes and give the money to the poor, or tell us to become a rigid, narrow Christian,[3] (or an Episcopalian, or Catholic, or Charismatic or whatever would be scariest to you).

Our worship is pure or defiled inasmuch as we entertain true of false thoughts of God. It is therefore worthwhile to examine who we think God really is. But in so doing we need to look beyond what we know intellectually and examine what is in our hearts.

> Our real idea of God may lie buried under the rubbish of conventional religious notions and may require an intelligent and vigorous search before it is finally unearthed and exposed for what it is. Only after an ordeal of painful self-probing are we likely to discover what we actually believe about God. [4]

We may find that the thoughts about God hidden in our hearts actually portray a god who is earthbound, as distorted in love as our own earthly parents. Our real beliefs about God may actually fall under the category of idolatry.

> The idolatrous heart assumes that God is other than He is – in itself a monstrous sin – and substitutes for the true God one made after its own likeness. Always this God will conform to the image of the one who created it and will be base or pure, cruel or kind, according to the moral state of the mind from which it emerges...Wrong ideas about God are not only the fountain from which the polluted waters of idolatry flow; they are themselves idolatrous. The idolater simply imagines things about God and acts as if they were true. [5]

Without a willingness to trust God and His mercy, we will not be able to let go of the false consolation of our sexual cycle and its mesmerizing preoccupations. This will always require walking in the dark, where we can see very little at first. We need to honestly look at our beliefs as they are held up in the light of the scripture and destroy those beliefs that are treasonous. We must take false ideas about God off the throne and seek out the truth. This is an essential element in turning our lives over to Him.

Learning to Discern

As we open our minds to direction from above, we will also need to learn to discern God's voice from our own urges. Our ability to do so grows as we spend time with the Lord. Time spent with Him in worship, studying His Word, and dialoguing with Him will refresh us, sustain us, and cause us to grow in discernment. We should also regularly ask Him to give us a heart purely for Him, and to pour out discernment and wisdom upon us. The more serious we are to obey Him, the more He will speak to us; we should not expect God to tell us things if we have no intention of taking what He says seriously. The more we concern ourselves with His purposes and His will, the more we will enjoy the pleasure of holy conversation with Him.

Feedback from our accountability group is essential as we walk this educational path. We will be able to learn discernment if we do it in the context other Christians who have gained experience in their own trek.

Developing Personal Boundaries

Once you have given up control to God, it will mean that you have also given up controlling the people around you. It is important to note that one or more people may step into the power void and attempt to control you. If this is true, you will feel very vulnerable unless you develop healthy boundaries.

A boundary is an invisible, protective barrier that keeps others out of your places of privacy. Boundaries are physical, emotional, and spiritual lines of demarcation. When working properly, they protect us from getting hurt, or compromising our moral belief systems in our relationships with others. When boundaries are established in relationships, they keep us from intruding into the personal space of others. They help us to take responsibility for the things in our own lives, and help us to be gentle with others, careful not to reach into their arenas of responsibility without prior permission.

An example of setting a boundary is the refusal to act upon someone's attempt to motivate us through guilt. Another example that has obvious relevance to us is that of setting sexual boundaries. We are trying to establish sexual boundaries as the practical outworking of this class. Our hope is that our sexual boundaries will match those that are established in the Word of God for marriage, singleness, and gender. Many of us will need to learn how to respect the sexual boundaries of our wives. She may have boundaries on the frequency, variety, and prerequisites to love making.

Boundaries are not the same for all the people in our lives. They are based on trust, the type of relationship, and the constraints of morality. Your feelings, once you get in touch with them, will be a good barometer for whether or not your boundaries are being broken. Listening to others and caring about their feelings will help you understand and establish boundaries for relationships. Loving others as yourself is a good axiom to use as a guideline.

Boundaries are not walls – they are flexible, interactive and tempered by love (as opposed to lust). At first, your boundaries may be more like walls and feel more like anger than love. But, as you grow you will become increasingly successful at setting assertive boundaries with love.

Conclusion

Surrender is a change of attitude, a change of heart. Surrender is a spiritual activity which goes beyond religion and releases our precious bastions of self-will into the hands of God. In giving ourselves over to God, we die to the idea that our life is our own. We reckon with the fact that we've been bought by the blood of Jesus, and that we are therefore to spend our lives for Him. This reality, when taken seriously, will radically alter our priorities. If we see Him truly, as little creatures looking up to our great Creator, the humble, natural response will be to give Him our full attention. He justly deserves all that we have to give Him, and He will be sure to guide our lives far more effectively than we can.

Surrender means coming to a crossroads and a life change. To try to surrender our lust while hanging onto addiction won't work. All must be given over to Jesus and begin to allow Him to be the center of our inmost being. We look to God to give us the boundary lines that are to protect us from harm — we listen to Him so as to know what to do, and what not to do. Then, we die to our desires in obedience to Him. Our only hope is to enter into deeper communion with the Lord, and to learn what He wants us to do (because His plans are the only truly effective ones). We will discover this inasmuch as we seek Him in His Word, in prayer, and through His body, the church.

References

[1] *Sexaholics Anonymous* (Simi Valley: SA Literature, 1989) 37.

[2] Gerald G. May, M. D. , *Addiction and Grace* (San Francisco: Harper & Row Publishers, 1988) 139.

[3] J. Keith Miller, *A Hunger for Healing* (San Francisco: Harper Collins, 1991) 242-243.

[4] A. W. Tozer, *The Knowledge of the Holy* (San Francisco: Harper & Row, 1961) 3.

[5] A. W. Tozer, *The Knowledge of the Holy* (San Francisco: Harper & Row, 1961) 4-5.

Homework

Homework

For those of us who are genuine about wanting to recover from our sexual addiction,
there must be a progressive realization of our powerlessness over sin that is accompanied by a
growing awareness of personal unmanageability. The following questions are designed to reveal both
of these conditions in us. Invest the time and energy in doing these for
maximum growth.

1. List continual or excessive feelings over which you are powerless.

   List recurring fears:

   List recurring anger (list associated actions which accompany anger):

2. Describe guilt and shame regarding: any areas of not being "perfect",
   your failures with God, or men in authority:

3. Describe your powerlessness regarding avoiding intimacy
   (describe how loneliness feels):

4. Describe powerlessness regarding other feelings (self-pity, sadness, pain, jealousy, numbness):

5. List any food, drink, or medicine that you keep eating or drinking or taking even though you do
   not want to:

6. Name any compulsive actions that continue in your life such as gambling, taking financial risks
   you can't afford, spending, exaggerating stories, lying, controlling others, fixing people, etc.

7. Describe the areas of your sexual life that are out of control.

8. List any significant events of your life that you would have done anything to avoid but were powerless to stop.

9. List specifically any ways in which your life has become unmanageable that you have left out until now.

10. What have you lost due to the unmanageability of your life (relationships, money, job, relationship with God, health)?

11. Do you agree with this statement?: I admit that all my old ways of coping have not worked and will not work in the future. I admit that the control that I have had is not more than an illusion. I recognize the pervasiveness of sin in my life - specifically sexual sin - and its destructiveness to my life. I confess my powerlessness over sin and that my life is not manageable without God's Spirit working in me.

    Yes _____   No _____

12. Describe your trust level with God. What hinders a complete surrender of your life to Him? (Give 'gut' feelings, as opposed to an intellectual response.)

13. Give an example of your "insanity. " For example: Things that you have done that were crazy, even though you knew the consequences could be harmful to you. It might be ignoring medical or dental problems, financial responsibilities, compulsive or self-defeating behaviors, relational problems that were destructive to others or yourself.

14. What messages or 'tapes' do you live by that empower your self-sufficiency? List them and describe where they came from.

15. What might happen to you if you put God in control of the rest of your life?

16. Discuss your boundaries. How do you cross over the boundaries of others? Write about any fears that you have about your boundaries being violated if you give up controlling others in relationships. Do you currently have boundaries that keep God at a distance?

17. Fear of surrender may be rooted in your childhood. Describe any memories, events, interactions, etc. that may have been contributors to an inability to totally surrender to God.

18. What is the next one thing that you can commit to doing in the process of your recovery?

19. Prayer of commitment:

God, I offer myself to you–to build me and do with me as you will. Relieve me of the bondage of self, that I may better do your will. Take away my difficulties, that victory over them may bear witness to those I would help through your power, your life, and your way of life. May I do your will always. (From the *Big Book of Alcoholics Anonymous*).

If you are ready to pray this prayer earnestly before God, rewrite it in words that fit your heart's cry – add to or subtract from it, then sign and date it.

Signature: _____ Date: _____

Confession: Discovering the Cross in Community

Chapter Seven

The work Jesus did on the cross is powerful, but we must choose to access it. We have done this by faith in Jesus' work there, and were therefore saved. We must continue to access its power if we want to grow, by choosing to live in the light through confession. There, we die the painful death entailed in being honest about our secret, shameful lives.

Then those who feared the Lord talked with each other, and the Lord listened and heard. A scroll of remembrance was written in His presence concerning those who feared the Lord and honored his name. They will be mine, says the Lord Almighty, in the day when I make up my treasured possession. I will spare them, just as in compassion a man spares his son who serves him. And you will again see the distinction between the righteous and the wicked, between those who serve God and those who do not. (Malachi 3:16-18)

True Community vs. Pseudo-community

What is the purpose of God's exhortation to community? Essentially it is a call for life, which comes as we move closer to God and each other. We were wounded through the relationships of our lives, and so it is through redemptive relationships that healing will occur. God calls us together and empowers us to become a community of faith, hope and love. He enables His people to heal and enrich each other.

Also, the Lord's community is for our purification. Already created in His image, we are destined to become conformed to the likeness of Christ. The presence of healing and growth in Christ is a critical mark by which the Church can be recognized. The Church, when it is living the Gospel in a healthy fashion, gathers always around the cross. Receiving the word of Jesus' atoning death for our sins, we believe and are redeemed. Then, no longer trusting in our own works to earn salvation, we are enabled to be honest with God and one another.

Knowing that we don't have to perform extraordinary works or holy deeds to gain grace, we are freed to be truthful about our own desires, inclinations and sins. We can be truthful with one another; knowing that the truth sets us free, we learn to be lovingly honest. Honesty in our gatherings breaks the grip of our addictions. Together, constantly growing in freedom and love for one another, we are also growing in gratitude to the Lord who made community possible by His cross and rising. He has made us acceptable to the Father and, as a result, we can lay down showy masks of social virtue.

In contrast to this, there are many Christian congregations where the Word preached is not adequately lived-out in the communal fellowship. In pseudo-community no one fellowships around the cross. No one asks what the Lord is doing in the other's life. There may be good works, there may be quoting of Scripture, there may even be feeding the poor, but there is no change in the inner life of the believer.

Pseudo-community lacks power to change our inner lives because it lacks the life-giving confrontation with truth made possible through the cross. Community is for the process of increasing the life of God in us. We see in the Scriptures that, far from a mere "me and Jesus" way of life, the Christian walk is meant to be a powerful encounter with Christ directly and indirectly, as He meets us through our brothers and sisters in the faith:

Confess your sins to one another and pray for one another that you might be healed. (James 5:6)

Therefore, each of you must put off falsehood and speak truthfully to his neighbor, for we are all members of one body. (Eph. 4:25)

If we walk in the light as He Himself is in the light, we have fellowship with one another. (1 John 1:7)

You also ought to wash one another's feet. (John 13:14)

Accept one another. (Romans 15:7)

Encourage one another. (Romans15:7)

Carry one another's burdens, and in this way fulfill the law of Christ. (Gal 6:2)

Let each of you regard one another as more important than himself. (Phil 2:3)

These are precisely the characteristics and activities that describe the focus of an effective accountability group. Effective Christian community helps its members break through to God.

Since therefore, brethren, we have confidence to enter the holy place by the blood of Jesus, by a new and living way through the veil, that is, His flesh, and since we have a great priest over the house of God, let us draw near with a sincere heart in full assurance of faith, having our hearts sprinkled clean from an evil conscience and our bodies washed with pure water. Let us hold fast the confession of our hope without wavering, for He who promised is faithful; and let us consider how to stimulate one another to love and good deeds, not forsaking our own assembling together, as is the habit of some, but encouraging one another; and all the more as you see the day drawing near. (Hebrews 10:19-26)

We embrace the cross-centered activities of the community and begin to understand that our access to the holy place was opened to us by the broken body and shed blood of Jesus. Christians cannot be fully transformed outside of a Christ-centered community. If we fail to gather together with our spiritual family as God commands, we cannot expect to enjoy the full life and freedom He promises. In order to affect change, godly community must inspire faith, courage and hope in becoming like Christ. Let us, therefore, not give up meeting together.

Pseudo-community skirts around the central issue of the cross and so fails to transform the members' lives. It has a form of godliness, but lacks the power of His presence.

The Importance of the Fear of the Lord

The fear of the Lord is foundational to being transformed and sanctified before Him. The fear of the Lord has to do with looking to God rather than man for our justification. That is, we base our status as "acceptable" on God's verdict for those who put their faith in His Son, and then live accordingly, rather than live in such a way as to solicit the approval of others for our sense of value. Thus, God's will motivates us more than what any individual man or woman might. The fundamental point regarding the fear of the Lord is that God's ways bring life, blessing and prosperity, and disobedience brings death and destruction. If we understand this truth with our hearts, there is healthy reverence for developing an awareness of God as we walk out our daily lives.

The fear of the Lord is the beginning of knowledge, but fools despise wisdom and discipline. (Proverbs 1:7)

The fear of the Lord is the beginning of wisdom; all who follow His precepts have good understanding. (Psalm 111:10)

Wisdom and knowledge start with this 'fear,' which aligns us with the truth about God's perspective on reality, and focuses us on Him as our Source. If we fear Him, we love His discipline because it roots or centers us in His character and truth. The fear of God properly places us on the path of life, where God's Spirit causes us to be conformed to the image and likeness of God. Only on the path of life do we encounter the One who can fill the gaping cavity in each person's heart, the Lord of Heaven.

The fear of the Lord brings eternity into our hearts, and is connected to loving respect and awe for the One who paid for our lives. If we fear the Lord, we are more concerned about pleasing God and delighting in Him than our temporal reputation. This is the one basis for our obedience. We want to hear, "well done" when we see Him face to face. We do not want our sin to separate us from Him – we begin to hate sin because we have a true perspective regarding its effects on our relationship with God. This holy fear brings intimacy and closeness with God.

The fear of man subverts the fear of God. It causes us to hide, and prevents us from doing what the Scripture commands with regard to community. Bowing down in the fear of man, therefore, deadens the fear of the Lord. To look acceptable to men, we must hide the weak and shameful parts of our heart. Further, to be acceptable in the sight of others we go along with what they do, even when it offends the Lord. Soon, as we continue walking in this darkened state, we lose touch with the realities of our heart and can no longer open our hearts to God. We become disconnected, lukewarm, and lapse into a powerless existence.

Community operates best when there is a corporate, healthy fear of God. It increases our awareness of a Holy God living within us.

Walking in Darkness vs. Walking in the Light

If we want to walk in the fear of God, then we must walk in the light. God is light. If we spurn the sinful fig leaves of our own making, then our true selves are freed, exposed to the light of God and others. As we choose to confess what's in our hearts to others, the barriers that hide us are destroyed. Our connection to God happens in that light. As we see in the scripture that follows, He has made the strength of our fellowship with Him dependent upon the sincerity and truthfulness with which we relate to other people in the Church.

This is the message we have heard from him and declare to you: God is light; in him there is no darkness at all. If we claim to have fellowship with him yet walk in the darkness, we lie and do not live by the truth. But if we walk in the light, as he is in the light, we have fellowship with one another, and the blood of Jesus, his Son, purifies us from all sin. If we claim to be without sin, we deceive ourselves and the truth is not in us. If we confess our sins, he is faithful and just and will forgive us our sins and purify us from all unrighteousness. If we claim we have not sinned, we make him out to be a liar and his word has no place in our lives. (1 John 1:5-10)

If we say we have fellowship with God but will not confess our sin to one another, then we lie because we are still hiding. The truth is not in us yet. One who fears God wants to be cleansed from any unrighteousness that separates him from God and others, even if the cleansing hurts. He delights in the only true covering — that of the blood of Jesus. He is willing to die the painful death involved in confessing to another, in order to please God and liberate himself.

The Destructiveness of Walking in Darkness (Denial)

Walking in darkness is simply pretending that we have no sin in our lives. It is denying that we are inordinately attached to things other than God, and thus that we do not have the purity of desire for God that we should. It is, for example, walking with God for ten, fifteen, twenty years and thinking, "God is pretty much done with me." This is denial. The truth is that the closer we get to God, the weaker and more sinful we feel. It is probable that most of us who are sexually addicted and have reached the point of seeking help are in touch with our need for God. However, we may still be hiding the deep issues of the heart that need exposure to the healing light of God. Many of us are likely in the beginning stages of cleansing and confession. If we ever get to the stage where we doubt our need for cleansing, then we are back into our pattern of denial and are sinking back into the mire of darkness.

The paradox of our addiction is that it robs us of our desire for God, but gives us the opportunity to understand God's grace. As we bring our broken lives before Him, there is the opportunity to experience a deep work of His love within us.

Specific disadvantages to walking in denial:

Sin continues to have power in our lives

Walking in the darkness of our own strength and provision prevents God's power because we have not done 2 Cor 9:12: we have not gloried in our own weakness so that God's power through the blood of Jesus can be manifested in our lives.

Sin prevents the fear of the Lord

If we are out of touch with our need of God, then we simply do not fear Him or give Him priority in our lives. The Psalmist's words ring true:

An oracle is within my heart concerning the sinfulness of the wicked; there is no fear of God before his eyes. For in his own eyes he flatters himself too much to detect or hate his sin. The words of his mouth are wicked and deceitful; he has ceased to be wise and to do good. Even on his bed he plots evil; he commits himself to a sinful course and does not reject what is wrong. (Psalm 36:1-4)

David may well have been writing about the patterns of a sexual addict as he begins the morning with the preoccupation stage of his cycle.

Self-flattery is necessary for the addict because he must walk in denial if he is to continue in his sexual sin. His pride keeps him from humbly accepting his need of God's deliverance.

Sin keeps us attached to dead objects

Our denial keeps us from seeing clearly how we use broken cisterns to fill ourselves with polluted, sickening waters. Yet, because we are blind, we do not notice that we are wasting away. Without light, we remain enslaved to dead things.

How Confession Activates the Power of the Cross

God made Him who had no sin to be sin for us, so that in Him we might become the righteousness of God. (2 Cor 5:21)

Dying on our behalf, Jesus became sin, and then died. Jesus died with all of our sin and its effects, and then rose to new life, now free of sin's power. By sending His Spirit to live within believers, we can increasingly share in His resurrection life.

Because He became sin for us and now lives in us, we can now become the very righteousness of God. Jesus has made possible a glorious exchange – we receive His righteousness in exchange for our sin. Notice, however, that Jesus' work on earth *bound suffering and glory together*. Part of the message of His death and rising is that we do not have to go through what He did, because He did it for us. The other part, however, is that it is necessary to imitate Him, when it comes to sin. We must metaphorically do what He did literally – we must die to sin. And, like Him, we will only find glory (freedom and peace) to the extent that we've died to sin.

In other words, we can grow in Christ and allow His personality and character to be expressed in and through us. This work of sanctification occurs as we embrace the rhythm of Kingdom life, *death unto resurrection*. Jesus only came to resurrection life after a painful death; like Him, we must die in order to be resurrected. To die to sin and evil means that we must turn from it so thoroughly that (by God's grace), it is as though sin has the same power it would have over a dead person.

Like His death, ours feels long and painful. But afterwards, His Spirit raises us to new life in Him. Then, free from our slavery to sin, we are liberated to enjoy the Lord and His work in and through us.

Confession accesses the power of the cross

If we walk in the light as He is in the light, we have fellowship with one another, and the blood of Jesus, his Son, cleanses us from all sin. (1 John 1:7)

The rhythm of *death unto resurrection* only occurs within the church, the body of Christ. In particular, God gives much grace for new life as we confess our sins to one another. We would like to confess only to God so as to hide our sins, but that circumvents an essential part of our death to sin.

The work Jesus did on the cross is powerful, but we must choose to access it. We have done this by faith in Jesus' work there, and were therefore saved. We must continue to access its power if we want to grow, by choosing to live in the light through confession. There, we die the painful death entailed in being honest about our secret, shameful lives. Fearful of rejection and judgment, we nevertheless admit our wrongdoings. Then, through the love of our brothers and sisters in Christ and through prayer, we receive new life. Dietrich Bonhoeffer writes:

> He who is alone with his sin is utterly alone. It may be that Christians, notwithstanding corporate worship, communion, prayer, and all their fellowship in service, may still be left to their loneliness. The final break-through to fellowship does not occur because, though they have fellowship with one another as believers and as devout people, they do not have fellowship as the un-devout, as sinners. The pious fellowship permits no one to be a sinner. So everybody must conceal his sin from himself and from the fellowship. We dare not be sinners. Many Christians are unthinkably horrified when a real sinner is suddenly discovered among the righteous. So we remain alone with our sin, living in lies and hypocrisy. The fact is that we are sinners. [1]

Elsewhere, Bonhoeffer continues:

> The cross of Jesus Christ destroys all pride. We cannot find the cross of Jesus if we shrink from going to the place where it is to be found, the public death of the sinner. And we refuse to bear the cross when we are ashamed to take upon ourselves the shameful death of the sinner in confession. [2]

Confession is a critical part of putting off the *old man* (see Ephesians 4:22). One cannot simply put off the old man by trying to convince oneself that he is gone. The old man only dies at the cross through the revelation of God's love and confession of sin. God's love enables us to confess because we are looking to Him to call us into our new identities. The resurrected man comes only from the tomb of the old man.

Confession heals our isolation and loneliness

Confession is the Christian's final frontier. The one who confesses dares to leap the chasm of isolation that prevents genuine communion between the saints. As we expose our brokenness to others, and as they then mirror back to us the mercy and love of God by extending Christ's forgiveness, we have the experience of being loved. Shame and the fear of intimacy are broken.

We Crucify the Old Self (the Flesh) in Confession

By confessing our sins one to another, we die a painful death. Despite the discomfort, that death yields precious rewards that are immediate.

Confession dismantles our fig leaves

We enter the light through confession, and the blood of Jesus cancels sin and destroys false coverings. Thankfully, we don't need to have the total picture of what our fig leaves (ways of hiding) look like. None of us are that smart anyway - the heart is deceptive and wicked. But God can lead us, one step at a time, through the maze of unforgiveness, false beliefs, and defensive vows that have been shelters for our bruised souls.

Confession makes us die to the "social saint"

How can you say you believe when you receive honor [approval] from one another and you do not seek that honor from the one and only God. (John 5:44)

Our humanity teaches us to look to others for approval. In the secret places of our hearts we hope the acceptance of others will reach beyond our social selves into the deep place of our insecurities, pain, and neediness. Yet we live in conflict. Becoming known is risky. Most of us can relate to one man who said, "I have this tiny little heart and whenever I bring it out somebody shoots it." Addicts, like most people, experience opposing desires that war within them (see James 4:1). We need to become honest to feel connection and acceptance from others, but we fear we could be rejected and hurt.

What is the solution to this dilemma? Ultimately, it is to look to God as the main source of our value and justification. With the acceptance of Jesus as the center and source of our acceptability, we can more easily reveal the truth of our sins to others. Still, our first efforts to tell the truth about our past are usually very difficult. Our fear of confession reflects the fact that, in our hearts, we actually want honor from man and not from God. The scriptural command to confess our sin to one another forces to light the issue of where our allegiance will lie.

As confession is made in front of others, the strongholds of our worldly and unstable justifications are abandoned, and justification by God through the blood of Jesus is acknowledged at an emotional level. Confession allows our hearts to experience the truth that Jesus loves and forgives us. Through confession, fear of man is gradually broken.

Having Crucified the Flesh, God Resurrects the New Self

While the purifying fire may have hurt badly, we walk out of it surprised to discover that we've been mightily refined, in a number of ways. We discover that we've been raised to new life in Christ.

Confession acknowledges God's power over sin

If we are trying to overcome our addiction through self-will, then we are not living as a Christian would; we are living as Pharisees.

That which I do not want to do I do - that which I want to do I do not. (Romans 7:15b)

This is Paul's description of powerlessness. We do not have our own power over the law of sin and death. The power to overcome sin only comes by the Spirit of God through grace.

In confession we proclaim our powerlessness over sin. We finally admit that we cannot conquer our separation from God's life through our performance. When we hold out our weakness before God, then His grace can give us power over sin's grip. We begin to recover.

Confession makes the truth of the gospel concrete in our souls

As a result of confession, we feel more centered in the Lord, more real. God's love begins to define us and form our identities in Christ.

God does not dwell in the mask of our social selves. He thrives on contact with the real person. Through confession, we continually put the mask off. When we do this in the presence of another person, we are confident that it has been done. The exposure is real.

About this, Bonhoeffer states that:

> in confession a man breaks through to certainty. Why is it that it is often easier for us to confess our sins to God than to a brother? Why should we not find it easier to go to a brother than to the holy God? But if we do, we must ask ourselves whether we have not often been deceiving ourselves with our confession of sin to God, whether we have not rather been confessing our sin to ourselves and also granting ourselves absolution.[3]

God gives us the certainty that we have been heard through our brother. It is for this reason that God gave His disciples the authority to proclaim and minister the forgiveness of sin.

As we confess our sins to one another, we feel closer to each other because we feel God's grace and love in our midst.

No one has seen God at any time; if we love one another, God abides in us, and His love is perfected in us. (1 John 4:12 NASB)

Christian community contains a paradox. To be healed we need to abandon idolatry of persons and other created things in favor of God. Yet we need people acting as God's representatives (demonstrating His love) in order to free us from the belief that all exposure is unsafe. (Freedom from this belief is crucial to the success of truly intimate relationships.) The love present in cross-centered community provides an atmosphere where the bruised reed will not be broken and the smoldering wick will not be snuffed out. In truth we experience God's love in a powerful way when it is moving through others. People can be "Jesus with skin on."

As we confess our sins in the presence of loving others, we discover who we really are. With masks cast aside, we escape the emptiness of a survival self, and finally enter the loving community we've desired for so long.

The secrecy of sin forces a man to stand by himself. The more isolated a man or woman has chosen to become, the more destructive the power of sin is over him or her. Confession bridges the lonely gap to fellowship.

Through Confession we begin to live in peace, serenity and humility

As we confess our sin we can begin to relax. We not longer have to be on guard so as to continually try to look good and acceptable. As Keith Miller puts it, we no longer bear the weight and complexity of "keeping all the image balls in the air." We can give up perfectionism and accept the fact that we are imperfect. We can humbly embrace ourselves right where we are.

Confession breaks through our pride. It forces us to admit that we are not God and increases our dependency on Him. Through confession, we acknowledge our finitude.

Confession purifies our inner lives

You blind Pharisee, first clean the inside of the cup and of the dish, so that the outside of it may become clean also. (Matthew 23:26)

We so often try to live our Christian lives by attending to external appearances. In this we still walk in blindness. As we deal honestly with our hearts and confess our sin, our outer selves will automatically become clean.

Through confession, the body of Christ is healed

Through confession, we take the logs out of our own eyes so we can clearly see our brothers and sisters in Christ. After God does surgery on our hearts, we are less likely to judge others, project our issues onto them, or go through the psychological maneuvering of putting them down so that we can feel better about ourselves. As we come to accept ourselves, we no longer envy others, and strive to prove ourselves worthy of their acceptance. In short, there is more unity in the body of Christ. Confession is an equalizer – none of us are God. Together, we begin to look to Him and not ourselves. We begin to see that all are sinners and in need of His grace. This has the potential to create tremendous unity as the brethren work together to pull one another from the mire.

Confession clears our formerly-impaired thinking

As addicts, we are used to flattering ourselves – distorting ourselves and our situations so that we can justify living in sin. We've let our thinking become darkened so that we can make sexual sin work for us.

As we confess our sin, our thinking becomes clear. The lies of our hearts are made visible in the light. A wider range of choices becomes possible as we see our deceptive thinking for what it is. Through total honesty we begin to see God, others, and ourselves more clearly.

On the other side of the cross is God's rest and refreshment

The only true rest occurs when we cease from our unaided efforts to overcome the power of sin.

Repent, therefore, and return to God, that your sins may be wiped away, in order that times of refreshing may come from the presence of the Lord. (Acts 3:19)

On the other side of the cross our life is "hidden with Christ in God." If we can embrace our own death at the cross, then we can begin to submit our sinful tendencies to Christ and let His power live in us. This is the premise of being "crucified with Christ." As we learn to live through the cross, Christ can begin to dwell in us and manifest His power.

On the other side of the cross, our will can rest in, and be empowered by, the greater and more powerful will of Christ. Indeed, the other side of the cross is where we will find the true empowering of our will. We must "let go and let God." Although it may seem like a trite saying, it is based in a powerful truth. When we learn how to let our will rest in the greater will of Jesus Christ, then we will find ourselves walking in true empowerment.

God is patient, but...

Jesus is our advocate with the Father. Through Him God has infinite patience with our sincere efforts to let His power rule and reign in us. If we are willing to participate in the principles that God has laid out for our redemption He will attend to the the garden of our heart and cause it to bear fruit. The advocacy of Jesus is demonstrated in the parable told in Luke 13:6-9.

Refusing to go the way of the cross in community

A certain man had a fig tree that had been planted in his vineyard, and he came looking for fruit on it, but did not find any. So he said to the vineyard keeper, 'Behold, for three years I have come looking for fruit on this fig tree without finding any. Cut it down! Why does it even use up the ground?' And he answered and said to him, 'Let it alone, sir, for this year too, until I dig around it and fertilize it. If it bears fruit next year, fine! But if not, cut it down.' (Luke 13:6-9)

This passage is a parable representing the fact that the Father is willing to discard a tree that is bearing no fruit. Thankfully, Jesus is willing to take the time to nurture the tree and give it the opportunity to bring forth its fruit. The parable is a picture of an ongoing Kingdom tension. The Father is waiting for us to bear fruit. Yet, as his people, we continue to sin. I can imagine Jesus standing before the Father asking for an extension of time so that we can be redeemed from our sinful state through the power of the Holy Spirit.

God is merciful and patient with us as we struggle to get free from our addiction. But we dare not tread on His mercy.

If we deliberately keep on sinning after we have received the knowledge of the truth, no sacrifice for sins is left, but only a fearful expectation of judgement and of raging fire that will consume the enemies of God...A man deserves to be punished who has trampled the Son of God under foot, who has treated as an unholy thing the blood of the covenant that sanctified him, and who has insulted the Spirit of grace...It is a dreadful thing to fall into the hands of the living God. (Hebrews 10:26-31)

What Should I Confess?

"What should I confess?" Everything past and present that still has power to shame the individual. At first this statement may seem shocking and impossible, especially for the long-term sexual addict. There are many who object to such an approach, quoting 2 Corinthians 5:17. But this passage refers to a positional truth about our justification in Christ. It is not an excuse for ignoring the effects of past sin on the soul.

From practical experience, I can say that confession of past sin, especially sexual sin, has a powerful effect in lessening the pull of lust. I think the Holy Spirit should be sought so He might reveal the specifics of confession, but the addict will be certain of some of the things that need to come into the light, namely the things that (s)he is afraid to tell others. Usually these events are very painful and carry a lot of shame. Telling someone else about such events in an atmosphere of grace cleanses the heart and breaks the power of the enemy's ability to work in dark and hidden places.

I suggest that the addict think and pray about the following two categories with the intent of bringing anything not previously confessed into the accountability group for confession:

Significant past sin, especially sexual sin

It is very helpful to confess past acts of sin even if they happened before you were a Christian and didn't "know better." These sins include both those done with others and when alone. Be careful not to use the rationalization, "I was alone, it didn't hurt anyone else." It hurt you and shame has a grip on your soul.

Current sexual sin and other ongoing sin

Sometimes we are tempted to think, "This is just one slip-up. I can handle it. I don't need to confess it." Sexual sin has something in common with eating potato chips. One act leads to another. Confession breaks the cycle. Confess every fall.

Conclusion

Confession of sin is an integral part of Christian community. It cannot be forsaken if we are going to have a vibrant community that demonstrates the transforming power of God.

Practically speaking, this means we will have to confess our sin to one another in the context of accountability groups. Breaking old patterns of hiding and fear involves risking vulnerability with one another in order to actualize the cleansing and healing of God. God is waiting, ready to wash our minds, hearts and bodies, but we need to take hold of His great grace through the confessional. Trying to live any other way results in death. In the garden God took away the fig leaf covering that Adam and Eve constructed for themselves. We must let him dismantle ours also.

There are many coverings, but only the blood of Jesus covers completely – it is the only adequate covering. The life of Jesus only comes through the power of His blood, the experience of His love, and the transforming power of the Holy Spirit – all experienced in His community through confession.

Your love, O Lord, reaches to the heavens, your faithfulness to the skies. Your righteousness is like the mighty mountains, your justice like the great deep. O Lord, you preserve both man and beast. How priceless is your unfailing love! Both high and low among men find refuge in the shadow of your wings. They feast on the abundance of your house; you give them drink from your river of delights. For with you is the fountain of life; in your light we see light. (Psalm 36:5-9)

Personal

References

[1] Dietrich Bonhoeffer, *Life Together* (San Francisco: Harper & Row, 1954) 110.

[2] Dietrich Bonhoeffer, *Life Together* (San Francisco: Harper & Row, 1954) 114.

[3] Dietrich Bonhoeffer, *Life Together* (San Francisco: Harper & Row, 1954) 110.

Homework

1. Make a list of things that you have never confessed to anyone else and that seem to have significance in your sexual history.

2. Make a list of "sin against you" that has caused a change in the way you think or feel about yourself.

3. Make a list of sexual sin that has occurred in the last six months.

Key Action Step: Begin to confess these things to your accountability group.

Practicing the Presence of God

Chapter Eight

Where can I go from your Spirit? Where can I flee from your presence? If I go up to the heavens, you are there; if I make my bed in the depths, you are there. If I rise on the wings of the dawn, if I settle on the far side of the sea, even there your hand will guide me, your right hand will hold me fast. (Psalm 139:7-10)

Loneliness is Separation from God

All of our growth in the Lord, and all of His benefits to us, issue from the reality of "Christ in us, the hope of glory." It is Christ working in us "both to will and do" His will which makes us full participants in what He has done.

Loneliness is a state of emptiness in which we ache and thirst for the company of another. This is true whether we're disconnected from His Spirit, or from those created in His image. Addiction is a restless course, one in which the addict attaches to something in a false and instantaneous way. This false bond substitutes for the authentic attachment of intimacy (with God or other people), which takes time.

God saw the potential for the intense pain of loneliness when He created man as a relational being. That is why He said, "It is not good for the man to be alone; I will make a helper suitable for him" (Genesis 2:18). God knew that neither animals nor even God (by Himself) would be enough for Adam. He needed someone who, like him, was created in the image of God. So God created Eve.

Then the Lord God made a woman from the rib he had taken out of the man, and he brought her to the man. The man said "this is now bone of my bone and flesh of my flesh; she shall be called woman, for she was taken out of man." For this reason a man will leave his father and mother and be united to his wife and they will become one flesh. (Genesis 2:22-23)

The basis for sexuality, sexual attraction, and the spark of romance between men and women is the fact that woman was taken out of man. Man now yearns for his complement in woman, and she for her complement in man. In finding the other, God intends for the sexes to bring fulfillment to one another. This is why Adam, after God separated Eve out of him, felt considerably different. He began "looking for his rib." Something was missing and was now found in Eve.

It is my belief that it is normal for man to feel a sense of "loneliness" when he is not in relational union with woman. The reverse is also true. This loneliness and sense of emptiness is painfully exaggerated when, for example, man has developmental wounding which leaves him deprived of early-life feminine love and nurture. In such a case, the man's drive for completion may become exaggerated and excessive. Sexual contact is used as an attempt to fulfill the unmet need.

When not in committed sexual and emotional union with woman, man needs even more than usual to get his needs met in the presence of God, as well as through friendships with others. God calls us to seek Him as our primary Source, as the only One who can complete us. However, we are also created to enjoy the fellowship of other people. But, because sin divorces man from the true state of his heart, he may try to solve the problem of his loneliness through illicit, sexual encounters with women.

Theologically speaking, evil comes out of being separated from the life of God that is continuously available to us as believers (Eph 4:18). Our loneliness motivates us to quickly quell the pain of loneliness, often through sin.

> Born lonely, we try hard to fit in, to be the kind of person that will cause others to like us. Craving and needing very much the affirmation of others, we compromise, put on any face, or many faces; we do even those things we do not like to do in order to fit in. We are bent toward the creature, attempting to find our identity in him. Slowly and compulsively the false self closes its hard, brittle shell around us, and our loneliness remains. [1]

Many of us have lived entombed by a secretive and isolating mask – the false self. Living out of this self, in separation from God, we have tried to find our completion through sexually addictive activities. This painful and lonely existence can ultimately be healed only by entering, and remaining in the presence of God.

The Work of God is to Know Him

The healing of our separation from God has been accomplished by Christ's work on the cross. We have been given free access to the Father's presence through the blood of Jesus. This access was accomplished as the temple curtain was torn in two. Simultaneously, Jesus uttered His last words, *"It is finished"* (John 19:30). At that moment, the Spirit of God was released from the Holy of Holies in the Temple. Since Pentecost, every believer has become a home to Him, and so He is continuously with us.

Even though our access to the Lord is secure, problems remain. For one, there is still evil in ourselves that we must overcome. We can only begin to access the presence of God within us when we are willing to step out of our false, sin-bent selves, and instead live from our true selves (the new selves God created when we were saved). This involves accepting our weaknesses, as discussed in previous chapters. Only then can God begin to change our identities, cleanse us from the guilt of our sin, and begin to empower us for holy living. We must expose the hidden strongholds (habitual ways of thinking and perceiving, and acting) of fear, love-deprivation, judgments, envy, unforgiveness, and idolatry, etc., so that we may die to them and thereby allow Jesus to clothe us in clean garments. Our work is to know God, and to live in His presence. That was the primary focus of Jesus when He walked the earth.

In John 4, we see that, one day, Jesus apparently had not eaten for awhile, prompting concern in His friends. The disciples said, "Rabbi, eat!" Jesus' meaningful reply said much to them and to us: "I have food to eat that you do not know about...My food is to do the will of Him who sent me, and to accomplish His work" (John 4:32, 34). When Jesus was asked what the works of God were, He replied, "This is the work of God, that you believe in Him whom He has sent" (John 6:29). God desires for us to believe in Him and His love for us not only with our intellects, but deeply in our hearts as well. We must have a heart-knowledge of the resurrection of Jesus in order to walk in new life. God wants, most of all, for His Kingdom to be established in the hearts of His people.

God's Kingdom flows out of His presence. All of our growth in the Lord, and all of His benefits to us, issue from the reality of "Christ in us, the hope of glory." It is Christ working in us "both to will and do" His will which makes us full participants in what He has done. If we want to "live and move and have our being in Christ," we must purpose to spend our time in His presence. We must make it a deliberate "work" of our lives.

The truth about the transforming nature of God's presence answers an important question! If we are indeed powerless over our sin and addiction, then what are our wills to be used for? Simply stated, we need to choose to be present to God, to let Him be present to us. We use our wills to be with God, and offer ourselves to Him, so that His Spirit can change the things that we are powerless to change for ourselves.

Incarnational Reality

The term "incarnational reality" merely refers to the fact that Jesus came in the flesh – God became a man and lived with the people He created. After His death and resurrection, He sent His Spirit to form the Church, in which He perpetuates His incarnation – His Spirit living within our mortal bodies. Because His Spirit now indwells believers, we can be in continuous fellowship with Him. Also, we can access His power, and thereby be freed from our addictions.

Christian reality is incarnational reality. We access the ever-present power of Jesus with and within us by choosing to die at the cross. We die to the old self (the flesh, or inclination to sin) with its diseased attitudes, and receive new life through the power of God's presence reigning in us.

I do not nullify the grace of God; for if righteousness comes through the law, then Christ died needlessly. O foolish Galatians! Who has bewitched you, before whose eyes Jesus Christ was publicly portrayed as crucified? Let me ask you only this: Did you receive the Spirit by works of the law, or by hearing with faith? Are you so foolish? Having begun with the Spirit, are you now ending with the flesh? (Gal. 2:21-3:3)

We must not nullify the grace of God by trying to overcome addiction as though our own strength was sufficient. If we think our strength is sufficient, then we are saying that Christ died needlessly. Exercising moral effort is very important but by choosing to obey, we are choosing to access God's power, and to allow His strength to be expressed through us. So, while our strength is insufficient, we choose to obey in the knowledge (through faith) that our wills will be fueled by the might of the God who indwells us.

Our hope is reflected in Paul's prayer recorded in Ephesians 3:16-20:

I pray that out of His glorious riches He may strengthen you with power through His Spirit in your inner being, so that Christ may dwell in your hearts through faith. And I pray that you, being rooted and established in love, may have power, together with all the saints, to grasp how wide and long and high and deep is the love of Christ, and to know this love that surpasses knowledge - that you may be filled to the measure of all the fullness of God. Now to him who is able to do immeasurably more than all we ask or imagine, according to His power that is at work within us, to Him be glory in the church and in Christ Jesus throughout all generations, forever and ever! Amen.

Incarnational reality, the fact that Christ is with and within us, means that there is abundant power available to deliver us, not only from sexual addiction, but from all that is ungodly.

Humility Prepares Us for His Presence

Truly, there is Another who is with us, and He does the work – if we are careful to do (and keep on doing) the one work the Father has given us to do: that of believing 'in the One whom He has sent.' We can go right on celebrating our smallness while leaning joyfully and heavily on the Son's greatness and love. We learn to practice His Presence. We trust Him to be, always, our adequacy. [2]

In the face of the shame and other negative feelings we have towards ourselves, God wants us to acknowledge our weakness, finiteness, and smallness so that we are acutely aware of our need for Him.

If we know beyond a shadow of a doubt that we need Him, then we can joyfully welcome Him into those areas of weakness. Our pride will tell us to stay in hiding, but this prevents us from knowing the power of God as it comes through others. The self-sufficient man is one who has become a friend of the world, according to a worldly "wisdom." But God's wisdom is quite different:

You adulterous people, don't you know that friendship with the world is hatred toward God? Anyone who chooses to be a friend of the world becomes an enemy of God. Or do you think scripture says without reason that the Spirit He causes to live in us tends toward envy, but He gives us more grace? That is why scripture says: 'God opposes the proud but gives grace to the humble. Submit yourselves, then, to God. Resist the devil, and he will flee from you. Come near to God and He will come near to you. Wash your hands, you sinners, and purify your hearts, you double-minded. Grieve, mourn, and wail. Change your laughter to mourning and your joy to gloom. **Humble yourselves before the Lord, and He will lift you up.**
(James 4:4-10)

God desires jealously to complete the sanctification of our hearts by means of His indwelling presence. He gives grace to those who are able to rejoice over their neediness and smallness before Him. We may feel miserable, grieve, and be gloomy for a time as our laughter gives way to the reality of our aching souls. But if we are willing to humble ourselves and seek the presence of God, He will lift us out of the mire.

Then, in our weakness, His power will have an outlet through which to be expressed.

How to Practice God's Presence

Practicing the presence of God is an act of faith. It is depending on Someone unseen. To practice His presence merely means that we think on the fact that the One who is accompanying us is the transcendent God who has the power to change us.

Practicing the presence of God is seeing with the eyes of our hearts. It is a refusal to depend on our past experiences as a barometer for truth. It is pressing into the supernatural realm through an act of our wills, based on faith.

The head/heart split

We have previously considered the devastation of the Fall of man and its effect on man's ability to live from his true self. As a result, man becomes consumed with activities (doing), and fails to enjoy the rest (being) that refreshes and gives meaning to activity. Unable to live out of his true center in God, a man in this condition has a split between his head and his heart. The head (rational, logical self) is inflated, and busy beyond necessity. Meanwhile, the heart (the intuitive self which communes in love with another, the self that relates) is weakened or inactive. Connection with the Spirit of truth is lost since man cannot be with the Lord. We may, in such a state, know much about God, but yet have very little relationship with Him. Failing to relate to Him, our sensitivity to Him and our knowledge of Him is impoverished. Instead of communion with the Lord, life becomes filled with uninspired doing.

We fix our eyes not on what is seen, but on what is unseen. For what is seen is temporary, but what is unseen is eternal. (2 Cor 4:18)

Again, the practice of the presence of God is the discipline of intentionally setting our minds on the reality that God is always with us. In the presence of God, the true self emerges and begins to be renewed in His image. Our intellectual knowledge of Him gradually becomes the heart-level knowledge of one who has spent much time with his Friend. About the practice of His presence, Frank Laubach writes:

> It is so simple that a child could practice it. This simple practice requires only a gentle pressure of the will, not more than a person can exert easily. It grows easier as the habit becomes fixed. Yet it transforms life into heaven. [3]

Laubach explains his experience in practicing this skill:

> Now what shall I call it? More than surrender. I had that before. I cannot find the word that will mean to you or to me what I am now experiencing. It is a will act. I compel my mind to open straight out toward God. I wait and listen with determined sensitiveness.
> I fix my attention there, and sometimes it requires a long time early in the morning.
> I determine not to get out of bed until that mindset upon the Lord is settled. [4]

Practicing the presence of God is an invitation to draw God into every situation, every location, and every fallen desire that we find ourselves experiencing. It is looking up, out of ourselves, as opposed to looking down and into ourselves. When we feel trapped by the overwhelming force of addiction, we must fix our eyes on the Holy God who has purchased us with His blood. We must invite Jesus into our shame so that His love can change our hearts and attitudes.

Practicing the presence of God is a form of prayer

Practicing the presence is meant to be a part of our prayer lives. All Christians, addicts especially, need to regularly spend time with the Lord. Only then can we enjoy Him and grow in Him, and only then can we reasonably hope for our full deliverance from addiction. The practice of the presence of God is a good starting place if you don't have a prayer life, as well as a good way to nourish the one you may already have.

> Some folks, thinking they are being honest, suffer from the notion that to practice the Presence is an exercise, not in faith, but in mere credulity (inclined to believe on a small bit of evidence). But to acknowledge the Presence of the God who is really there, is actually a form of prayer — a way of praying always as the scriptures exhort us to do. When we do this, the eyes and ears of our hearts are opened to receive the word He is always speaking. We enter into a path of obedience, perhaps unknown to us before, where we joyfully acknowledge 'Jesus is Lord.' But the acknowledgment that God is always with us — even when in our sensory being we are least aware of it — is not always easy. It requires discipline. [5]

In learning this skill, we must realize that we will often have no feeling of God's presence with us. It is His presence with us that changes us, not our sensations of that presence.

As we learn to more regularly spend our time in His presence, our behavior will be radically affected. It will be very difficult to watch a pornographic video in the presence of God!

Resymbolizing our hearts

Practicing the presence of God is crucial in order to bring an end to addictive cycles *When we become aware that we have been triggered, we can invite Jesus into our cycle*. It is for this reason that we must become aware of our triggers. The practice of the presence of God, in the midst of our cycle, is a resource that we cannot afford to ignore.

We can also resymbolize places that are triggers for us. For example, for a man who habitually masturbates in the shower, the shower is a trigger. It represents a place where he can submerge himself in sexual fantasy and euphoria. He is triggered by association with this place which has sexual meaning for him. He has a choice to either stop taking showers or to change the way he sees the stall. Once he sees objectively that the shower is a trigger, he can begin to resymbolize the shower as a place of prayer by making an active decision before he gets to the bathroom every morning. Over time, the shower stall will become a place of abiding in God. Initially, as he begins to feel the stimulus of the water on his skin, he may have to go through the (sometimes difficult) process of inviting Jesus into the ache of not indulging himself in masturbation. He may instead need to face feelings of isolation and loneliness.

The addict must face the pain of giving up his idols and be willing to stand in the fire, looking toward God as the one that can give him the life that he desperately needs. Substituting the life-giving practice of God's presence for heart-hardening cycles of masturbation is essential to the healing of sexual addiction.

Listening for the healing word of God

Practicing the presence of God also involves listening for the words of truth that God is always speaking to us. As we grow in our awareness of God's presence, we will hear Him speaking to us about our adoption (sonship or daughtership) and our value to Him. We will hear the healing words that are able to pull down the strongholds of lies that veil our true identity in Christ, and which impede the transformation we desperately need. In order for this to occur, we must be renewing our minds through study of the word of God, in addition to practicing His presence.

Hindrances to Practicing God's Presence

Slothfulness

Many of us are guilty of spiritual slothfulness or laziness. We have never developed spiritual disciplines. We are not in the habit of presenting ourselves to God so that He can transform us.

How long will you lie down, O sluggard? When will you arise from your sleep? 'A little sleep, a little slumber, a little folding of the hands to rest' – Your need will come in like a vagabond, and your need like an armed man. (Proverbs 6:9-11)

Surely one of the reasons we stay in spiritual and psychological poverty is because we do not work hard enough at practicing God's presence in our lives.

Unbelief

Although we profess faith, some of us do not believe that prayer will actually change things. We lack the faith to depend upon an unseen God. Our unbelief and pride keep us in the sin of prayerlessness. We need to confess the sin of unbelief and regularly ask God to help us to pray.

Idolatry

Much has been said about idolatry in the course of this book. Hanging onto any substitute for God will prevent us from being present to Him. He cannot come in if our hearts are set on other things. We cannot abide in Him if we are abiding in something else.

Intellectualizing

Intellectualizing calcifies the split between head and heart. A man must understand reality and engage it with both his head and his heart for the gospel to have power to transform him. The Pharisees had knowledge, but their righteous acts only amounted to a deadening religion. It is the inside of the cup (our hearts) that needs cleansing (Matt 23:25-26). In many churches, and in many of our hearts, conceptual knowledge about God has become the mainstay, replacing the practicalities of knowing how to walk with God.

Introspection

Introspection has to do with an obsessive, inward gaze, where one hopes to gain enough self-knowledge so as to solve one's problems. While the introspective person thinks this mental activity will yield fruit, in fact, it is a form of abiding in one's own self, instead of in God. It is a death-spiral when one practices the presence of the fallen self rather than the presence of God. To practice the presence of ourselves, as Leanne Payne puts it, is to spiral down into darkness and confusion. Rather than seeking to figure ourselves out, we need to look to the Lord who alone can heal us.

The paradox of emotional healing is that one must look outside oneself in order to be healed within. We must face our true and damaged selves, yes, but only with the cross plainly in view. Only God has the power to tell us who we are as His sons and daughters. We cannot successfully rename and restore ourselves.

The Power of God's Presence in Us

To have the powerful presence of God within us means that a transformed heart is available for the taking. As the old self is put off in the light of God, the true self is raised up and empowered to live life by the Spirit of God.

Then I will sprinkle clean water on you, and you will be clean; I will cleanse you from all your filthiness and from all your idols. Moreover, I will give you a new heart and put a new spirit within you; and I will remove the heart of stone from your flesh and give you a heart of flesh. And I will put My Spirit within you and cause you to walk in My statutes, and you will be careful to observe my ordinances.
(Eze 36:25-27)

References

[1] Leanne Payne, *The Broken Image* (Westchester: Good News Publishers, 1981) 139.

[2] Leanne Payne, *The Healing Presence* (Westchester: Good news Publishers, 1989) 21-22.

[3] Frank Laubach and Brother Lawrence, *Practicing His Presence* 26.

[4] Laubach 6.

[5] Leanne Payne, *The Healing Presence* (Westchester: Good news Publishers, 1989) 23.

Homework

Homework

Please respond to the following questions as honestly and thoroughly as you can.

1. How do I think and feel about the concept of practicing the presence of God?

2. How often do I intentionally set my mind on God?
   What plans do I want to make to change this aspect of my life?

3. What tendencies do I have toward introspection (if any)?
   How can I begin to take to the cross that which I find in my heart?

4. What triggers (places, events etc.) can I identify that could be 'resymbolized' through prayer and practicing God's presence?

5. Which, if any, of the hindrances mentioned in the lesson would stop me from practicing the presence of God?

6. Read the following statement:

   I have made a decision to look at Jesus Christ as my resource and to practice opening my heart to Him and the incarnational reality and truth available in His presence. I will begin to daily focus deliberately on developing a conscious awareness of His presence.

If you agree with the above statement, rewrite it into a prayer that reflects your heart's cry for freedom. Then please date and sign the prayer.

_____   _____

Name   Date

Disciplines

Seeking God Through Spiritual Disciplines

We cannot circumvent this process by having someone perform miraculous healing prayer. To be sure, God has miracles He is eager to do in our lives. Nonetheless, we take hold of His grace by listening to Him. All of us must walk the path of relating to God who is personal and specific with each of us. It is this unique, personal, and individual relationship with God that changes our hearts.

Chapter Nine

So I say to you: Ask and it will be given to you; seek and you will find; knock and the door will be opened to you. For everyone who asks receives; he who seeks finds; and to him who knocks, the door will be opened. (Luke 11:9-10)

The Necessity of Involvement with the Holy Spirit

Man was separated from God's presence and life when he fell away. Immediately God set into motion His plan to reconnect man to Himself. The first step was to set up the law, which had a double function. Its demands foreshadowed the fruit of the Holy Spirit while, at the same time, it exposed and defined sin. The Law was a provision, a temporary measure until the coming of the Spirit. No man could live up to its standards while he was still separated from God.

Having given the law, the next step in His plan was to qualify those who believed in Him to be partakers of the life of God. He did this through the atoning sacrifice of Jesus on the cross. As we receive that sacrifice and submit our lives to the lordship of Jesus, God considers us righteous (in right standing) to receive His promises.

One of the most significant of these promises appears in Ezekiel 36:26-27:

Moreover, I will give you a new heart and put a new spirit within you; and I will remove the heart of stone from your flesh and give you a heart of flesh. And I will put My Spirit within you and cause you to walk in my statutes, and you will be careful to observe My ordinances.

God sent the Holy Spirit into the world to change our hearts. If our hearts are changed, we are able and willing to conform to His laws because we are inwardly inclined to do so, not merely because we are following rules. It is the Holy Spirit who gives us power to walk a godly life (Eph 3:16, Gal 5:16). It is through the Holy Spirit that we experience the love of God and His presence in our lives (Romans 5:5). It is the Spirit of God by which we experience God's adoption and are moved to seek Him and know Him as Father.

For you did not receive a spirit that makes you a slave again to fear, but you received the Spirit of sonship. And by Him we cry 'Abba, Father.' The Spirit himself testifies with our spirit that we are God's children. Now if we are children, then we are heirs - heirs of God and co-heirs with Christ, if indeed we share in His sufferings in order that we may also share in His glory. (Romans 8:15-17)

We who are enslaved by sexual addictions have a desperate need to know the Father's love and to incorporate His word and power into our hearts. Through the power of the Holy Spirit, we can live a life of love, rather than using others at a very high cost to their souls and ours.

The Living Word

The letter kills, but the Spirit gives life. (2 Cor 3:6)

The word of God can be a terrible burden when we do not have the personal resources to obey its mandates for our lives. Our consistent failures remind us frequently that sin and death are with us. We toil under the burden of knowing what we are supposed to do, while lacking the empowering of the Spirit.

The Holy Spirit is able to write the word of God on our hearts. This process is called "illumination." Once we are illuminated by the word, it has far more power to change us. It becomes powerful, active, and penetrating in our lives, even giving us discernment about what is carnally motivated and what is motivated by the Holy Spirit. The word empowered by the Holy Spirit has the qualities described by the writer of Hebrews:

For the word of God is living and active. Sharper than any double-edged sword, it penetrates even to dividing soul and spirit, joints and marrow; it judges the thoughts and attitudes of the heart. (Hebrews 4:12)

Meditation on the word of God is one of the principle ways that we open ourselves up to receive God's illumination. Thus, meditation is a means of experiencing God's grace.

The Necessity of Meditating on the Word of God

By meditating upon the word of God, the riches of His wisdom are opened to us. This blesses our personal relationship with God, but it also protects us from others' wickedness. We are thus preserved in ways we wouldn't have otherwise been protected.

Blessed is the man who does not walk in the counsel of the wicked or stand in the way of sinners or sit in the seat of mockers. But his delight is in the Law of the Lord, and on His Law he meditates day and night. He is like a tree planted by streams of water, which yields its fruit in season and whose leaf does not wither. Whatever he does prospers. Not so the wicked! They are like chaff that the wind blows away. (Psalm 1:1-4)

Oh, how I love your Law! I meditate on it all day long. Your commands make me wiser than my enemies, for they are ever with me. I have more insight than all my teachers, for I meditate on your statutes. I have more understanding than the elders, for I obey your precepts. I have kept my feet from every evil path so that I might obey your word. I have not departed from your laws for you yourself have taught me. How sweet are your words to my taste, sweeter than honey to my mouth! I gain understanding from your precepts; therefore I hate every wrong path. (Psalm 119:97-104)

Meditation is the act of spiritual evaluation

Meditation is a form of Christian prayer (completely unlike non-Christian forms of meditation). Meditation involves reading the Bible and then pondering the meaning of what's being said. We consider what the Lord is saying to us personally through the text, and how we might personally apply it to our lives. Instead of merely skimming through the text, we wrestle with it, and prefer to take in smaller amounts of text so as to deeply understand and profit from them. If God's word was food (which it is), meditation would be the act of chewing it up into smaller pieces so that it could be absorbed into the body.

One form of meditation is to keep a portion of the word of God before the conscious mind so that it can be pondered from different angles. The reader might consider its different parts, asking the Holy Spirit to illuminate the meaning He wants us to derive from it. This process may be ongoing throughout a day, or even for weeks until the richness of a text is realized. We see the psalmist with this kind of intensity in Psalm 119:147-148:

I rise before dawn and cry for help; I have put my hope in your word. My eyes stay open through the watches of the night, that I may meditate on your promises.

Meditation is that act of spiritual application

Therefore putting aside all filthiness and all that remains of wickedness, in humility receive the word implanted, which is able to save your souls. (James 1:21)

When our meditation leads to application, we can stop the addictive habit of hearing and not doing, thus deceiving ourselves. Pondering how to put the word into action sows it deeper into our hearts. Doing the word anchors it even more deeply.

Do not merely listen to the word, and so deceive yourselves. Do what it says. Anyone who listens to the word but does not do what it says is like a man who looks at his face in a mirror and, after looking at himself, goes away and immediately forgets what he looks like. But the man who looks intently into the perfect law that gives freedom, and continues to do this, not forgetting what he has heard but doing it - he will be blessed in what he does. (James 1:22-25)

Meditation is working the ground of our hearts

In Mark 4, Jesus tells a parable about the word of God. He compares it to seed being thrown on a field, and tells of the ways that the seed is removed from the field and thus fails to germinate. The obstacles can be many: the force of the Enemy against us, the cares of this life, the deceitfulness of riches, the desire for other things and the pull of our addiction can all pluck the word away from the soil of our hearts.

Frequently, it is the hardness of our hearts that keeps the word from taking root. Often our hearts are like hard, rocky ground in which the word cannot take root, unless it is plowed and watered by the Holy Spirit.

Meditation is plowing up the ground of our heart. It is tilling the soil of our hearts so that the seed of God's word can take root and grow. One big hindrance to this tilling is a lack of discipline in taking the time required. We must slow down with regard to the word of God, take bite-sized portions, and chew. When the illumination comes move on to the next bite. Many of us try to chew whole chapters or books at a time.

Waiting on God is an aspect of meditation

Time is a big factor in the illumination of the Word. Jesus described this process by using the analogy of how a plant grows in Mark 4:26-28:

The kingdom of God is like a man who casts seed upon the soil; and goes to bed at night and gets up by day, and the seed sprouts up and grows - how, he himself does not know. The soil produces crops by itself; first the blade, then the head, then the mature grain in the head. (Mark 4:26-28)

Being transformed by God's word involves patiently waiting for the life of the word to grow in us. If we do not keep His word before us, Satan may seek to abort its life before it produces fruit. Endeavor to walk in the way of the psalmist:

I have chosen the faithful way; I have placed your ordinances before me. I cling to your testimonies, O Lord; do not put me to shame! I shall run the way of your commandments, for you will enlarge my heart. (Psalm 119:30-32)

Christians ensnared in sexual addiction are involved in a war for the possession of their minds. All of us lose battles, but we must fight the temptation to become discouraged, give up, and lose the war. If the word of God loses its centrality in your life for a time, be tenacious to re-center it. Continue to meditate upon His word. His holy seeds will grow as we are faithful.

Petitionary Prayer Brings the Rain of the Holy Spirit

Just as the prayer of meditation breaks up the fallow ground of our hearts, prayer of petition invites the runoff of the Holy Spirit that nourishes the plant and causes it to grow. When we pray, we open ourselves up to the presence of God. We draw close to Him so that He can breathe upon us and place His word within us. Many of us do not ask, and so we do not have what we need (James 4:2b). Prayer is a simple mystery that requires only that we humble ourselves before God, laying our needs before Him. Dick Eastman writes:

> Prayer is the divine enigma - that marvelous mystery hidden behind the cloud of God's omnipotence. Nothing is beyond the reach of prayer because God Himself is the focus of prayer. E.M. Bounds agreed when he wrote, 'Prayer is the contact of a living soul with God. In prayer, God stoops to kiss man, to bless man, and to aid in everything that God can devise or man can need.' Charles Spurgeon adds, 'Prayer is the slender nerve that moveth the muscles of omnipotence.' [1]

Prayer, the humble request of a needy soul, opens the floodgates to the power of God's love. Without it, not much gets done. In Luke 18:7-8, Jesus makes it clear that God the Father is willing to come quickly with answers to our prayers. He goes on to ask the rhetorical question, "When the Son of Man comes, will He find faith on the earth?"

Faith in God is naturally expressed by a life of prayer. A man of faith knows that without prayer he is left with his own lame efforts. Do you seek to be freed from your sexual addiction? Then stand before God and ask Him to send his power into your weaknesses. Make a conscious effort to do so, often.

In prayer we utter God's word back to Him, laying the hopes and desires of our hearts before the One who can do something about them. Through prayer we become vulnerable to God as we give Him permission to reign over and through our lives. That is why the humble man prays. He knows that God is the Author of life who alone has the power to change him, and that his own efforts are as filthy rags.

Developing a prayer life

Prayer has many expressions. There are many books on prayer that can be read in order to gain more knowledge on how to pray (such as Richard Foster's book, aptly titled *Prayer*). But the most important thing is that one start praying. Here are some suggestions for those beginning to pray:

• Start with short times of prayer, 5 to 10 minutes, and gradually increase your time in prayer.

- Develop a routine for your prayer life. It is helpful to pray at the same time and in the same place each day so that it becomes a part of your daily schedule. Those of us who are addictive are good at rituals. Getting rid of bad rituals is insufficient: lasting change happens as we replace unhealthy rituals with healthy ones.

- Pray the promises of God and the prayers of cleansing modeled in the scripture. The scripture says that we know that God hears us if we pray according to His will. His will is revealed in His word. The word of God has many good prayer outlines in it. Of special help to us is Eph 1:17-23, 3:16-21, James 4:6-8, Psalm 19:7-14, 51:5-17 and 139:23-24. Of course there are many more, but these will be a helpful start.

- Pray to God with an honest heart. If we lie to Him, we lie to ourselves. He knows all things. Avoid telling Him only the things you think He wants to hear.

- Pray in an upright position, otherwise you may find yourself sleeping!

- If you notice you have stopped praying - start again. Refuse the lie that you cannot be a person of prayer.

- Routinely ask the Holy Spirit to help you pray.

Listening prayer

For out of the heart come evil thoughts, murder, adultery, sexual immorality, theft, false testimony, slander. These are what make a man 'unclean'. (Matthew 15:19-20a)

Though often non-obvious, our hearts are just as Jesus has said – full of much darkness. In the case of the sexual addict, the thoughts lodged in the heart are diseased and reflect deep self-loathing which prohibits the addict from accepting himself. Thus, the addict has difficulty accepting the truth about his new position in Christ.

If we were to journal, we could probably fill up pages with thoughts that reflect what we truly believe about ourselves. Our hearts store painful feelings and thoughts of unworthiness, rejection, failure, and isolation. We have been falsely named over the course of our history – deceived about who we really are, and about what we're like. This occurred both directly and indirectly, by the words and actions of others that had authority in our lives. It is the pain of this hidden belief system that drives our addiction.

Listening prayer is a critical practice in the healing of the soul. Merely identifying these feelings cannot change our wayward heart; however, letting the Holy Spirit bring them up is the first step to entering meaningful dialogue with God. We must be aware of our heart's attitudes and repent of them. We must also wait for God to speak into our hearts the truths that can remove the sting of painful memories, labels and false beliefs that have been heaped upon us through the experiences of our life. But we will miss His voice if we are unwilling to wait before Him in prayer.

The discipline of solitude is an essential ingredient if we are to change. We cannot hear God if our constant activity keeps us distracted from His voice. We must purpose to find a quiet place where we can be alone to rest in Jesus. In prayer and meditation, we wait for His healing words and the help of the Spirit. The Holy Spirit, our Advocate and Counselor, is faithful to bring us to repentance regarding the lies of our heart and to show us the truth which replaces old falsehoods. The prophet Isaiah understood the value of solitude when he wrote:

This is what the Sovereign Lord, the Holy One of Israel, says: 'In repentance and rest is your salvation, in quietness and trust is your strength.' (Isaiah 30:15)

God's "speaking" might be done through scriptures, impressions, waves of consoling love, visions or pictures. He may speak through otherwise ordinary events. These communications will not contradict God's truth in scripture, which is the standard He has established to help us discern truth from error.

As God speaks truth into our hearts, we will begin to loose the false center of the "old man" and experience a new solid-footedness or centering in His love. We can participate in this process by taking our false beliefs captive, by confessing them to God and leaving them at the foot of the cross.

We conquer sexual addiction through a continual process of putting off the old man, and by allowing the Holy Spirit to anchor us in the new self. This happens as we listen to Him. This process is what Leanne Payne calls the 'mystical wedding' of the human soul to Christ:

> That is what happens when we quit listening to the voices of the world, the flesh and the devil - when we rightly discern and refute them where necessary and start really listening to God and receiving from him. [2]

We cannot circumvent this process by having someone perform miraculous healing prayer. To be sure, God has miracles He is eager to do in our lives. Nonetheless, we take hold of His grace by listening to Him. All of us must walk the path of relating to God who is personal and specific with each of us. It is this unique, personal, and individual relationship with God that changes our hearts.

Be sure to schedule time with God. Allow the Holy Spirit to bring to the surface any pain within you. Write down what He brings up on paper. Give Him your pain; renounce any lies He shows you and nail them to the cross. Then wait for the Father to speak the healing words of truth that you need to hear. This form of prayer involves listening and learning to hear, not only God, but also your own heart. As the scripture says:

Listen, listen to me, and eat what is good and your soul will delight in the richest of fare. Give ear and come to me; hear me, that your soul may live. (Is. 55:2b-3a)

Cautions in prayer

The first thing to keep in mind when learning to pray is not to be too hard on yourself. It may be that your mind wanders, or you have impure thoughts. Answers don't come right away, and you may fail to keep your intended schedule. The enemy hates it when we seek God in prayer, especially if we do so regularly. We may find that he brings an unusual number of distractions to us when we take time with the Lord. Spiritual growth is a process of learning which involves the discipline of seeking God. Part of your growth will come from making mistakes. Welcome them as learning opportunities.

Most Twelve-Step programs suggest that we begin to receive God's guidance when we relinquish to Him our own agendas about how and when we think He should heal us. We must acknowledge that we have a history of being self-centered and blind to our hearts' condition. My suggestion for a prayer agenda is to pray, above all, for the knowledge of His will and the power to carry it out. We need to be cautious that we are not asking God to heal us our way, according to our plan. We need to let Him be God so that we can be His followers.

Don't demand open visions, bolts of lightning and the audible voice of God. God's communication will probably come in the form of a small nudge or an impression. Respond to these in the best way that you can. You will learn to discern His voice by trial and error.

Thanking God as a Spiritual Discipline

That attitude of being grateful is like taking spiritual vitamins. I feel so much better and become even more grateful and serene when I express gratitude. [3]

The man who thanks God for what he has reinforces the notion that God wants to provide for us, and is therefore able to hope for more. The man who looks only to what he does not have becomes discouraged and soon becomes weighed down by cares. This is one reason that thanksgiving is so important as a part of our prayer life. Thanksgiving acknowledges the work of God in our lives and gives us energy to look for the next thing that He will do.

Thanksgiving helps us focus on God's faithfulness. It is an integral part of our prayer and watching.

Devote yourselves to prayer, keeping alert in it with an attitude of thanksgiving. (Col 4:2)

Conclusion

We must seek God and ask Him to be an active force in the healing of our lives. It is true that we must look at the strongholds deep in our hearts that keep us in pain. But working recovery steps and receiving inner healing are only part of the equation that produces our healing. These things must be seen in the context of our search for God, our quest to know and serve Him more. Our healing and recovery is important to God, but we advance them best when we make Him, not our own well-being, the focus of our hearts.

Participating in regular spiritual disciplines greatly enables the word of God to grow within us and produce fruit in our lives. If we make an effort to abide in Christ, He promises to come and abide in us. Some of the ways that we present ourselves to God are meditation on His word, prayer, and thanksgiving. In these activities we become more aware of God's presence in our lives and healing.

References

[1] Dick Eastman, *The Hour That Changes The World* (Grand Rapids: Baker House Publishers, 1978) 11.

[2] Leanne Payne, *Restoring the Christian Soul* (Wheaton: Good News Publishers, 1991) 61.

[3] Keith Miller, *A Hunger For Healing* (San Francisco; HarperCollins, 1992) 189.

Homework

Homework

1. Describe your current prayer life and its level of satisfaction to you.

2. What hinders you from giving your time and attention to God? What keeps you from allowing Him into your world? In what ways are you afraid of God?

3. What would you like your prayer/meditative life with God to be like?

4. What ways have your prayers reflected self-centeredness as opposed to God-centeredness?

5. I will begin to incorporate the following action steps into my life:
   - A place of prayer; time of day, duration, frequency
   - Meditation - what method
   - Listening prayer
   - Accountability
   - Motivation
   - Goals
   - (add you own thoughts)

I am ready, through prayer and meditation, to seek God, to improve my conscious contact with Him, and to pray for knowledge of His will for my life coupled with the power to carry this out.

Signature_____

Date_____

Understanding the Addictive System

*Chapter Ten

When the addict is still running from his own pain, he has not embraced his weakness. He does not yet understand God's mercy and kindness at a heart level. The addict's shame prevents him from receiving the grace of God.

See to it brothers, that none of you has a sinful, unbelieving heart that turns away from the living God. But encourage one another daily, as long as it is called today, so that none of you may be hardened by sin's deceitfulness. Hebrews 3:12-13

The Addictive System

Up to this point, we have been looking at various aspects of the addictive cycle. We have seen how triggers launch the sexual addict into preoccupation with sex, ritualized patterns of acting out, a flash of ecstasy and, finally, guilt and despair. This is the process described in James 1:14-15: desire leads to sinful acts, and those bring emotional and spiritual death. As mentioned before, this cycle has everything to do with idolatry and is an attempt to bury underlying pain by using the addictive process as a mood altering high. As the addictive cycle is interrupted, the underlying roots can finally be exposed.

We are now ready to talk about the deeper aspects of the addict's heart. The diagram on page 88 of this chapter shows the components that work together as a system to drive sexual addiction. At the center of this system is the human heart. The realities of its unrenewed state are what the addict is running from. The spiritual surgery that must occur there will greatly aid the addict in finding freedom.

The different boxes in the diagram represent different aspects of the addictive experience. As the addict continues around the cycle, it is as if he were running around the borders of a walled city. As long as he keeps running, the city gates will not open. In fact, he will not even notice that they are there. It is the same with the gateway into the addict's soul. As the addict stops running, the cycles slows and the doors to the unrenewed self will begin to open so as to reveal what was previously hidden from sight.

The Shame Core

Shame is a sense of personal "badness" that results from negative messages about oneself, received over the course of one's life. Over time, the negative messages have become interwoven with the person's identity. This painful image of self is gradually submerged as the false addictive self is built on top of it. Shame is the emotional machinery that drives the addictive system, much like an engine drives a car.

Prior to healing, the components of shame continue to refute the truth of what God's word and Spirit say about the addict.

The solid, heart shaped, area in the center of the diagram labeled "Shame Core" represents the emotional wall formed by the addict's avoidance of his painful sense of himself. Shame is healed as the addict gives God access to his wounded core. Then, with God's help, the addict can work through the illusions trapped within, until he eventually is able to whole-heartedly internalize his true identity in Christ. Then he will walk fully empowered by the Spirit of God. As shame is healed, the addictive cycle becomes an empty shell and loses much of its power. Thus, the healing of shame is an essential path for the addict.

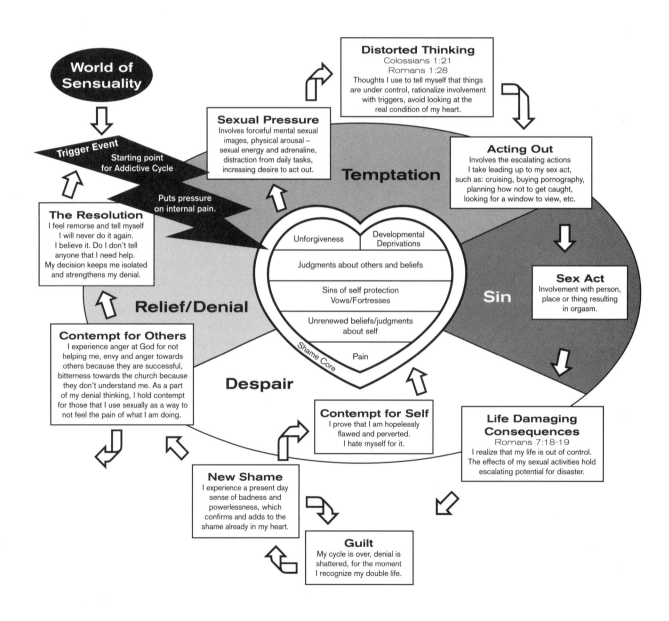

Diagram 3: The Addictive System

Components of the shame core

Feelings of pain

When the addict first begins to get in touch with his heart, he will likely feel fear, pain, and torment (separation from God). It is important to pay attention to these feelings because they are powerful motivators, especially with respect to relationships. The fear of rejection, for example, hinders true intimacy and motivates emotionless sexual contact. Painful feelings are connected to a broken identity. The addict's heart has yet to receive the truth about his acceptance in Christ and his new identity as a beloved son. Acknowledging pain is particularly important because a major factor in staying sober is the ability to face and walk through pain, rather than running from it into addictive activities.

Feelings are important, but not the focus of healing. When a trigger event begins to put pressure on the walls of the addict's heart, powerful negative feelings begin to surface. He then runs from these frightening emotions toward the object of his addiction. To avoid pain, the addict has often run toward sexual sin. If unwilling to face pain, the addict will return to sin again.

Barriers to relationship

Other words depicted in the "shame core" represent various areas of brokenness. They can be addressed to the extent that the addict repents of those defensive strategies adopted to survive his early relational history.

The topics of *unforgiveness, judgements, false belief systems, sins of self-protection* and *developmental deprivations* are all addressed in other chapters. It is only important to note here that they all contribute to the sense of shame that the addict carries.

How the Parts of the System Work Together

We have already discussed the more tangible stages of the cycle from beginning to end. This diagram of the addictive system has several new boxes not yet discussed. Although these are the less obvious contributors to the system, they are integral parts of what keeps it in motion.

Life damaging Consequences

The end result of the addictive cycle is shame and despair, which leads to another cycle of acting out. As the cycles repeat and increase in intensity and frequency, the addict's life becomes unmanageable, the activities of his addiction more damaging. He may get caught in adultery, which will threaten his family life and relationships. He may get AIDS or some other sexually transmitted disease. He may become ineffective at work and loose his job as sexual preoccupation overwhelms him. Or he may get arrested, as his behavior becomes more victimizing. Whatever form the life-damaging consequences take, the resulting exposure increases the addict's pain and shame – he continues to trade a fruitful existence for a consuming, chaotic sexual life. His losses will inevitably push him one of two ways – towards help, or towards greater isolation, despair, and enslavement to his addiction.

Contempt for self

If the addicted person has not seared his or her conscience, each cycle faithfully brings true guilt over sexual sin, and despair over his powerlessness. These painful feelings mingle with anger toward self as each cycle reconfirms that the addict is hopelessly flawed and perverse. One addict said:

> In the end I had no morals, no conscience and I had compromised all my values and integrity. I was willing to do, and indeed did, anything and everything that I needed to continue on in my addiction – unable to stop myself. So I became the person I hated, and had behaviors that I despised and loathed.

The failure to live a moral life dredges up and reinforces old judgements about self, reasserting the messages of the shame core. The addict may even repeat contemptuous words spoken to him by significant childhood figures. He goes beyond condemning his actions and attacks himself as a person. Some addicts even get sloppy with acting out, leaving a trail that eventually brings painful consequences, as a way to punish themselves and confirm their sense of worthlessness.

Self hatred encourages the addict to sink further into denial. His sin nature resists and hates the truth about the inner vulnerabilities that distort his relationships. Anger at self provides a hidden energy that repels conscious awareness of his fears, insecurities, and tendencies to use others. Self hatred keeps him from honestly facing his need for true love; he disdains that need and represses it.

Distorted thinking

To survive the pain of his addiction, the addict lies to himself about reality, telling himself things are really not that bad. Self-deception allows for him to keep acting out. Over time, the sexual addict's thinking becomes impaired, his reality distorted.

Denial and rationalization are present throughout the addictive cycle. They appear in the diagram of the addictive system between the arrival of sexual pressure and the acting out activities *because they provide the bridge between temptation and the act of sexual sin*. For example, one addict said:

> When I am cruising around looking for something sexual to do I play all sorts of mind games with myself. First of all I won't acknowledge to myself that I am really cruising, that would be unchristian. I won't let myself openly choose to go to a topless bar. I need a rationalized excuse. One of my little rules says that acting out is understandable if I get triggered into it. The trigger makes it not my fault. So I drive around until I see a provocative movie poster on a bus stop marquee, then I feel justified in moving on to the next step. Then it is not my fault. I know it is crazy but that's how I work out the conflict.

In this example of rationalization, the addict deems it acceptable to place himself in the path of temptation. When temptation arises, he can give into it as he has been overwhelmed by sin's power. This is how addiction works. He chooses to believe that he can't help it if this evil world is full of sensual trappings. He thinks, "Even a well-meaning but weak Christian will fall when assaulted by such forces." But, in fact, he is denying that he is actually looking for the trigger. He deludes himself by thinking that he is a well-meaning Christian and that sinning wasn't really his choice.

Much of the addict's thinking is distorted in order to conceal his flight from true relationships. Consider the following passage from a man we'll call "Stuart," who describes the thought processes surrounding his sexual acting-out:

> A small, nondescript, young man, Stuart, with his horn-rimmed glasses, white shirt with a pocket full of pens, and sensible shoes would be unlikely to draw a second look from most people-which may be why he finds exposing himself so satisfying. 'The woman would gasp', Stuart recalls vividly. Her eyes would open wide, and I would be thinking, 'Wow, I really got to her. Man, did I get a thrill or what!?' By then I would have high-tailed it out of there, ducked behind a building, gotten away in my car or whatever, but my mind was still going a mile a minute. I'd tell myself, 'She must think I'm really exciting. I bet she's thinking about me right now. I bet she wants me so bad.' And all the time, I'd be going over the whole flash in my mind, every step, especially the look on her face. Then I'd think, 'Man, I'm so high. This is so great. I've got to do it again.' [1]

Stuart's escapade is narcissistic – his perception of the event revolves around the pleasure he derives from it, without any sense that his victims more likely experience horror than feeling thrilled. His thinking is entirely egocentric: the other peoples' feelings are ultimately a non-issue to him. Stuart's warped thinking allows him to escape ugly reality by entering an imaginary scenario to cope with his poor self-image. His projects imaginary, positive responses onto the victimized woman in order to minimize the damage of what he has done. "I bet she wants me so bad," really means, "I have such incredible, irresistible sexual appeal that she has come under my power just by seeing me. I am so desirable women go crazy over me. I am very special." He also builds himself up with that which he values most – sex. The whole transaction works in Stuart's favor because of how he thinks about it.

In order to begin to recover from his addiction, Stuart must acknowledge that the woman was not blessed by seeing his genitals, but rather repulsed. She felt victimized – not excited. One exercise that might help Stuart to grasp the reality of his victimizing behavior would be to reflect upon times of being victimized himself. He could consider the pain and wounds he suffered as a result. In this way he might gain empathy for those he is currently victimizing.

Contempt for others

Another kind of distortion that often accompanies sexual addiction involves judgements about others. In the aftermath of acting out, the addict believes that God is angry with him and is punishing him by not changing his circumstances. Prior to coming out of denial, many Christian addicts use their anger at God as an objection and an excuse to avoid walking through inner pain. It is common to find statements such as John's:

> God could take away my addiction if He wanted to. He holds the universe together. I know this guy who had been using alcohol for nineteen years and God took away his cravings instantly after one prayer session. Sometimes I feel like I should just walk away from my faith in God if He isn't going to heal me. What is the point? He heals other people – Why doesn't he heal me?

Hidden in this thinking is anger about God's alternative to a quick healing fix. In his mercy, God usually waits patiently for the addict to submit to the pathway of personal sanctification. It is of much greater value for the addict to gain the wisdom and character that emerges as he walks through the dark valley of his brokenness. In that valley, he will learn to trust God and others. On that journey he will realize with his heart that God accepts him unconditionally. On that pathway he will acquire the courage to trust in God's sufficiency as he faces his inner darkness. But if he decides to stay angry with God, he need not take the scary and narrow path into the valley of painful reality. He can blame God for his failure. Thus his contempt for God and His ways keeps him on the broad path of the addictive system.

Another example of contempt for others would be a man who hides his fear of women behind anger, as he tells himself that no women are trustworthy, or that all are good for being used. Or he may rationalize his lack of involvement with the church by asserting that all the members are hypocrites and that nobody will understand him. Contempt and distorted thinking work together as the addict uses them to further account for his avoidance of real relationships.

The resolution

The resolution, as described in chapter four, is another form of distorted thinking. At the end of the cycle, feeling remorse and despair, the addict often tells himself, "Now I really know that what I am doing is wrong. I don't need to tell anyone because it is not going to happen again. This is the last time. I clearly see that I need to stop tempting myself and giving in." He may then confess his sin to God, ask forgiveness and plan not to act out again. At this point the delusion is strong and the resolution not to act out again is really an exercise in magical thinking. He believes his resolution, even though everything in his history should indicate that he has no reason to believe it. But inwardly he is too fragile to confess to himself that he is still trapped in his own addictive system.

In later stages of the addiction, resolutions to not act out may disappear. In some cases this means that the addict is beginning to realize that he is powerless over his sexual sin. He may be coming to the end of his rope and may be close to enlisting the help of others. On the other hand, the disappearance of resolutions may mean that he has become resigned to acting out again. He knows he is powerless but he has yielded to hopelessness and has hardened his heart.

The reader should ask himself, "Do I recognize the voice of my resolution?" It will sound something like, "No need to tell anyone. I can overcome this addiction on my own." Recognizing and owning the falsity of our resolutions to not act out can be a turning point in the addictive system. Our resolutions are schemes to stay isolated, not real interventions. After having recognized this truth, we can resolve to dispense with our resolutions. Instead, we can choose to enter into community by confessing our sin to others and becoming accountable to the body of Christ.

If this form of distorted thinking remains in place, the addict is bound to move into another cycle of addiction, all the while telling himself that he is doing fine. His world may come to reflect Romans 1:28:

And just as they did not see fit to acknowledge God any longer, God gave them over to a depraved mind, to do those things which are not proper.

With the passing of time, the addictive system increases in intensity and perpetuates the addict's enslavement to sin.

Spiritual Intervention

The starting point for spiritual intervention is the healing of shame. Healing shame is a process in which the addict comes to understand and receive God's justification at a heart level. Understanding justification by grace means that we give up the notion that we can do anything to better ourselves in the eyes of God. Once the addict can grasp this truth, he can relax and accept his imperfections and weaknesses. Change will then come through his interaction with the Holy Spirit, as he divulges his deep heart with all its flaws.

When the addict is still running from his own pain, he has not embraced his weakness. He does not yet understand God's mercy and kindness at a heart level. The addict's shame prevents him from receiving the grace of God. Healing the addict's shame, therefore, must be a priority for restoration.

For we also once were foolish ourselves, disobedient, deceived, enslaved to various lusts and pleasures… But when the kindness of God our Savior and His love for mankind appeared, He saved us, not because of righteous things we had done, but because of His mercy, by the washing of regeneration and renewing by the Holy Spirit, whom He poured out upon us rightly through Jesus Christ our Savior, that being justified by His grace we might be made heirs according to the hope of eternal life. (Titus 3:3-7)

Personal

References

[1]   Dr. Ralph Earle and Dr. Gregory Crow, *Lonely All The Time* (New York: Simon Schuster Inc., 1989) 58.

Homework

Homework

First, read Appendix D

1. List the events of your past and present life that contribute to your "Shame Core" as described in this chapter's material.

2. Describe how you know when you are feeling sexual pressure.

3. Describe the role that your distorted thinking takes in enabling you to move around your addictive cycle. Use specific examples of how you think.

4. Do you make a resolution not to act out again at the end of your cycle? Write out the words that you use to convince yourself that you don't have to tell anyone what just happened.

5. Do you experience contempt or anger for self? Write out the words of that contempt.

6. Do you experience contempt or anger towards others surrounding your addiction? Describe the words that give voice to that anger.

Allowing God to Remove Our Defects

A humble man is able to receive God's estimation of who he is. His heart is contrite (broken, supple, moldable) and trembles at the words of his Father in Heaven.... If God says that he is loved, his heart responds with thanksgiving and joy. The humble man receives love and value from the One who can name him and give him significance by calling him a son. Self-hatred is the enemy of humility.

Chapter Eleven

Search me, O God, and know my heart; test me and know my anxious thoughts. See if there is any offensive way in me, and lead me in the way everlasting. (Psalm 139:23-24)

Inner Vows

As he thinketh in his heart, so is he. (Proverbs 23:7, KJV)

In the King James version, the word "thinketh" is a translation of the Hebrew word *shaar*. *Shaar* is often used to communicate the image of a gatekeeper of a walled city, the watchman who ensures that no evil forces enter the communal dwelling. We could rework the Proverb to read, *"As a man keeps the gate of his heart, so is he."* In other words, like a sentry atop a city wall, each person determines what comes into his heart (and therefore into his life). Based on what he chooses to close the gates of his heart to, and what he chooses to let in, so shall the life of his "city" be determined.

Sometimes, decisions we've made long ago continue to keep certain good things out of our lives. If we don't reverse these decisions, we prevent good things from coming to us. This is sometimes what happens in the case of "inner vows."

> An inner vow is a determination set by the mind and heart into all the being in early life... [and is] usually forgotten. Our inner being persistently retains such programming, no matter what changes of mind...may later pertain. [1]

The will is a powerful faculty. We can make choices early in our lives, such as to reject certain relationships or kinds of people. "Inner vows" made in childhood become like policies by which our lives are governed. To be set free of them, we must deliberately choose to break them in prayer.

Consider the example of a common vow, such as the decision to not need other people, to be self-sufficient. Vowing to be self-sufficient is a denial of God's intention for humanity, since He has made us to be relational beings. Such a vow might prevent certain sorts of hurt from occurring, but it would also prevent a person from rightfully relying on others.

In emotionally damaging families, children make inner vows both consciously and unconsciously. These vows are protective in nature. They are made to prevent future emotional injury in relationships. Initially, vows may help children survive their families of origin, but later these same vows will stand in the way of healthy interaction and intimacy in relationships.

One example of a vow as an obstacle to intimacy occurred in a young woman; her legalistic father often withheld good things from her as a form of discipline. In return, she made a vow never to expect good things from her father. This vow kept her from painful disappointment. Later in life, the vow manifested itself when she discovered that she could not believe in, nor receive good things from, God the Father. She could not experience His presence. In order to begin receiving the love of God she had to repent and, in prayer, break the vow that she had made long ago.

In another example, a ten-year-old boy lost his father to an incurable disease. The loss was traumatic and painful. As a defense against further pain, he refused to let family or friends step in as father figures, vowing never to be hurt by men again. He thought that refusing to receive love from a sort of emotional surrogate father would protect him. This vow worked against him by closing his heart off to the nurture of men. Even so, his heart was always yearning for an earthly father. He simultaneously wanted love, and yet refused to be open to receive it. Therefore he could not receive from God the fatherly love that was available to him. In the end, he had to repent of both the protective vow and the distorted fantasy of finding an earthly father so he could begin to receive the love of God.

Vows take many forms but are always relational. A man may vow never to be vulnerable to women as the result of a harsh relationship with a specific woman. This can be the motivation behind a string of sexual encounters that lack commitment. Such a vow might also be expressed through difficulty in committing oneself to the opposite sex.

One very common vow is the choice not to feel anymore. This vow chokes the heart, making relationship with others very difficult. Healing is also difficult because the split between head and heart has rendered the person trapped in his intellect (unable to feel) and detached, so that nothing touches the heart.

Specific vows are almost always generalized. For example: vows made in reaction to mom can become vows against women; vows against dad can become vows against all men and God the Father. If the barriers in our hearts remain standing, they will likely keep God out. He will not be able to cleanse our wounded selves. The emotional effects of our sin will remain. Vows will keep us from obeying Jesus' second great commandment, to love others as we love ourselves. Therefore, confessing and repenting of our vows is very important. Once confessed and renounced, we can then break the vow through prayer. It is also beneficial to ask God to restore the original functioning of the heart and pray His blessing and love into it.

Defensive Detachment

Defensive detachment is a specific type of inner vow, wherein the person's heart determines that "in order to stay safe, I am not going to allow you to be emotionally close to me." A child will often make this kind of vow as a result of continuous wounding, or even a single severe wound by a parent. When a child defensively detaches from his parent(s), he is choosing to close his heart to their wounding. But because he closes the doors of his heart to them, their goodness and love cannot penetrate him any longer, either. His identity, therefore, will bear the marks of the broken relationship. The detachment may give rise to belief systems that are generalized towards whole genders, where all men are seen to be like the father, for example.

Some distortions that issue out of defensive detachment are:
• fear of rejection

• fear of intimacy

- fear of confrontation
- compulsive, inappropriate intimacy outside of marriage
- emotional isolation inside the marriage
- sexually connecting without commitment
- sexually addictive affairs
- narcissistic masturbation
- fear of initiating sexually
- sexualized anger
- misogyny (generalized hatred of women)
- misandry (generalized hatred of men)
- homosexual and lesbian tendencies

Once inner vows are revealed in the recovery process, the addict must repent of his unconscious decision to play it safe. He must learn to risk again in relationships. Since it is likely that the detachment was in relation to a parent, this repentance must be coupled with forgiveness towards the parent, for whatever his or her sins were. Forgiveness will free the person to see others more clearly. It will also free him to acknowledge and accept the parts of himself that are like the one from whom he detached. Then, with the ability to recognize and accept those part of himself like the offender, he will be able to grow to be more like what God has always intended him to be. (We will focus more specifically on forgiving others in Chapter 18.)

Fortresses

For though we walk in the flesh, we do not war according to the flesh, for the weapons of our warfare are not of the flesh, but divinely powerful for the destruction of fortresses. We are destroying speculations and every lofty thing raised up against the knowledge of God, and we are taking every thought captive to the obedience of Christ. (2 Cor 10:3-5)

A fortress is a house of thoughts, a mental structure composed of related thoughts, perspectives, and feelings. The fortress is created to protect us. While the vow is a defensive decision made to protect from pain in relationships, the fortress is a belief system that gives the person a place to hide. For example, the belief, "No one would love me as I am," is a lie.

This lie both exalts itself against the truth that God loves the sexual addict, and also serves as a hiding place which gives him an excuse to not risk in relationships. If he clings to this belief, he can rationalize his occasional sexual sins as ways of easing his loneliness, without having to involve his heart. He has chosen to believe that true relationship will only end in rejection, and his choice to believe the lie causes it to become a self-fulfilling prophesy.

Another fortress exists around those who construct an image which they present to the world, as if to say, "If I can appear perfect, people will not reject me." This hiding place prevents the addict from letting others see his imperfect and wounded self. He hides from all people, including Jesus. He demands much from himself, and also hides from his own weaknesses, accepting the grandiose notion that his own works can buy the acceptance of God. He therefore cannot be humble, contrite, and real, since he will not face the fact that he is finite, limited, and needs God's help.

Fortresses come in all shapes and sizes. The addict must ask the Holy Spirit to identify the deadening belief systems under which he lives in order to protect himself from pain in relationships. This insight will often come through the accountability group or accountability group leader, as he is sharing. It is important to note that *taking thoughts into captivity* is an on-going process. The thinking of our hearts which is contrary to the

Gospel will most likely be uncovered in layers. Fortresses will be destroyed a little at a time. This discovery process may take place through journaling, prayer, and feedback from others.

The healing goal in discovering and throwing off self-made fortresses is to securely hide the vulnerable places of our heart in the shelter of God's acceptance. If our hearts live in the love of Jesus, no one's sin or rejection will be able to remove our sense of worth. The Psalmist seemed to understand this truth as he wrote:

How great is your goodness, which you have stored up for those who fear you, which you bestow in the sight of men on those who take refuge in you. In the shelter of your presence you hide them from the intrigues of men; in your dwelling place you keep them safe from accusing tongues. (Psalm 31:19-20)

Disassembling mental fortresses can be very frightening, even terrifying, for the addict. He knows in his head that Jesus has been designated by God as his true Fortress, but he has never had the experience to back it up. There may be a frightened child within who is terrified at the thought of placing himself in the hands of an unseen "Father" figure.

Belief Systems

You were taught, with regard to your former way of life, to put off your old self, which is being corrupted by its deceitful desires; to be made new in the attitude of your minds; and to put on the new self created to be like God in true righteousness and holiness. (Ephesians 4:22-24)

When Adam and Eve fell, their first response to their sin was to notice their nakedness and to be ashamed. All of us share their legacy, to some extent or another; we all feel some shame. We can break out of our shame by allowing God to show us the thoughts and attitudes that we hold towards ourselves which are untrue. Some of them are:

- I'm worthless
- I'm stupid
- I'm a failure at relationships
- I'm not loveable
- I'm a bad person
- I'm ugly
- My life will never amount to anything
- Everything I touch turns to disaster
- I'm not masculine. I'm not feminine
- When things go wrong, it's always my fault
- God can't forgive me

Such attitudes enshroud us in darkness, so that the light of who we truly are to God is concealed. This can be one reason why we read the word of God and intellectually agree with it, yet find that it only touches us superficially.

The scripture tells us that we are to actively put off these attitudes by the renewing of our minds. One thing we can do to change is to study and meditate upon scripture, to discover who we are in Christ. The Holy Spirit will illumine us as we read the Word, and will displace old beliefs. Also, we can ask the Holy Spirit reveal our diseased attitudes, in order to repent from them and replace them with the truth. Also important is healing prayer for the areas of woundedness that may cement these lies into our hearts.

Hurtful interactions with significant people in our early lives are often at the root of shame-filled self-perceptions. These attitudes were then incorporated into our hearts. The actions of parents or others implied negative things about us, which we simply accepted as true. Over time, we began acting on these negative beliefs about ourselves and, in some cases, unconsciously set up situations so as to confirm the beliefs. Shame gave birth to a kind of self-fulfilling prophecy, and was reinforced repeatedly. Our parents may have laid the foundation of skewed self-perceptions, but we took hold of what we received from them. By accepting lies about ourselves, we engaged unknowingly in self-sabotage.

To be set free, it is necessary to acknowledge and repent of our faulty belief systems. Equally necessary is forgiveness: we will need to forgive those people who took part in forming old, false understandings about ourselves. By forgiving them we cancel their debts. This sets us free to no longer demand the love from them that we never received. We release them and, in turn, release ourselves from bondage.

Some of the faulty beliefs that sexual addicts hold are more central to their specific sexual problems. This is the case with four core beliefs that have been articulated by Patrick Carnes:
• Sex is my most important need
• No one would love me as I am
• My needs will never get met if I have to depend on others
• I am basically a bad, unworthy person [2]

Authors Earle and Crow identify a fifth belief,
• If I have to depend on my social skills to get close to anyone, it will never happen [3]

Judgements

Judgements are generalized beliefs about others; they automatically color our mindset before we actually know anything about a person or group of people. These preconceived notions can be held toward genders, races, personality types, professions, or any other kind of group. Judgements can also be rendered against oneself. (If you look back through the beliefs above, some of them are judgements.)

When judgements are hidden and established in the heart, they lock-in fears and other barriers toward relationships. These bind us to jaundiced expectations about the outcomes of involvement with others. As a result, the one who holds the judgements reaps bitter fruit in relationships in accord with the destructive seeds sown in his heart.

Do not judge, or you too will be judged. For in the same way you judge others, you will be judged, and with the measure you use, it will be measured to you. (Matthew 7:1-2)

Without even being aware of it, the addict's judgements will bring about the negative relational outcome(s) that his heart expects. Some of the most serious judgements for the addict are about what will happen if he becomes emotionally vulnerable with another person. Some examples might be:
• All (wo)men are evil and will play with my mind
• All (wo)men will reject me
• If I get close to (wo)men they will leave me
• All (wo)men are needy and will suffocate me
• (Wo)men are shaming and hurtful
• (Wo)men are emotional monsters that consume little boys/girls
• When (wo)men find out who I am they won't want me

It is easy to understand how an addict with judgements of this type would consciously or unconsciously avoid committed, intimate relationship. Such fearful expectations kill off relationships with others before ever giving them a chance to begin.

Judgements about others were often formed in primary relationships and then generalized to the whole world. They need to be treated seriously by the addict as he progresses with his healing. Just as with faulty belief systems, judgements need to be identified, acknowledged, and repented of. People who were participants in the formation of our judgements must be forgiven.

Facing Self-Hatred

In the Twelve Steps, Step Seven states, "We humbly asked Him to remove these shortcomings." The key and most significant word in this sentence is *humble*. A *humble* man is able to receive God's estimation of who he is. His heart is contrite (broken, supple, moldable) and trembles at the words of his Father in Heaven. If God says he is justified, then he forgets his guilt. If God says that he is loved, his heart responds with thanksgiving and joy. The *humble* man receives love and value from the One who can name him and give him significance by calling him a son.

Self-hatred is the enemy of humility. Where there is self-hatred, the addict must live behind a mask or false self, which has been constructed over many years in order to stifle the pain of his self-rejection. As Leanne Payne puts it, such a person "walks alongside of himself;" full of self-hatred, he looks at, analyzes, criticizes and picks himself apart, always having himself in view. The man with self-hatred is turned against himself because he is still in agreement with the negative messages that he received in his youth. He agrees that he is bad and contemptible, unworthy of love. He, therefore, experiences feelings of shame and self-pity that have nothing to do with the conviction of the Holy Spirit.

We cannot say that we are ready for God to remove our defects and hate ourselves at the same time. Self-hatred is evil and needs to go. We must decide to repent of the sin of self-hatred and renounce it.

Embracing self-acceptance as we face the cross

Self-hatred has a bearing on the addict's ability to love others. According to Jesus, the second great commandment is to *love your neighbor as yourself*. This command is a problem for the man who hates himself. In fact, this is precisely the problem with the world. It is full of people who "love" others in exactly the same way that they "love" themselves.

The goal of accepting and embracing our wounded selves is a worthy one – not just for our own healing, but also so that we might reflect the love of God and let it shine out to others. Self-acceptance is not the same as self-actualization, which involves people accenting and developing themselves apart from God. Self-actualization does not work. Only Jesus can raise the new self to its full stature. The new self in God does not come as a result of introspection and self-analysis. It will only come when a person looks outside of himself to Jesus and grasps the truth about himself. He receives and walks in Jesus' perspective on himself.

The process of coming to accept oneself is that of dying to the selfishness and pride that refuses to receive the truth of God. Attaining the Christian virtue of self-acceptance involves the work of the cross in our lives. The first barrier that needs to go is the self-flattery that often prevents the addict from detecting his self-hatred; though full of self-hatred, he does not see it. As with many other areas of his life, he is in denial. We break the power of self-hatred when we embrace our weakness and admit that God's grace is the antidote to our striving toward acceptability. To receive God's grace, we have to give up.

When we are willing to drop our masks and begin to acknowledge the true center that comes with the new birth, we embrace those life-giving attributes and abilities that have been pushed away and lost. As a man is cleansed, he may begin to feel new spontaneity, creativity, ability to feel, and ability to bond with others. He begins to "change and become like a child," gaining entry into the Kingdom of God. God cannot dwell in a covering that man builds for himself. He can only begin to break into the soul when a man is willing to have his pride exposed and agrees to give up the faulty attitudes that call him something other than God's son.

Renouncing Self-Hatred

But whenever a person turns to the Lord, the veil is taken away…Therefore, since we have this ministry, as we received mercy, we do not lose heart, but we have renounced the things hidden because of shame, not walking in craftiness…For God, who said, 'Light shall shine out of darkness', is the one who has shone in our hearts to give the light of the knowledge of the glory of God in the face of Christ. (2 Cor. 3:16, 4:1-2a, 6)

If we are still living in agreement with vows, fortresses, and strongholds that exalt themselves against His love, there will be a veil over our hearts that prevents us from walking in the truth of God. We will be doomed to live in the negative feelings and shame that come with them.

For this reason, we must start the process of gaining self-acceptance by renouncing our self-hatred, as an act of the will. We make the decision to repent knowing that our present feelings will be unreliable and a reflection of diseased attitudes. A *prayer of renunciation* might go something like this:

> Lord, I acknowledge that, in my heart, I have not agreed with Your assessment of me as revealed in Your Word. I have agreed with the negative messages of my youth and have lived from a false self, not the true self that You created me to be. I acknowledge that I have hated myself. I repent for having indulged myself in this sin. Please forgive me Lord, and cleanse me from this sin. Through the power of Your grace in me, I renounce the sin of self-hatred, and I refuse its power over me. Lord, break off of me the longstanding effects this sin has had on me. I choose and determine to live from my true self. I choose to deal honestly with sinful attitudes by bringing them before You and acknowledging the work of Jesus on the cross. I ask You to reveal issues that have been hidden to me because of shame, and I ask You to do an ongoing work in my life. Please continue to cleanse me of self-hatred, Lord, until I am fully free from its effects. Amen.

As a man renounces his self-hatred, he breaks through what Leanne Payne calls "the first great barrier to wholeness in Christ." It will take time and struggle for the truth to be felt at the level of the heart, especially for those who have been entrenched in sin and perversion for years. As we persevere, God will be faithful to deliver us.

References

[1] John and Paula Sandford, *Transformation of the Inner Man* (So. Plainfield: Bridge Publishing, Inc., 1982) 192.

[2] Patrick Carnes, *Out of the Shadows* (Minneapolis: CompCare Publications, 1983) 120.

[3] Dr. Ralph Earle and Dr. Gregory Crow, *Lonely All The Time* (New York: Simon & Schuster, 1989) 19.

HOMEWORK

1. Ask the Holy Spirit to show you any vows that you have made that are affecting your relationship with God, others or yourself. List them and explain how they are affecting your life.

2. Ask the Holy Spirit to show you any strongholds that you have erected for protection in relationships. List them and explain how they are affecting your life.

3. Do the same for strongholds that constitute beliefs or judgments that you have about yourself or others that do not mirror God's truth, and need to be repented of.

4. Are you aware of any negative words/attitudes that you hold toward yourself that would constitute self-hatred? Write them out in sentence form.

5. Write a little about your beliefs on humility. What does it mean? What will you have to do to begin operating in humility?

6. Write out a statement for yourself (if you are ready!) regarding your willingness to let God remove all of your defects. Sign and date it.

Signature _____ Date _____

Key Action: Plan to share answers to questions 1 and 3 with your accountability group:

Date _____

Embracing Loss as a Way of Gain

Embracing

In walking the path away from our old lifestyles, we may experience overwhelming feelings of shame and sadness. The truth which God is pouring in will illuminate the destructiveness of our actions. Remorse may be a part of getting a real picture of what our lives have become.

Chapter Twelve

I called on your name, O Lord, from the depths of the pit. You heard my plea: "Do not close your ears to my cry for relief." You came near when I called you, and you said, 'Do not fear.' (Lamentations 3:55-57)

Count All Things Lost

But whatever things were gain to me, those things I have counted as loss for the sake of Christ. More than that, I count all things to be loss in view of the surpassing value of knowing Christ Jesus my Lord, for whom I have suffered the loss of all things, and count them but rubbish so that I may gain Christ, and may be found in Him, …that I may know Him, and the power of His resurrection and the fellowship of His sufferings, being conformed to His death. (Phil 3:7-10)

Paul here records his very real experience of loss for the sake of his relationship with Christ. What did Paul lose as he made Jesus his sole source of life? He gave up the affirmation and status gained from his peers through legalistic performance as a Pharisee. He no longer took pride in his lineage of the tribe of Benjamin. He gave up being seen in the marketplace as a successful religious man with much power.

Forsaking addictive activities in pursuit of an undivided heart is not so glamorous. Yet, we must lose these activities if we are to gain Christ. There are some important principles to grasp in what Paul says.

Count Our Addiction as Lost

In the process of "losing" our addiction, we must define and name specific actions *as being lost to us*, declaring with certainty that we can never return them.

To avoid the pain of loss, we may try to bargain our way around the reality that we must lose our addictions for good. Because we are accustomed to walking in denial and the darkness of our distorted thinking, we will be tempted to entertain thoughts such as:
- "Masturbation is not so bad – it's not really an addiction."
- "I'm just a partial addict; I'm not as bad as the other guys in my group."
- "It's only in my mind – I'm not really acting out."
- "I need to test and see if I'm still addicted."
- "I've been good – I'll just treat myself."

Avoiding the finality of our loss is a certain way to re-enter the addictive cycle. The temptation to turn back to old ways may be compelling for some because of feelings of alarm, panic, and terror that can accompany a heart-felt decision to stop acting out. It is not uncommon for the sexual addict to think that he has made a horrible mistake as he faces life without his addiction. Yet if he allows himself to compromise, he will surely find himself back in it.

Counting Our Addiction as Rubbish

Ask yourself these questions, and then answer them, preferably on paper:

- Do I really see the destructiveness of my addiction?

- Do I hate what it does to my life?

- Do I see it as bad only because God says it is, and yet still cherish my addictive ways in my heart?

If you answered "yes" to the third question, you will return to your addiction.

We must ask ourselves hard questions if we are going to count our addiction as loss. To arrive at honest, genuine answers to these questions, it is helpful to meditate on the destructiveness of our addictions and their effects on our relationships with God and others. Rather than lie to ourselves, we need to be brutally honest about whether we've been choosing our sexual addiction or knowing Christ. It will be impossible to love Christ if we still love our addiction.

Be Found in Christ

Jesus said, "I am the true vine" (John 15:1). By this He indicates that there are many other vines – false vines that do not bear fruit. If we are abiding in the vine of sexual addiction, we will not bear godly fruit – we will not experience the surpassing knowledge of Christ. Jesus goes on to say:

Abide in Me, and I in you. As the branch cannot bear fruit of itself, unless it abides in the vine, so neither can you unless you abide in me. (John 15:4)

If we are still nurturing addiction, we cannot feed on the life of Christ. We must be honest about where we abide, and then do something about it.

Knowing the Fellowship of His Sufferings

When we think of giving up our addiction, we cannot help but fear we'll suffer with feelings of emptiness as we resist the temptation to act out. We fear that we won't be able to withstand the underlying pain that arises. As we entrust ourselves to Jesus, we rely on His strength to help us finish the race.

Let us also lay aside every encumbrance and sin which so easily entangles us, and let us run with endurance the race that is set before us, fixing our eyes on Jesus, the author and perfecter of our faith, who for the joy set before Him endured such hostility by sinners against himself, so that you may not grow weary and lose heart. You have not yet resisted to the point of shedding blood in your striving against sin. (Hebrews 12:1b-4)

As Jesus resisted the temptation to flee from the "cup" of suffering and death that the Father had given Him, He experienced so much anguish that He sweat drops of blood. We know, therefore, that He can sympathize with our sufferings as we resist sin. He is able to abide in our pain with us and does not shrink back from it. If we are willing to look for him there, He will become the strength of our hearts.

Contrary to what we might feel, we can survive more pain than we think. We have been running from the pain in our hearts for so long that it has become a monster; we believe that monster has the power to devour us if we let it arise.

Out task is to face the cross of Christ as we walk through the death of the old man. Only by entering into the fellowship of His sufferings can we experience the resurrection life of Christ. There is life *on the other side* of the cross. If we want to be free of our addictions, we must be conformed to His death. Dying to one's old or false self is a painful process.

Grieving the Loss of Our Addiction

In order to gain Christ, you must lose an old friend. If you are angry, that is normal. Anger is a normal part of losing something that has been "nurturing" your life. Every time you are ripped from the comfort of your "friend," you may feel angry – that's all right. But it's important not to displace your anger onto someone else. Be angry that you are losing something and acknowledge that loss. God wants to hear from you about your feelings; you don't have to hide them from Him.

Anger is a normal part of the grieving process that you will go through as you give up your addictive activities. As you reckon with the loss of your addiction, you may feel angry at God for allowing the situations that predisposed you to addiction. You may become angry at others who expect you to try harder. You will probably become angry at yourself for letting your life get so out of control. God wants to use these opportunities to help you – anger can be welcomed as a source of energy that will help you extricate yourself from attachments that have kept you bound to your addiction.

As a general rule, it is unproductive to stay angry for long with those who are trying to help, such as God and your support people. Instead, we can use the anger as an ally, *embracing the anger* as a friend in battle and turning it against sin. The anger can motivate and fuel our fight, whereas before we felt anger there was only apathy.

Anger can also inspire us to create new, healthy emotional distance between ourselves and those people connected with our destructive lifestyles. It can give us strength to fight lies wedged in our hearts, such as those related to self-hatred.

In walking the path away from our old lifestyles, we may experience overwhelming feelings of shame and sadness. The truth which God is pouring in will illuminate the destructiveness of our actions. Remorse may be a part of getting a real picture of what our lives have become.

We may be tempted to live in self-pity, which stomps its childish foot and refuses to humbly accept responsibility for past actions. It also refuses to acknowledge the provision and forgiveness of God. Self-pity is a detour back to addiction, an excuse to binge which must be brought swiftly to the cross. This can be done through gratitude, thanking God for the many good things He has provided and which He promises to continue to provide.

In giving up their addictions, most addicts experience other feelings besides those already mentioned, such as undefined pain, loneliness, fear, anxiety, and depression. Feelings like these can surface from our hearts, which has been anesthetized for years by restless acting out.

You may already recognize, some of the following signs of grief as you begin to count your addiction as loss:

- Confusion about how to act, and what to do

- Feelings of alienation

- Fantasies about how things could have been

- Sadness over unfulfilled expectations and wasted months and years

- Desire for a quick fix

- Feelings of exposure and vulnerability

- Failure to take care of oneself

- Uncontrollable emotions

- Dark thoughts about death, which may or many not include suicidal thoughts

- Sudden, accident-prone behavior

- Fear that the pain will not go away [1]

The process of grieving is important to find freedom. It cannot be sidetracked or avoided. It is the natural process by which we accept the loss of something which we held dear. It is also the process by which we kick idols out of our hearts. On the other side of the pain, as the pain of grief flows up and out of us, is resurrection life. This life can gradually replace the places formerly taken-up by grief in our hearts. This will happen as we abide in Christ and do not switch to other types of addiction.

The Importance of Feelings

Our feelings are very important. They motivate us, and comprise the energy that gives us passion for God. Our feelings make us vital and "real." A man without feelings will not find much enjoyment in life. In fact, a serious clinical depression is one that has gone further than mere sadness, and which has become a deep numbness, an inability to feel. This is experienced by many to be a sense of deadness, emptiness, and meaninglessness.

In order to cut off our feelings, we must harden our hearts. Hardening our hearts also cuts off the life of God. We cannot connect with God without giving Him our hearts, and He cannot connect with us profoundly if we avoid our feelings.

As we begin to open up to our feelings, we will find some of them to be painful. This is because we have spent a lifetime stuffing what was uncomfortable to us. But, as we remain open, positive and joyful feelings will accompany the negative. *The capacity to feel (one capacity of the soul) is not like a supermarket where we have the power to pull whatever feeling off the shelf we like. Gaining access to the heart is more like coming upon a field where a variety of plants grow together.*

Experiencing darker feelings can lead us to false beliefs in our hearts. Negative feelings may be attached to the diseased belief systems which drive our addictive behavior. As we experience our feelings afresh, we can connect them to the deeper beliefs and corresponding memories that need to be healed. Our painful feelings may point to sins, ours and those committed against us by others, which need forgiveness. Learning to name and feel our feelings is, therefore, a necessary part of the healing process. Many of us need help with this activity because we came out of families that did not allow us to talk about or value feelings.

Stand in the Furnace of Separation

If we are going to survive our decisions to die to our addictions, then we must have the same attitude demonstrated by Shadrach, Meshach, and Abednego (see Daniel, chapter 3). Their story illustrates the experience of trusting God. In Daniel 3, King Nebuchadnezzar demanded that they bow down to a large gold-plated idol. (For our purposes, we can imagine the idol as a pornographic video, or whatever we've been bent toward). He said to the three Israelites:

If you are ready to fall down and worship the image I made, very good. But if you do not worship it, you will be thrown immediately into a blazing furnace. Then what god will be able to rescue you from my hand? (Daniel 3:15)

Like these three, we must choose between our God and His rivals, the idol gods we once served. If we choose our God, then we must face the pain of our emptiness. If we refuse to bow down and feed our hunger through sexually addictive activity, then we may be left with an awareness of our pain and the inability to hide from it. We may feel the deep deprivation that has been driving us. This is the fiery furnace, and it is no less awful than the one the three Israelites faced in Babylon. At this time we must cease bending toward addictive idols. Instead, we look up towards Heaven and invite God into our pain. If we will wait on Him, He will heal us and be our Comforter. But if we choose friendship with sensuality and prefer its false comforts, we remain earthbound. Our souls will succumb to death. To become perfected in love, we need the attitude of the three Israelites:

O Nebuchadnezzar, we do not need to defend ourselves before you in this matter. If we are thrown into the blazing furnace, the God we serve is able to save us from it, and He will rescue us from your hand, O King. But even if he does not, we want you to know, O King, that we will not serve your gods or worship the image of gold you have set up. (Daniel 3:16-18)

As we likely know, Shadrach, Meshach, and Abednego were thrown into the furnace because they refused to bow down to the idol. In the furnace, a fourth man (Jesus) was seen among them, and saved them. Having been willing to suffer for God, they chose rightly. Happily, they came out of the furnace and were delivered from the evil king's power.

I believe that this story is a promise to us from God. We need only the courage to stand with Him in the furnace, and we will be delivered.

The Cost of Failing to Grieve

You may be thinking, "Isn't there some way to get around facing the furnace, the pain of the grieving process?" I believe the answer is no. In fact, there is a cost for those who refuse to grieve.

There are two types of losses to be faced in recovery. We have already talked about present losses. The loss of a loved one, the loss of a job, or the loss of an addiction can provoke grief. We have been talking about the present loss associated with giving up our addictive activities. The second type of loss is less obvious. It involves essential qualities of human contact lost long ago, and never acknowledged because these painful losses were buried in the depths of the heart. These losses are often less concrete and do not begin to hurt until the truth about early wounding is uncovered and acknowledged. Examples of this type of loss are:

- The loss of warmth and affection from a healthy mother, leaving a sense of emptiness

- The loss of wisdom and guidance from a father who may actually have been absent, harsh, or emotionally distant

- The loss associated with a lack of affirmation and, instead, receiving abuse and rejection

- The loss of personal dignity, having been used for someone else's purposes

- The loss of personal uniqueness

- The loss of ability to trust in intimate relationships – instead we hate our need to be deeply connected to someone, because it has always caused pain

All of the losses listed above reflect a loss of love. Many of us never received the input of nurturing caretakers. Because we were young and lacked sophistication, we couldn't process our pain at the time. We only knew how to survive. Since then we have used our addiction as a way of keeping these losses at bay.

What happened when we did not process our losses? Simply put, our hearts stayed sick because we never learned how to live in reality. In order to avoid acknowledging our losses, we continued to hope in illusions. For example, the eight year-old boy whose father died, circumvented grieving through hoping to find another earthly father some day. As long as he kept looking, he did not have to face his loss. Similarly, the sexual addict has hoped that sensuality would replace his need to learn how to be truly intimate. As a result, he continued living a life with many external contacts, leaving him empty and lonely on the inside. In both cases, the addict hoped for what he would never find. He put his trust in a strategy that could not give life. False hope actually keeps us in a continual state of loss. Proverbs 13:12 states:

Hope deferred makes the heart sick.

Failing to grieve keeps us in a state of longing for things that cannot satisfy. If we grieve, we make room in our hearts for a real solution, and embrace a foundational longing. Only one thing can fulfill our deepest needs – knowing the God of love. As we grieve, we will be able to understand clearly what the psalmist says:

Why are you downcast, O my soul? Why so disturbed within me? Put your hope in God, for I will yet praise him, my Savior and my God. (Psalm 42:5)

The Problem of Painful Memories

The history of your life is important. Though you live in the present, your life is composed of the tapestry of memories in your heart, the quilt of remembered experiences. You are the only one with those memories, all of which are recalled from your perspective. All of your past, and how you've dealt with it, is summed up in the person you are today. Your memories, in other words, are very important. David Seamands writes,

> In Scripture, memory is considered one of the most important aspects of both God's mind and ours. It is central to God's nature as well as to forgiveness, salvation, and righteous living. God's ability to remember or not remember is a part of the divine mind or knowledge which filled the biblical writers with awe. Since we have been created in the divine image, we too have this ability. Though ours is limited, the biblical writers considered this human [faculty] a reason for wonder and praise. [2]

Your childhood experiences in an imperfect family left emotional scars, which exist in your memories. Pain and suffering that you experienced colored your view of reality. These emotional scars established "lenses" through which you now view your life. To the extent that perspective has been shaped by your experience of evil in this world, it will not reflect *God's assessment* about who you and others truly are. The result is a heart that thinks, feels, and perceives in distorted ways, and which has difficulty receiving the truth of God's word.

In our youth, we experienced and recorded memories from a child's vantage point. It is not surprising that we drew unsophisticated conclusions and raised strong internal boundaries against towering, godlike adults.

"I hate mom became I hate women." We formed internal judgements that kept our wounded heart from being hurt again. Now as adults, those judgements imprison us. Our judgements distort reality and color our expectations about relationships.

Our childhood survival techniques do not work in a grown-up world. Defensive and mistrustful, we struggle with mutual, giving relationships. Our memories hold old lies and distortions in place. David Seamands writes:

> Many of us have hurtful memories which we try to push out of our minds. Such memories cannot be healed by the mere passage of time any more than an infected wound could be. The infection turns inward and actually worsens because it spreads to other areas, affecting and infecting them. So it is with certain painful experiences, especially those that happened during the important years of early childhood and teenage development. [3]

In a very real sense that child within us is still perceiving parental figures in the outside world and reacting according to fears about being rejected. As children, we had no choice but to make broad generalizations, because that's how children think. Children miss many nuances that are obvious to adults. In many cases, those generalizations are still in place. To the degree that original wounds were never resolved, we find that our inner world is still bound to old realities. As a result, our ability to move into new types of relating is hampered. In a very real sense, sexual addiction is a way of avoiding our inner strongholds.

One of the ways that God heals is to revisit old memories. With the light of the Holy Spirit and the truth of His Word, He helps us sort the wrong beliefs from the true ones. He helps us break the unhealthy vows, so that we might newly make good, life-giving choices. He also delights in revealing to us how we have transferred beliefs about our parents' flaws onto Him and others, thus closing off the inflow of His real love.

Part of revisiting our memories will be feeling the painful feelings associated with them. When we revisit memories and experience the pain, we know we are in touch with our hearts. When we ask God to heal us there, expect that He will!

Helpful Hints for Memory Exploration

In the healing process, God will often bring memories to mind. If God calls memories to mind, it means He wants to heal wounds that occurred at that time. Sometimes we may not feel much as they come into our awareness; other times, we are flooded with feelings. As we discuss our experiences with the Lord, He may answer questions we've long wondered about. He may change our perspectives, so that we can see what happened from an additional viewpoint. He may ask us what we are feeling; He frees us to feel what we couldn't feel then.

If we are certain of nothing else, we can know that He wants to heal us, so that we are no longer shaped by what happened to us in the past. One important thing we can do to receive His healing is to forgive those who've hurt us, or towards whom we've been bitter. Before forgiving, He may first call us to deal with the pain.

In working through memories with the Lord, it's important to keep a number of things in mind:

- Earlier memories usually are more core, foundational, and powerful in the healing process. We form our primary personality strategies before the age of six. Wounding before that time becomes very deeply seated.

- When healing memories, the memories must be specific. Forgiving generally is not as powerful as forgiving specifically. Often specific memories can be representative of many others like it, but forgiving for specific events is much more manageable than forgiving for a whole life time.

- During times of healing prayer focus on the clearest part of a memory. Often you will only get bits and pieces at a time. Do not make things up. Allow the Holy Spirit to bring up what needs to be healed in His time. He does it in an orderly fashion and takes into His consideration what we can handle.

- The memories must be yours, coming from inside of you. Be on guard against taking on a memory told to you by a relative, unless it connects with something within you.

- Attach a feeling to the clearest part of the memory. Often, pictures come first. Begin to allow yourself to feel.

- Feelings often lead to memories. Be willing to feel painful feelings without memories and allow the memories to come back in that context. Sometimes memories will be first; sometimes feelings will come first.

- Be wary of memories not accompanied with feelings. Sometimes, what we think are memories can be imagination. Usually the feeling of being in the memory will not come up if the memory is imaginary. We may have feelings of concern about whether or not the memory is true, but that is not the same as having feelings that come from the memory.

The objectives of processing a memory

What are we trying to do when we process a memory? The overall objective is to remove the inner life structures that block our ability to risk in relationships. These have already been discussed in-depth in the chapter titled, "Allowing God to Remove Our Defects." Our inability to risk blocks intimacy. In developing early strategies for protecting ourselves from further wounding we began a partnership with the law of sin and death working in us. Our reaction to the sin of others became our sin.

Here are some of the general relational barriers that we are trying discover and resolve in revisiting a memory:

- Any negative attitudes toward, faulty beliefs about, or rejection of any aspect of ourselves that we have disowned.

- Release any stored up emotion that never got expressed regarding painful events or significant losses.

- Acknowledge damage incurred as we were hurt by others – our reaction to sin. Take responsibility for our sin of self-protection.
    1. Beliefs about self
    2. Judgments about others, including expectations about how they will act towards us
    3. Vows of protection made to stay safe in the future
    4. Dysfunctional beliefs about how we should live or organize our lives.
       For example, "Sex is the most important thing about life and can meet all my needs."
- Forgive others specifically for what they did to us.

Notes

Personal

References

1   Patrick Carnes, *Contrary to Love* (Minneapolis: CompCare Publishers, 1989) 168.

2   David Seamands, *Healing of Memories* (SP Publications, Inc., 1985) 251.

3   David Seamands, *Healing of Memories* (SP Publications, Inc., 1985) 270.

Homework

On a separate piece of paper:

1. Write down those events in your life that are associated with anger and pain, beginning with the most recent memories and working your way back through your life.

2. Draw a box around each memory with an arrow indicating the flow from the most recent memory to the earliest. (You may want to make a rough draft letting your memories flow freely without putting emphasis on chronology in the initial stages of the exercise.)

3. In each box that you have drawn list:

   who hurt you

   what happened

   how you felt

   how the memory effected what you believed about yourself

   how you changed your life

Note: Be as brief as possible.

You may want to get prayer for some of these memories in your accountability group.

If your feelings get too intense, or you begin to feel panic, it is all right to stop. However, do expect this exercise to be uncomfortable and feeling-oriented.

On the following page are some trigger words and phrases that may help stir up memories. Think about them and ask the Holy Spirit to help search your heart. Read through the lists once, and begin with what is sparked inside of you. Continue to go through the lists and stop where you feel stirred.

Feeling Word List

Low Energy

Bashful	Beaten down	Bushed	Dull	Exhausted
Feeble	Groggy	Listless	Lukewarm	Pensive
Shy	Tired	Unlively	Washed out	Waterlogged
Weak	Wilted			

Affectionate

Amorous	Cozy	Grateful	Loving	Moved
Passionate	Romantic	Sensitive	Sexy	Tender
Touched	Warm			

Afraid

Aghast	Anxious	Apprehensive	Bewildered	Boxed-in
Burdened	Confused	Dismayed	Distressed	Fearful
Fluttery	Frightened	Guarded	Hard-pressed	Horrified
Horror-stricken	Jittery	Locked-in	Nervous	Overwhelmed
Panicky	Paralyzed	Queasy	Quivery	Shaky
Shocked	Squeamish	Tense	Terrified	Timid
Trembly	Up-tight	Worried		

Unhappy/Uncomfortable

Aching	Agonizing	Ashamed	Chagrined	Cheerless
Cold	Crushed	Dark	Dejected	Depressed
Desperate	Despondent	Disconcerted	Discouraged	Dismal
Down-in-the-mouth	Down-in-the-dumps	Down cast	Downhearted	Frowny
Gloomy	Glum	Grief-stricken	Grieved	Heartbroken
Joyless	Lonely	Long-faced	Morose	Mournful
Murky	Pained	Sad	Sullen	Weepy
Whinny	Wistful			

Common Verbal Expressions

I'm fed up

I've had it

I'm sick and tired

You're driving me crazy

I'm ready to explode

I'm disappointed

I'm down in the dumps

I'm blue

You hurt me

I don't know

Physiological Disturbances

headaches

ulcers

arthritis

colitis

fatigue, etc

When a need is perceived and the body experiences a state of arousal of energy, a person can identify the need and meet it or dispel the energy without the need of satisfaction. The following are expressions which do not effectively meet human needs:

Bringing up subject then dropping it, "forget it"

Abuse, drug, alcohol, people, food, etc.

Pacing	Nail biting	Giving up
Smoking	Name calling	Hassling
Biting	Leg shaking	Prejudice
Hitting	Rebelling	Sarcasm
Kicking	Abandoning	Biting humor
Scratching	Running away	Non-responsive
Withdrawing	Insulting	Trailing behind
Stomping out of room	Teasing	Accident proneness
Slamming doors	Tickling	Rape
Breaking things	Gossiping	Violence
Crying	Procrastinating	Vandalism
Holding their breath	Sulking	Murder
Pulling hair	Shining	Suicide
Twisting hair	Clinging	Wish another dead
Thumb sucking	Demanding	Promise and forget
Laughing at	Arguing	Depression
Finger tapping	Hoping	Irritation
Hopelessness	Waiting	Harried
Helplessness	Wanting to die	Annoyance
Paranoia	Insomnia	Refusal to learn
		Headaches

Early grade school teachers

Conflict	Embarrassment	Shaming
Power	Longing	Abusive

Early neighborhoods/ houses

Hiding places	Accident	Rituals
Basements	Gangs	Clubs
Initiation	New kid	Doctor

Childhood moods

Fearful	Quiet	Passive
Angry	Sexual	Gross
Terror	Abandonment	Blank
Gray	Sad	Sickly
Powerless	Self pity	Loner
Manipulative	Scariest experience	Dread
Claustrophobic	Enmeshed	

Early peers

Left out	Odd	Peer pressure
Neighborhood	School	Secrets
Delinquent	Coercion	Physical fights
Shame	Conflict	Masturbation
'Post Office' game	Girlfriend/boyfriend	Rejection

Miscellaneous

Significant place	First sexual experience	Most powerful sexual experience
Controlling others	Being controlled	Perverted acts
Something I never told anyone		

Family events

Absent: emotionally, physically, protectively, provisionally

Special outings	Birthdays	Vacations
Christmas	Broken promises	Bad touch
Sibling sex	Violence	Words
Incest	Sexual innuendo	Pornography
Mother	Father	Siblings
Spankings	Discipline	Parents fallible
Perfectionism	"I give up"	Bedrooms, middle of the night

Notes
Personal

Family
Origins of Addictions

Chapter Thirteen

Because of thirst the infant's tongue sticks to the roof of its mouth; the children beg for bread, but no one gives it to them. (Lamentations 4:4)

Origins and Escalation of the Addict's Cycle

Sexual addicts travel along a common path. This shared addictive cycle can be broken down into six phases. Patrick Carnes, author of *Contrary to Love*, labels them as follows: the initiation phase, the establishment phase, an escalating and a de-escalating contingent phase and, if the cycle progresses, the chronic and acute phases. As an addict moves through the different phases, the sexual activity becomes more violating to others and more risky to the addict.

In this session we will attempt to give a concise and introductory picture of what sexual addiction looks like. Most sexual addicts have a pattern of sexual sin that has been established over a lifetime. It is very common for this same pattern to run through the history of the addict's family.

"The Initiation Phase"

This stage is hard to distinguish from normal sexual development, with its corresponding curiosity and experimentation. The average person passes through his first sexual experiences in adolescence with an appropriate amount of guilt. He recovers well enough. For him, sexual experimentation does not trip him up and remain a focus. The addict, on the other hand, often had intense sexual experiences early in grade school, from which he did not recover. With these early experiences began a life of secrecy and self-doubt, with undue importance placed on sex. Even during early experimentation, most addicts reportedly used self-stimulation to deaden pain.

Typically, as the addict reminisces, he portrays his early sexual life as a collection of shameful memories, rather than events from which wisdom was gained. Those events became like behavioral grooves along which later events followed, a set of ritualized patterns for coping with life. Although this is the most common scenario, not all addicts report this history. Some who have had a relatively "normal" childhood used sex to deal with stressors in life. We see here the power of repetitive sin to produce death.

Abandonment events, such as childhood loss of parents (or other significant relationships), abuse, neglect, and harsh discipline are closely related to deep-seated rejection issues. As we have already noted, rejection is one of the triggers for the addictive cycle. Besides abandonment-related events, sexual addictions can result from early sexual stimulation, such as molestation. Such events can awaken confusing feelings which tie sexuality to acceptance and closeness.

Two things in early family life can contribute to the genesis of an addiction: catalytic **environments**, and catalytic **events**.

Catalytic environments, or environments that foster sexual addiction, are often a part of the initiation phase of the addiction. The most common catalytic environment is one in which there are high demands for performance and achievement coupled with little or no encouragement and nurture. A classic environment for the sexually addicted Christian would be a church setting with a high demand for holiness, yet which had neither practical teaching to inform one's attempt to maintain the standard, nor a warm fellowship of believers. The resulting feelings of helplessness produce secrecy, hopelessness, rebellion, and possibly even excitement about engaging in the forbidden acts which became an addiction. This rigid type of church environment mirrors many addict-producing families.

Different family environments empower addiction in different ways. The chaotic family, for example, sets up unpredictable, non-accountable crisis situations that require adrenaline to survive. This damages children in two ways: 1) Nothing ever gets accomplished, so child does not learn stable problem solving skills; 2) The family lacks a set of values and beliefs that unite them. Therefore, the child learns the value of not being responsible for the crisis (especially his sexual addiction). Both the rigid family and the chaotic family generate children dependent upon an exterior structure in order to organize their inner worlds.

Addictions issue from a need to find something dependable that meets previously unmet emotional needs. When children's needs are not met through the rigid family, or when they are left with chaos because of their crisis-oriented families, the children conclude that they must depend on themselves to survive. Patrick Carnes describes the emotional dynamics that are produced in such environments:

> Note that anxiety and control are common aspects of these experiences. The uncertainty of mastering unknown, uncertain, or extreme environments and the inability to ensure acceptable outcomes, are cornerstones of all addiction. The addiction supplies a temporary solution by allying anxiety and giving momentary purpose to the self, but ultimately it compounds life's problems. [1]

Fear of emotional intimacy is basic to non-committed sexual contact.

Catalytic events are also a part of the sexual addict's formation. They take two forms: **abandonment events** and **sexual events**. Abandonment events, such as childhood loss of parents (or other significant relationships), abuse, neglect, and harsh discipline are closely related to deep-seated rejection issues. As we have already noted, rejection is one of the triggers for the addictive cycle. Besides abandonment-related events, sexual addictions can result from early sexual stimulation, such as molestation. Such events can awaken confusing feelings which tie sexuality to acceptance and closeness. These feelings are then acted out inappropriately in later life.

The following summary of characteristics of the initiation phase is taken from Patrick Carnes' book, *Contrary to Love*: [2]

Characteristics of Initiation Phase:
- Coping with stress or tension through sex
- Determination to find ways to maximize opportunities for sexual behavior
- Episodic periods of excessive acting out, or abusive sexual behavior
- Concerns, disappointment, or guilt about sexual behavior

- Loss of faith in oneself, feelings of unworthiness and distrust, while living in a behaviorally-extreme environment

- Incongruence between exhilaration and degradation

- Catalytic events which correspond with first episode of sexual excess

- Perception of behavior as experimental, occasional, or short-lived, when in reality it is regular, periodic, or increasing in frequency or intensity (denial is involved)

- Feeling exhilarated while sexually acting out, while there is real danger from the act itself, or from the possibility of detection (real danger is denied and hidden from conscious awareness)

During the initiation phase, the addict's sexual exploits shift from isolated, spontaneous events to a predictable cycle. This cycle becomes the organizing principle of his life. As previously stated, this cycle has four distinct parts:

- Preoccupation

- Ritualization

- Sexual Compulsivity

- Shame and Despair

The machinery which allows the cycle to operate is a belief system which is more difficult to detect than the visible events of the cycle. This belief system is intertwined with the heart-level attitudes of the addict. This belief system drives and hardens the addictive cycle. The most noteworthy sign of these faulty beliefs is that the addictive cycle is actually increasing the addict's negative feelings about himself. As he continues to be out of control, his shame grows.

"The Establishment Phase"

In this phase, distorted or impaired thinking is present – it serves to cover up the obvious depravity of the addict's sexual acting out. Yet despite his rationalization, self-righteousness, and blame of others, the denial will stop working. Eventually, the reality of broken family relationships, decreasing productivity of work, and the violation of his own values break through the addict's defensive barriers. He is forced to realize that his life is unmanageable. When sexual addiction has been established, the addict is living a double life: one is that of living the "good" Christian life, the unseen other a shameful life of sexual addiction. He embodies what Paul describes in Romans 7:15:

For what I am doing, I do not understand for I am not practicing what I would like to do, but I am doing the very thing I hate.

Robert Louis Stevenson seemed to understand the dynamics involved in living a double life. He captures both the split in the self, and the growth of the split, when he describes how a potion-induced monster began to occupy more and more of good Dr Jekyll's life:

> Whereas in the beginning the difficulty had been to throw off the body of Jekyll, it had of late gradually but decidedly transferred itself to the other side...I was slowly losing hold of my original and better self and becoming slowly incorporated with my second and worse self. [3]

Similarly, in the establishment stage, excessive sexual behavior has been established *as a way to organize the addict's internal world of pain*. The real person has begun to sink beneath a delusional self. Increasingly isolated and out of touch with reality, the addict has a Jekyll and Hyde existence; the external Christian shell, which is presented to others, and the inner man preoccupied with his compulsion. In the battle between the Spirit and the flesh, the spirit-man of the addict has long since atrophied.

As time goes on, the split between delusion and reality eats away at the addict's sense of self. This painful loss of faith in one's potential, originating in the catalytic factors in the addict's life, deepens with the regular repetition of the addict's cycle. It contributes negative emotional energy to core beliefs about his unworthiness.

> When the addictive cycle has become fully established, the addictive system becomes an autonomous, closed system, feeding upon itself, maintaining regularity and priority. [4]

"The Contingent Phases: Escalation and De-escalation"

In these phases, the addiction often vacillates and varies in intensity. For a period, the person's behavior may become notably more risky; at other times, acting-out may become less risky and less frequent. However, the internal belief system remains the same and so, even in significant times of de-escalation, the addiction remains. People sometimes mistake seasons of de-escalation for recovery. But recovery is only genuinely occurring when there is a de-escalation of behavior, accompanied by a dismantling of the addictive belief system. Without this dismantling of the belief system, what looks like recovery is only the de-escalation phase.

"The Acute Phase"

If the person reaches the acute phase, he becomes lost in his addiction. He breaks with reality, abandons his value system, and shrinks back from the significant people to whom he could be accountable. At this time, preoccupation with sex is almost constant. Acting out is extreme, and cyclical patterns have hardened into place. The conscience has been seared and a high state of denial enables sexual actions to become increasingly risky, disregarding societal norms. Usually the activities end only as a result of physical or social consequences, such as death or imprisonment. Or they may de-escalate if the addict substitutes one addiction for another or better yet, turns to God.

"The Chronic Phase"

The chronic phase of sexual addiction seems almost irreversible. Most addicts in this phase become institutionalized. Here, behavior abates only a result of limited opportunity. Fortunately, all things are possible for those who believe.

Levels of Addiction

The sexual activity of the addict can be measured by its intrusiveness and destructiveness to others. In general, the more entrenched the addict becomes in his activities, the more risk he is willing to take to satisfy his need. At times there is also escalation in the victimization of others. Appendix A shows the relationship between different types of sexual activity and their offensiveness to God and to society.

Sexual addiction tends towards increasing bondage, but does not always progress to the chronic phase. Also, addiction can be happening on many levels simultaneously. It may come and go in phases, or build to the establishment phase and then taper off. The latter case is what Carnes describes in his "contingent phases." We see in Appendix A that with increased levels of addiction often come increased severity of crime against others. As the addiction progresses, the addict deludes himself, and abdicates more of his true self.

Family — The Bigger Picture

Often, the sexual addict feels desperate and isolated, plagued by the belief that he must carry the weight of his compulsions alone. He believes that other Christians would never have this kind of sin in their lives. The truth is that he is a part of a much bigger picture that probably includes his family and ancestors.

Sexual addiction is so engrossing and overwhelming that it can span a person's entire life and spread through whole generations of a family. It is so insidious and toxic that it can survive in many environments, often becoming dormant - only to emerge at the least expected time. It is so deceptive and secretive that intimate family members can be in its presence and yet be unaware of its impact. Carnes writes,

> Addiction is a pathological system of great strength that envelops individuals and their families as it grows, drawing further strength from its environment. [5]

Family Secrecy

One of the characteristics of the addict's family of origin is secrecy and lack of genuine communication. Typically, the expression of feelings and negative thoughts were taboo. The addict's isolation is merely a reflection of the family's sanctioned no-talk rule. When the norm is to not talk about family events, the child must guess about reality. Usually he fills in the blank with the lowest common denominator - that he is somehow responsible for the family dysfunction. This uncertainty and lack of feedback eventually becomes so painful that the child learns not to feel, and certainly not to trust others with his true self, with all of its genuine emotions and reactions. Because of the family dysfunction, the addict never learns to trust; therefore, he is unable to test reality with others in relationships. He is then doomed to a lifestyle of hiding from himself and others, languishing in the despair of his personal, silent hell.

If the addict is married (let's say for discussion purposes, he is a man), he probably picked a wife who agrees to a no-talk rule in their new family unit. She, also a survivor of dysfunctional family with sick rules, does not deal with the addiction either. Rather, she chooses to deny or accept his sexual problems so that she can stay dependent on him. This family unit, which comprises a new generation, will move along with the same relational sin as the family units before it, unless intervention occurs. Until then, it will be a fertile environment for sexual sin to find roots in its new members.

If the addict chooses to change, it will force change in the family equilibrium. Disrupting the status quo of the family can be a painful process, but it is necessary for healing. As change begins, everyone in the family system will feel himself or herself being pushed out of what has been normal and comfortable family interaction. It is important, therefore, for the wife (and sometimes the children) to be a part of the healing process. The wife's involvement in the unmasking of the dysfunctional family system will require that she be willing to look at how she contributes to the dysfunction.

The only way out of sexual addiction is to break the pattern of secrecy. The addict must begin walking in the light, both personally and with respect to the generational sin of his family.

Generational Sin

You shall have no other gods before me. You shall not make for yourself an idol in the form of anything in heaven above or on the earth beneath or in the waters below. You shall not bow down to them or worship them; for I, the Lord your God, am a jealous God, punishing the children for the sin of the fathers to the third and fourth generation of those who hate me, but showing love to a thousand generations of those who love me and keep my commandments. (Deut. 5:7-10)

Sexual sin is frequently generational sin. As the addict begins to come into the light, he often learns that what he thought was unique to him is really a part of a longstanding pattern. His sexual sin is empowered by an inheritance of psychological/spiritual forces that are the working-out of sins' consequences.

To some extent, this process is a mystery. We don't know exactly how it works, but must concede that it is real because "punishment" for ancestral sins is clearly stated in scripture. Further, it can be observed as we look into the history of our own families. Our disobedience brings destructive consequences. God will let us reap what we've sown, both the good and the bad. In letting us reap the consequences of sin, God is mercifully forcing us to wake up to reality.

One consequence of sin is that it continues beyond us, reaching the generations to come. Our sins will be passed on to our children, just as the sins of those before us have visited us. Having lived in sick families, our hearts became like emotional garbage dumps, infested by demonic forces like rats in a trash heap. These dark forces empower and perpetuate the curse of sin to following generations.

We see an example of this in scripture in the family line of Abraham, Isaac, and Jacob. In Genesis 12:11-12 , before having been renamed Abraham by God, we see Abram's sin of dishonesty, fear of man, and unfaithfulness to his wife. The story begins when Abram moves to Egypt to survive a severe famine. While there, Abram became afraid for his life because of Sarai's beauty. He feared the rulers of Egypt would kill him in order to have her, should they discover him to be her husband. To protect himself, he told them she was his sister. Abram's lie had the predictable consequence of Pharaoh innocently taking Sarah as his wife. God brought plagues upon Pharaoh because of Abram's deception and eventually Pharaoh figured out what was going on. He immediately sent both Abram and Sarai away commanding his men not to touch them.

Later, Isaac was born from Abraham and Sarah and, presumably, without knowledge of the incident with the Egyptians. As life progressed and Isaac matured, he was told by God to go to Egypt in order to survive a famine. There, he participated in the same sin of deception, calling his wife, Rebecca, his sister - and for the same reason (Genesis 26:1-11). King Abimelich, who reigned at the time, eventually saw Isaac caressing his wife, discerned the truth, and became furious because of the potential curse that could come down upon his government, should someone in his ranks take her.

The twins Esau and Jacob were born to Isaac and Rebecca. The scripture pointedly underlines the effects of generational sin. It is no surprise that the name Jacob means *supplanter* (which is to throw another down by force or trickery). In the third generation this sin of deception has become "full blown" in Jacob, and has been a way of life for him. Empowered through his mother's cunning, Jacob gains his brother's birthright and his father's blessing through deception. Later in his life, he, like his forefathers, was caught in deception surrounding his wives. He left secretly from Laban's estate lest he be killed by Laban, whom Jacob feared would try to keep his daughters (Jacob's wives). We can see how specifically this sin was carried on for three generations in Abraham's family.

In the family's fourth generation, the simple but contagious strain of deception has grown into something perverted, dysfunctional, and cruel. Deception takes on new dimensions as Jacob's children sell his son Joseph into captivity, telling their father his son is dead, then feigning to comfort him. Now deception has gathered to itself insecurity, collusion, and premeditated gain. When sin goes unacknowledged and God's intervention is not sought, it becomes more powerful, engrossing, and twisted as it infects the entire family tree.

Sexual addiction spreads along family lines, infecting generations of families that bow down to sin; in this case, we are concerned with the sin of sexual idolatry. The result is that our forefathers' sins have exacerbated our fallen, blind condition. More than would otherwise be the case, we fit Paul's description of our fallen state in Romans 1:24-16:

Therefore God gave them over in the sinful desires of their hearts to sexual impurity for the degrading of their bodies with one another. They exchanged the truth of God for a lie, and worshiped and served created things rather than the Creator – who is forever praised…Because of this, God gave them over to shameful lusts.

Breaking Generational Ties

Breaking generational ties has to do with disconnecting ourselves from our families' inheritance of sin. While we want all of the good things they've passed onto us, we must refuse the darkness that has plagued our forebears. It means taking family patterns of sin to the cross through prayer and applying the power of Jesus' blood. As the addict discovers generational patterns of sin through personal investigation or through revelation of the Holy Spirit, he must then renounce them; he can then assert the victory of Jesus' blood over the generational pattern. He must take a stand under the blood of Jesus as a new creature in Christ. There is spiritual power available to us as we stand in our inheritance as children of God. This is especially true for those of us who have been operating under generational curses and vows passed down through the generations. To effectively break generational sin, the addict should renounce the hold of his family's sin upon him, and receive prayer from the accountability group. The goal is to sever any demonic attachments that have had access to him because of generational sin.

Conclusion

As sin tightens its grip on man he often begins to seek relief from the accompanying pain. Hopefully, he looks back to God. If he does not, any sin (sexual or otherwise) can run rampant through his life and those of his descendants.

Investigating one's family history can give hope to the addict. By doing so, he can take note of and objectify the pattern of sin and death; this is the heritage of his old man. As he is willing to take hold of his new identity – the inheritance provided through the new birth in Jesus Christ – the true self can be reclaimed. By the power of Christ's love, he can choose a new way of life and renounce the old, deadening ways.

References

[1] Patrick Carnes, Ph.D., *Contrary to Love* (Minneapolis: CompCare Publishers, 1989) 55.

[2] Patrick Carnes, Ph.D., *Contrary to Love* (Minneapolis: CompCare Publishers, 1989) 58-59.

[3] Patrick Carnes, Ph.D., *Contrary to Love* (Minneapolis: CompCare Publishers, 1989) 72.

[4] Patrick Carnes, Ph.D., *Contrary to Love* (Minneapolis: CompCare Publishers, 1989) 72.

[5] Patrick Carnes, Ph.D., *Contrary to Love* (Minneapolis: CompCare Publishers, 1989) 45-46.

HOMEWORK
Homework

1. Reflect on your childhood home environment. Describe any ways that it could have been a catalytic environment for your addiction. In what ways did it foster the no-talk, no-trust, no-feelings rules? Describe the qualities of your family system which foster any of the following: performance, isolation of your true self, secrecy, excessive closeness, smothering, or abandonment.

2. List or describe any catalytic events (sexual or non-sexual) which you think may have contributed to your involvement with "sex as a drug." These events may be intense sexual events, sexual events equated to love, exciting sexual events, abandonment events, i.e. death, desertion, neglect, abuse (physical, emotional, or sexual).

3. Describe both 'personalities' of your double life (Dr. Jekyll and Mr. Hyde).

4. Begin to construct your genogram (a picture of your family tree). This genogram will later be shared in your accountability group. The focus of the genogram will be to help you see the forces and patterns of sin and brokenness in your family history. Identify all manifestations of sin, such as alcoholism, suicide, mental illness, abuse, womanizing, misogyny (hatred of women), pursuit of mammon, idolatry, divorce, etc., in addition to sexual sin. Note: you may have to ask some questions of family members to get necessary information. It is best to be non-judgmental and non-condemning as you break open family secrets. Continue to ask all members of your family (some will talk, others will not).

Spiritual Cleansing

Chapter Fourteen

*But if I drive out demons by the finger of God,
Then the kingdom of God has come to you.* (Luke 11:20)

Generational Sin

In the last chapter, we identified the generational nature of sin. We saw how patterns of sin slither around the family tree and influence the addict's life in ways that he does not fully understand. In spite of this lack of understanding, one who has been influenced by the power of generational sin needs to be cleansed of its effects.

This cleansing entails confessing and renouncing the sins of ancestors, then prayerfully choosing to accept one's new inheritance as a child of God. One may also need to forgive those in his ancestral line, and to receive the ministry of other believers to break the hold of any demonic activity. I believe that all sexual addicts should participate in the breaking of generational ties.

Curses

There are several types of curses in the scripture. The first is the curse described in Genesis 3 that was pronounced upon Adam and Eve as a result of the fall. God pronounced the effects that sin would have on the lives of all who followed Adam and Eve. Because of the disorder that began in the garden, God established the Mosaic law to help man walk uprightly before God and to declare sin's grip upon him (Romans 7:9-12). Anyone who did not walk according to God's law walked under a curse:

See, I am setting before you today a blessing and a curse: the blessing, if you listen to the commandments of the Lord your God, which I am commanding you today. (Deut 11:26-27)

This type of curse has much to do with the generational visitation of sin upon us.

Another type of curse seems to be connected to the authority that God has given to those whom He has established in a place of government, spiritually or prophetically. With this kind of "cursing," a man may pronounce a curse upon what God is cursing and it will come to pass. One story, found in Numbers 22, records

It is important to state here that the spiritual cleansing and deliverance that happens does not take the place of emotional healing that is needed, and does not eliminate the need to resist sexual temptations. Spiritual cleansing is only one part of the healing of sexual addiction.

the request of King Balak to Balaam the prophet to curse the sons of Israel, because he feared their power. Balaam inquires of the Lord and finds out that he may not curse the people because they are blessed. He, therefore, replies to Balak, "Though Balak were to give me his house full of silver and gold, I could not do anything, either small or great, contrary to the command of the Lord my God." The implication is that, if God would have allowed it, Balaam could have cursed the children of Israel.

Acts 5 records the story of Ananias and Sapphira and their lie to the Holy Spirit. After Ananias is judged by God for his deceit, Peter pronounced his coming death. With God's authority resting upon them, Peter's words came to pass.

God is the Authority over nations, and He has established the governments that guide them. The most fundamental form of that government is the authority that He has given fathers over their sons. It is my belief that the words of a father have authority to release the forces of the spiritual realm over their children. This can come in the form of blessing or cursing. We can see an example of this by looking deeper into the story of Jacob and Esau found in Genesis 25 and 27. After Jacob (spurred on by his mother) tricked Esau out of his birthright, he went on to deceive his father into giving him his blessing. Jacob, in contrast to Esau, knew the value of the father's blessing. He and his mother devised the plan to take advantage of his father's failing eyesight. Yet he was unsure that the plan would work and said to his mother, *"Perhaps my father will feel me, then I shall be as a deceiver in his sight; and I shall bring upon myself a curse and not a blessing"* (Genesis 27:12). His mother acknowledged the validity of the potential curse: *"Your curse be on me, my son"* (Genesis 27:13).

After Jacob stole his father's blessing, Esau discovered what had happened, and bitterly cried out, *"Bless me, even me also, my father"* (Genesis 27:34). But it was too late. Isaac instead pronounced a curse upon Esau, as recorded in Gen. 27:39-40. I believe that Isaac uttered this curse because Esau despised his birthright. I also believe that if Esau had turned to God, there would have been provision for him. Instead, he held a grudge against Jacob. Over time, the nation of Edom, which came from Esau, ended in destruction.

Then the house of Jacob will be a fire and the house of Joseph a flame; but the house of Esau will be as stubble. And they will set them on fire and consume them, so that there will be no survivor of the house of Esau, for the Lord has spoken. (Obadiah 18)

We cannot separate the father's spiritual authority, and the effect of his words on Esau's heart, both of which weighed heavily upon his future. The weight of the father's curse had the effect of hardening Esau's heart. This was also a curse from God (Lam. 3:65).

The words of our parents uniquely influence us in our childhood years. Their actions, words and body language all powerfully influence us, for good or ill, whether or not we're consciously aware of it. My belief is that God has built into us a principle that stores up words from our parents in our hearts, so that their positive contributions to our lives powerfully impact us. We therefore gain healthy identities, and emotional stability. In turn, their failures and sins against us negatively shape us.

When the words of our parents are needlessly harsh, and therefore do not reflect God's attitude toward us, they act as curses. The negative words of our parents make us vulnerable to the evil one and his condemnation of us. Our distorted *beliefs* about *who we are* may prevent God's word from entering in. Rather than feeling the joy of our true inheritance, we may be oppressed in our emotions.

Parents' negative pronouncements open children up to darkness from the spiritual realm. The misuse of parental authority over the child gives permission for Satan to come and fulfill the curse that is spoken out. In the New Testament, the word curse comes from a Greek word that means *to doom or execrate (invoke through prayer) evil upon someone else.* When we curse someone with our negative pronouncements or wishes, we do not think of this as praying. But to maliciously wish evil upon someone is to contribute to supernatural evil, at least in a subconscious way. There can be demonic attachments and empowerment in curses spoken over us!

Examples of Parental Curses

Below are examples of some of the curses I have come across in ministry to others. In each case, the pronouncement, or series of pronouncements, had profound and painful effects on the child.

- A mother's words, after finding her son touching his genitals: *"You are a horrible, nasty little boy."*

- A father berating his son when he turned away from a fight: *"You're nothing but a little girl."* As a punishment, the father put a dress on his son and paraded him around the neighborhood.

- A father's remark to his daughter after she flirtatiously responded to his sexual advances: *"I knew you were a little slut."*

- A mother to her son after he did a minimal job of cleaning his room: *"You'll end up a good for nothing like your father."* She said this many times during his childhood.

The addict must renounce any curses that have been spoken over him. It is also important to receive prayer to break the power of any demonic, psychological, or emotional power that the curse has over his heart. The addict must also forgive **and bless** the one who cursed him.

I say to you who hear, love your enemies, do good to those who hate you, bless those who curse you. (Luke 6:27-28)

This command by Jesus is more than a loving suggestion. It is a powerful form of spiritual warfare which will often help break the hold of a curse over one's life.

The final type of curse is the most overt type, those which are uttered in the form of witchcraft. Sometimes we may discern these by the Spirit. They, like the other kinds of curses, can be broken through prayer and the blood of Jesus.

Demonic Influences

The New Testament understands demons to be evil fallen angels (2 Peter 2:4, Jude 6, Rev. 12:7). Demonic oppression can exacerbate, or even be the cause of, some mental and physical illnesses. Demonic influence can range in severity, from full oppression, as in the Gadarene Demoniac (Mark 5), to mental influence and temptation.

The concept of "demon possession" does not appear in the original language of the Bible. Instead, differing states of demonic activity are described by a word that is more accurately translated "demonized," or demonically "influenced." This influence can vary, from mild harassment and oppression, to powerful bondage over a person's will.

The scripture has many accounts of human beings experiencing oppression by demons. Where sexual addiction is concerned, lust, perversion and various fixations can be demonically empowered and driven. Since some of the addict's drivenness can be demonically induced, healing may first require that the demonic influence is removed through prayer. See appendix D, "Renouncing Baal".

Access Points

Although many debate the issue theologically, Christians can be demonized. Demons gain access to us in a number of ways. Some of the most common for the sexual addict are:

- Prolonged submission of one's body to ongoing sexual sin

- Significant life trauma (especially sexual in nature)

- The taking on of a demon companion as a result of personal loneliness, a demonic visitation, and a bonding with darkness

- The result of a generational, familiar spirit

- Agreeing with various lies regarding the addict's sexual identity

Many people report having sexual encounters with spirit beings, and are plagued, mentally and spiritually, by repeated sexual violation. Historically, a demon that makes direct sexual contact with humans is called an *incubus* (the female counterpart) or a *succubus* (the male demonic form). Other demons seem to go by the name of the activity that they drive. Oftentimes, deliverance will be a part of the healing of the sexual addict. (See Appendix D, "Renouncing Baal.")

In praying for deliverance, it will be important to identify lies in the belief system. Also important to root out are unforgiveness and unconfessed sin, which give the demonic presence the right to attach to the one oppressed. All require repentance and the ministry of healing prayer in order for the demon to be expelled permanently. Depending on his history, the addict may have to renounce "friendship" with the demonic presence, and be willing to let go of whatever the presence is providing. He must receive the comforting presence of the Holy Spirit in its place. Demons may also spontaneously leave as a result of prayer for breaking generational sin.

Manifestations of Deliverance

It will be important for the sexual addict to be aware of certain manifestations within his own body during prayer. They may mean that the Holy Spirit is making known the presence of a demon. If the person receiving prayer is aware of these manifestations, then he can report them to whomever is praying, so that the prayer can persist until the oppression is over.

Possible Signs of Demonic Presence or Need For Deliverance Prayer

Tightness or pressure in the body may indicate demonic activity. Sometimes a person will feel pain or pressure moving around in their body during prayer. This can indicate demonic presence. Once noticed, the demon can be rebuked directly. Other times, the one receiving prayer may feel tightness or nausea in the stomach, such as a sensation that he is going to vomit. This should not be resisted because it is often the removal of some sort of bondage. The person receiving prayer may feel a pressure in the throat or chest that intensifies during prayer. This can be addressed in prayer.

The urge to cough, dry heave, burp or scream are often present. Sometimes coughing or burping is a part of release of oppression. At times, longstanding emotional pressure which has built-up in the person will manifest in a scream or shriek. This should also be allowed by the prayer team as a way for demonic attachment to be released. Sometimes, rather than a scream, the manifestation of exit will be a deflating sign.

I hesitate to be this plain about encountering demons because of the tendency of people to be frightened by them. If, however, a manifestation like this should occur in a accountability group, it is nothing to be ashamed of, but rather a chance to glorify God for His cleansing power. No one plans to have demonic attachments. But if they are there, it is a cause for rejoicing when they are driven out.

Renouncing Occult Involvement

It's important for the addict to try to recall any occult experience that he has willingly participated in, and then to confess and renounce these sins. Involvement with false religions and spirit-guides can leave a person with demonic attachments that oppress him. This is especially true of certain types of satanism that involve sexual sacrifice.

If the addict is a survivor of satanic ritual abuse (SRA), therapy is suggested. Therapeutic support will be essential to sort out the feeling and identity distortions that result from this type of abuse. It will be important for the SRA survivor to remember that, no matter what sacrifice or sexual acts they took part in, the blood of Jesus is a greater sacrifice, and is able to cancel all other blood pacts, dedications, and spiritual assignments. Once these occasions are remembered, he will need to pray through and renounce them specifically.

The prayer or renunciation can be as simple as the one that follows:

> Lord, I confess that I have participated in _____. I ask for your forgiveness, and renounce _____ in the name of Jesus. Amen.

Again, prayer from those who are experienced in the ministry of deliverance may be necessary for total cleansing. In addition to renunciation of occult activities, the addict may need to break one-flesh unions with any people with whom sexual contact was either welcomed or forced.

Breaking One-Flesh Unions

There is a spiritual and emotional tie that forms between people during sexual intercourse. This tie is implicitly spoken of in scripture in I Corinthians 6:12-20. It helps explain why many marriages are sexually unfulfilled and diffused by an illicit fantasy life.

Another thing you do: You flood the Lord's altar with tears. You weep and wail because He no longer pays attention to your offerings or accepts them with pleasure from your hands. You ask "why?" It is because the Lord is acting as the witness between you and the wife of your youth, because you have broken faith with her, though she is your partner, the wife of your marriage covenant. Has not the Lord made them one? In flesh and spirit they are His. And why one? Because he was seeking godly offspring. So guard yourself in your spirit, and do not break faith with the wife of your youth. (Malachi 2:13-15)

We know from scripture that when a man leaves his mother and father and is married, he clings to his wife and becomes one flesh with her. Not only is there intimate physical and emotional union, but also a mysterious spiritual one.

Scripture states that a man guards his spirit by keeping faith with the wife of his youth. How does he guard his spirit? He guards it against emotional and spiritual connections with anyone but his spouse. This is true, whether the union was before or after the marriage covenant was made. The act of sex not only consecrates a marriage, but also creates the spiritual and emotional tie in the marriage. It is not the marriage ceremony; it is the act of sexual intercourse that ties the couple together spiritually. This is why God does not allow premarital experimentation. He wants to prevent the pain of spiritual bonds which are then torn apart. He knows the agony caused when a person tries to sustain a monogamous marriage relationship with yet another partner.

A vivid example of breaking one flesh unions in prayer involved a forty-year-old woman who had been married ten years to her current husband. She enjoyed her marriage except for frequent, tormenting guilt that she felt over sexual longings for a man from her past. Many nights she awoke to the nearly tangible presence of a youth pastor who had seduced her when she was a teen. Although she hated the abusiveness of the memory, she clung to the sense of specialness that she felt during that time.

> During prayer to break the one flesh union, she saw a "vision" of Jesus come and cut a silver chord that connected her with the youth pastor. From then on she was free from her feeling of being visited at night.

A one-flesh union with past partners may explain why some men or women are not satisfied with their current mate – why they fantasize about others during love making with their spouse. That may also explain why they cannot bond sexually with their spouse at a deep level. Their spirit is torn and divided – connected with one or many others. This is why God says:

Do you not know that he who unites himself with a prostitute is one with her in body? For it is said, 'The two will become one flesh.' But he who unites himself with the Lord is one with Him in spirit. Flee from sexual immorality. All other sins a man commits are outside his body, but he who sins sexually sins against his own body. (I Corinthians 6:16-18)

Prayer for breaking one-flesh unions is a part of the addict's spiritual cleansing. There is both a spiritual and an emotional component to work with. Here is a prayer model that you may want to use:

- Bring each previous sexual partner specifically and individually before the cross. For those with many, even anonymous sexual contacts, you may need to do this in categories. In general, the more emotional connection with any given partner, the more in-depth the prayer should be.

- Confess any emotional or fantasy attachments to each partner. These may take the form of coveting body parts, personality characteristics, or willingness to do specific acts. Release them to the cross.

- Renounce the relationship, and ask God to break the spiritual tie. A prayer team can also pray to break the spiritual connections at this time.

- Forgive and release the person spiritually.

- Ask God to fill those places in your soul that were given to the other person and to repair any tearing-away or spiritual wound that had occurred in separation.

- Ask God to bless and restore the person released.

- Be willing to grieve any emotional loss that comes up with the giving-up of this tie. Do not minimize this step.

It is important to state here that the spiritual cleansing and deliverance that happens does not take the place of emotional healing that is needed, and does not eliminate the need to resist sexual temptations. Spiritual cleansing is only one part of the healing of sexual addiction.

Personal

Homework

Prayerfully prepare a list of names with whom you need to break one-flesh unions. Begin to think about your needs to release each person:

- Spiritually

- Emotionally

- With regard to idolatry

Eventually this list and your preparation will culminate in prayer for the breaking of one-flesh unions with your accountability group.

Action Step

I will finish this list by (date) _____

I will receive prayer to break one flesh unions on (date) _____

(This date is to be scheduled with your accountability group or prayer ministry at your church.)

Facing the Mother Wound

Chapter Fifteen

And yet, in Christ's fellowship woman is as essential to man as man to woman. If woman was made out of man, it is through woman that man now comes to be; and God is the source of all. (1 Corinthians 11:11)

Mother/Infant Attachment

The brokenness in the hearts of sexual addicts is often deep, going back many years. Surprising as it may seem, the roots of their struggles frequently originated in disruptions in early infantile attachment to mother. People are usually surprised to discover the result of pain experienced in the first year of life. Homosexual tendencies, heterosexual compulsions, drug addictions and deep interrelational dependencies are just a few. Often, the foundation of an addiction develops during the mother/infant bonding stage of psychological development. The tendency toward sexual addictions, fetish behavior, cross dressing, even fixation on erotic images can be rooted in these sorts of wounds.

Mother is our First Home

Our bodies are formed in mother's womb. If our mother is emotionally healthy (not riddled with stress and anxiety), the womb can feel like the safest place on earth for an infant. In healthy pregnancies, all the baby's needs are met. He is safe and attached. In the womb, the baby receives food, nurture and comfort; even the sound of the mother's heartbeat fills the child with security and a sense of belonging and comfort. Every beat reminds him that he is not alone, that his mother is with him. However, once the baby is born, "womb service" is over.

At birth, the developmental process is far from finished. In the same way that the organs and body are still not fully developed, there is much psychological development yet to take place. The phase having to do with the bonding of mother and child occurs during the first three years of life. The most critical stage occurs within the first year. It is then that the baby is able to take into his tiny world a sense of who he is, as one who is loved, and receive what is sometimes called a "sense of being."

A sense of being establishes in the child a foundation of security and confidence upon which the growth of his personality develops. When acceptance has been internalized... relationships with others do not revolve around whether or not others accept him. He is at peace with who he is. He begins life with the immense advantage of objectivity in relationships, of not fearing rejection or abandonment.

A "sense of being," a term coined by Frank Lake and popularized by Leanne Payne, could be described as a core sense of warmth that is connected to the baby's ability to peacefully exist, without feeling a need to earn his acceptability. It is a primary, psychological base of trust; this sense of being assures him that he is not in danger of losing love or significance, even though he is doing nothing to earn that significance. The sense of being goes far beyond head knowledge, because a pre-verbal child does not think in the same way that we do. As adults, we are able to reason because we have language; our thinking may or may not be full of feeling. A baby cannot be rational. In his primitive state, he experiences his environment as synonymous with his internal reality. Thus, as he begins to experience his new environment outside the womb, he begins to learn from it who he is.

In the first year of life, relationship with mother is the primary experience of the child. Successful bonding causes trust to be formed between mother and baby. She conveys acceptance and love through her eyes, her touch, her breasts, her cooing, talking and singing. The mother, if she has a sense of well-being, is able to intuitively sense the needs of her child, and to discern the meaning of his various cries.

The baby, contentedly feeding at the mother's breast, perfectly symbolizes the closeness, nurture, sense of warmth, and physical provision that conveys acceptance and value to the child, without having to strive to earn it. As all of his needs are met in the milieu of love, the baby receives a sense of well-being, peace, safety, and rest during early stages of attachment. This developmental reality is attested to in Psalm 22:9: *"Yet you brought me out of the womb, you made me trust in you even at my mother's breast."*

A sense of being establishes in the child a foundation of security and confidence upon which the growth of his personality develops. When acceptance has been internalized, the child has a sense of self; once he has a sense of himself, as an "I," he can enter into relationships with another person as other than himself. Relationships with others do not revolve around whether or not others accept him. He is at peace with who he is. **He begins life with the immense advantage of objectivity in relationships, of not fearing rejection or abandonment.** In other words, he has a basis for trust in relationships. He can therefore bond to others successfully, without anxiety.

Now you may be thinking, "What about the other stages of life? Can't other traumas affect trust also?" The answer is yes, but if early development has occurred successfully, the healing is not as hard to accomplish; the damage is not as deep. Conversely, if mother-infant wounding is a real issue and goes unaddressed, we ignore a crucial piece of the puzzle. Freedom may not come as easily.

It is likely that all of us have had some breach bonding as infants, and probably don't have conscious memories of it. After all, every mother has been affected by the Fall to some extent – a perfect mother who attends to her child flawlessly does not exist. But even without having conscious memories of this early stage of our lives, it is important to address it for the purpose of creating opportunities for healing. Knowledge of this wound is essential in order to heal it. Infant deprivation is a root wound and source of bondage in many people. If our sexual problems are at least partially rooted there, then we should receive prayer in that area. We may need to receive a lot of prayer from safe people, because this critical stage of development is the most fundamental building block in our lives. In asking God to heal this type of wound, we pray His love into the depth of the wound. Those who pray simply ask God to set-in a deep foundation of love, in place of the original one that was never established in the child.

How Breaches in Mother/Infant Bonding Can Occur

Breaches in mother/infant bonding occur for many reasons, some of which have to do with bad mothering and some have to do with bad circumstances. If a mother is absent, there will be a breach in bonding. Some mothers love their children very much but have lives that are not conducive to creating attentive, nurturing homes for their little ones. The mother may be depressed and withdrawn, have several other kids, or a husband who abandoned her, resulting in a great deal of stress and anxiety. The financial difficulties of the family may force the mother to work outside the home during critical stages of development. Or young parents may be unaware of the importance of what is happening developmentally in the child during this early stage of life.

What follows is a recounting of the testimony of one woman who experienced a need for this type of healing.

> In my own life, my mother was a wonderful woman. She was an operating room nurse in my growing up years. Her perfectionism was evident. I can remember how all through my childhood, my mother meticulously and medically cared for me. She went overboard with the care she took for me. I know every baby bottle in the house was completely sterilized.
>
> My mother grew up in the depression era — her parents were Polish immigrants and very poor. She grew up hungry. Since her parents both worked, she raised herself and often went to bed hungry. I believe that my mother never had nurturing herself. She never received a sense of being from her mother. Therefore, she was unable to convey one to me. Although she did all the right outward things, she was perfectionistic in them, and not nurturing.
>
> There is a life-giving quality that a woman receives into herself when she is nurtured by her own mother. When [mother] is whole enough, she is able to give this same nurture to her children. A lot of this giving has to do with a feminine intuition that perceives the needs of her little ones. God has given mothers the gift of being able to intuit the needs of their babies who are crying. It is not 100% accurate all the time, but a healthy mother will know why her baby is crying because there is a God-given, mysterious connection between them. In healthy mother/infant relationships, this attachment is secure.
>
> In my own life, my mother was not able to connect with me because that feminine quality within her was not intact. Because I did not have that bonding, there was a sense of emptiness, darkness, dread, and anxiety that became lodged in my soul and that I carried around for years. For me, that emptiness led to lesbian tendencies. The 'sense of being' deprivation became sexualized, and I sought to find completion in other women.

When Baby Does Not Bond With Mother

When the baby does not sense the emotional presence of the mother, he begins to experience distress. Based on the observation of many children, and through people's recollections as they relive this pain in therapy, we know what happens to a baby when his mother goes away and stays away too long. Frank Lake describes the experience of the baby:

> The severing of the essential relationship with the mother, seen and known to be present, which alone can give to the infant a sense of personal 'being' and selfhood,...cannot fail...to result in...the experience of 'dread'.... Subjectively, this is described by patients recalling it as 'getting to the end of my tether,' a dangerous waning of hope and expectancy, a certainty that one will not be able to last out long enough, a feeling that time passed in solitariness is equivalent to an imminent death of the spirit. [Also, there is] a mounting anxiety,...[called] separation anxiety. Aloneness is intolerable where the nature of the infantile organism at this phase is to find it as impossible to survive the loss of the living face as it would be within the actual womb to survive without supplies of oxygenated blood. Instead of continuing to feel like a proper human person, through access to the desired maternal source of personal being, the infant experiences a painful state of nonacceptance and rejection. It is an experience of being shut out from life as a person, cut off from 'being' itself. [1]

Perhaps Mom was actually physically absent, or just not *emotionally* present enough for the baby to feel connected to her. Whatever the case, the distress of the child can be very intense. Because young babies initially experience mother as an extension of themselves, separation from her loving care and attention for extended lengths of time can cause a profound sense of dread and anxiety.

The dread that an infant experiences at mom's absence in early life makes him feel as though he is ceasing to exist. It is felt as a profound fear associated with nonexistence, or existence apart from love. Perhaps it is like the experience of Hell itself, where persons are eternally separated from the grace and presence of God. Because infants are really just very small people, the dread that they feel when separated from mother powerfully overwhelms them, and is recorded as memories in their little bodies. A lot of this pain gets repressed. Later in life, the addict may still feel this pain as anxiety, fear, or depression. It may even be the root of his fear of intimacy. He may experience the prospect of being emotionally vulnerable to women as a subconscious dread of annihilation.

More than anything else, an adult man might fear the feelings of regressing into a state of emotional dependency in which he becomes an infant, vulnerable to the care of his mother. Becoming too intimately attached or vulnerable in a relationship with a woman might cause such a regression. Gordon Dalby put it well when he wrote:

> Such powerful mysteries of male sexuality are reflected in the very act of physical union. During intercourse, the man physically enters the woman's womb with his male-defining organ. In an emotional/spiritual sense, he is reentering the womb of his infancy – and thus re-encountering all the primal in utero fears of life-or death dependency...**Only one who fears death is compelled to seek and face it continually in order to reassure himself he has power over it.** Hence, the 'daredevil' model of apparent male courage and the playboy or demanding husband, who must constantly reenter the womb – and more importantly, leave – to prove he now has power to break the mother's confines. [2]

Early Origins of Obsession

Addictions and fetish behaviors, such as cross-dressing, can be related to an early mother wound. The root of both problems can go back to early bonding disturbances with mother.

To survive the discomfort of early separation trauma, the child must learn to defend against the anxiety that now comes up when he is alone. The first step he will take to get his needs met is to protest. The baby will scream and cry and, if he is old enough, he may rattle his crib to get mother's attention. If mother does not come soon enough, he will enter into a stage of despair. This despair is an infantile depression in which the infant loses interest in the environment around him, and becomes very sullen and withdrawn. If the despair goes on too long, the final stage is a detachment. The child actually erects an emotional wall between himself and his mother. Like all who are descended from Adam, sin is bound in the heart of the child. There is an automatic tendency to separate in relationships when they are experienced as painful.

When mother does come back, the baby , of course, is glad to see his mother. But emotionally, he will build a wall in his heart, so that she cannot hurt him as much again. That vital, life-giving connection to feminine love is now impeded. If this wound is not healed, the child will no longer be able to rest in his mother's love. It is as if the knot on the "sense of being balloon" has been tied prematurely. Now, no matter how much love is poured out upon the child, the compartment will remain shriveled and unfilled. Developmentally, the baby's capacity to be filled and motivated by love will be severely hindered.

One symptom of this type of wounding involves an inability to be still and quiet before God. An addict without a sense of being may not be able to receive love from God. He may hear the loving words of the Father but not be able to experience them in his emotional life.

Lack of Bonding Affects Moral Development

True morality is centered in love. It is concerned with wanting what's truly best for another's life – body, soul and spirit. When morality is founded upon a loving childhood, the individual will have a sense of the badness of relational sin, which is based on love for those outside of the self. That deterrent is a sense of remorse over hurting someone with whom he has a meaningful relationship. Godly morality is a motivation to do good, based on the maturing of both the intellectual understanding of right and wrong, and the feelings of connectedness to others.

Lack of remorse for sexual sin is one of the symptoms of most sexual addicts. One man related the following,

> I can't feel sorrow for what I've done to my wife or to God. I try, but it's just not there. Deep in my heart, I don't feel connected. So my main prayer right now is asking the Holy Spirit to fill me, and give me the capacity to be connected. If I could be emotionally attached to my wife, I don't think I'd have these problems.

This man's early detachment from mother had an effect on his moral development. As he continued to grow, he learned about good and bad, right and wrong. But because he was wounded in his capacity to carry love, his "obedience" was superficial and disconnected from his heart.

Fetish Behavior and Compulsive Attachments

Piaget discovered that after around 9 months or a year, an infant develops a sense of object permanence or object constancy. Once this capacity has developed, the baby can see an object and, after it is hidden, will continue to look for it. In other words, he will have developed evocative memory, the ability to evoke an image of something he saw, which he could not do before this time. Before this time, he would have forgotten about the object when it was taken from his field of vision; hence the idiom, "Out of sight, out of mind."

This capacity to visually recall something that's no longer present is important for an infant. It allows him to gradually grow out of his total dependence on Mommy. This happens by learning to take her with him mentally, even when she's not physically present.

If Mommy is absent, the baby may call up one of his pictures of her, upon which he can focus his attention. The result is peace. This mental snapshot may be of Mommy's nipple, her hair, or piece of her clothing. Infants grab an image in their minds and hold onto it as a substitute for mother when she is gone. If the mother leaves the room, the infant will comfort itself through evoking this mental picture. A child's use of such pictures is called *libidinal fantasy*.

An infant with no breach in relationship with mother will call on this image when the need arises. He will grow out of the practice of using it as he develops and becomes able to be in a relationship with mother as a whole person.

There is evidence that unresolved libidinal fantasy is often the root of lust toward specific body parts and compulsive fetish behavior. Sexualized libidinal fantasy may cause a man to see women, not as whole people, appreciating them in their whole beauty, but as a breast, hair, legs, or other body parts. Sexual arousal related to articles of clothing may be rooted in the confusion that occurs when clothing has been substituted for mother in a libidinal fantasy – the child may have taken in an image of her bra, for example, and bonded with it because Mommy wasn't sufficiently present. Frequently, cross-dressing compulsions may involve an attempt such as this to recapture closeness to mother, through dressing in women's clothing.

In a sense, the man with unresolved libidinal fantasy interacts with the world through a lens that highlights the objects in his environment which remind him of one of his favorite shapes. These shapes belong to the infant within who still retains a gallery of powerful snapshots that he transfers onto the environment. He thus attempts to gain a sense of peace and love, which he didn't fully attain in his mother's arms. As he walks down the street, through the bar or past the laundry mat, he unconsciously looks for something that can ease his sense of dread about being disconnected and alone.

> As these fantasies are part and parcel of a regression, pulling away from an unsatisfactory present, back and down a long-lost infantile past, they share with all the other dynamic patterns laid down in the first year an all-or-nothing quality. When such fantasies are haunting in force, they drive a man to absurd, impossible infatuations. That is to say, in a day when marriage vows were taken to be for life they [the vows, in light of the libidinal fantasy,] would be looked upon as impossible. They take no account of any other bonds or obligations. Unlike creative imagination, which helps a man to make adjustments to real life situations, libidinal fantasies, if translated into action, make adjustment to actual family ties impossible. [3]

Women can suffer painful sexual harassment as a result of these types of fixations. In what follows, a woman tells of her experience of being the object of such fixations:

> In my own life, I not only suffered from this separation anxiety because of the lack of bonding with my mother, but I suffered at the hands of men who could only see a part of me, not a whole woman.
>
> God made me with very large breasts. In my adolescent years, I began the hell of my life because of the size of my breasts and how they began to develop beyond the other girls in my school. The boys singled me out, and I would often hear obscene comments. For three years I experienced incredible sexual harassment from the boys in my class. Degrading comments also happened on the streets. Drivers would yell out the car window at me. When I would swim at the public pool, boys would jump in the water and gang-molest me. I have been in a mall or at a gas station where men have walked up to me and made crude, sexual comments.
>
> I was a Christian at the time and not giving off sexual signals. This abusiveness has been the most painful thing in my life. Two years ago I received prayer for the harassment and it has not happened to me since. I thank the Lord for that.
>
> Then one day I was ministering with Leanne Payne when she made an interesting comment to me. She said, 'You suffer the same root in you that men suffer from, which is separation anxiety from their mothers. That is why the men fixate on you.' The same root of my lesbian tendencies is the same root that causes men to see me as a part and not a whole woman. This revelation gave me compassion for my perpetrators because I know the pain of separation anxiety myself, and had to deal with it myself. You can see how these behaviors root back into early infancy.

Early separation has another component that is related to sexual addiction. The separation anxiety and dread which occur will often register in the genital area. Often a child will appear to be masturbating but really isn't. In early childhood, genital stimulation is more like massaging a foot to relieve tension than it is a sexual act. But, as the child matures, the stimulation becomes increasingly sexual in nature. As a result, adults with unresolved infantile anxiety experience adult sexual tension and genital anxiety that trace back to the primal separation issues with mother.

Many addicts have experienced what happens at puberty when a blossoming adult sexuality becomes affected by earlier genital anxiety, which was not previously sexualized. The marrying of two forces, that were not meant to be married, yields a sudden eruption of sexually driven behavior. Environmental stimuli and stresses can now become a trigger for sexual behavior. For instance, perhaps a boy has had an anxious day at school that is related to his feelings of infantile anxiety. Because he also has sexual energy, his body responds with an erection. Thus, having been triggered internally and physically, he may masturbate, or act out with a person, and be propelled into a cycle of acting out.

Around the age of puberty, the anxiety and dread become conscious to them. The adolescent, for the first time, is beginning to reason as an adult. He has a newfound awareness of his pain, and an ability to reflect upon it. It may be at this time, if not before, that a habit of masturbation develops, to avoid the anxiety and dread that otherwise threaten to break into awareness. This masturbation may then become compulsive.

Author and speaker Mario Bergner asserts that a man who is dealing with sexual addiction needs to separate anxiety from sexuality. The two are not meant to be connected, but for the sexual addict they are. Bergner suggests that when anxiety is recognized, one speak very gently to his or her body and say, "It's okay to be anxious. Anxiety is just a sign that something is amiss." We should ask the Lord to help us separate our anxiety from our sexuality. He can put our sexuality in the right perspective. It really has nothing to do with anxiety. Bergner also suggests that we get prayer concerning this issue, asking God to fill us with peace and to give us strength.

Hopefully, you can now see how someone struggling with unresolved libidinal fantasy, combined with genital anxiety, can be plagued with compulsive masturbation and fantasy life as an adult. It is clear that some aspects of our sexual brokenness can be rooted in this early relationship with our mothers.

Separation and Individuation

As a child gets a little older, he experiences separation and individuation. This occurs between the ages of 1 and 3 years. During the first year, an infant does not know he is separate from his mother. This is God's plan. Around the age of one, a baby starts to realize that he is an individual and starts to test his separateness. A healthy mother lets the child individuate from her. She can make the room safe so the child won't hurt himself, but will give him space to experience his separateness. She sets proper boundaries where they are needed, but she primarily serves as a home base, so that when the child goes over to the corner and realizes that he is alone, Mom is there to welcome him back. She doesn't clutch onto the child, so as to nullify his desire to explore, but does not reject him when he returns, either. A healthy mom facilitates separation and individuation.

A mother who never had mother/infant bonding herself, could over-indulge her attachment to the baby. When her baby begins to recognize that he is separate, she may not want to let go and may keep the child inordinately close to her, not allowing him to become separate. This scenario is the root of many adult boundary and relational problems. A man coming out of this childhood pattern may find himself demanding too much sex from his wife. At the same time he is unable to initiate provision outside of the relationship in areas such as vocation and spiritual life. His healthy sense of independence was overwhelmed by Mommy long ago, which produces an emotional dependency that reduces or masks masculine initiative.

The Engulfed Child

Lack of separation between mother and son can reach a more serious level when mother uses the child to nurture herself with his love. A still deeper invasion of a son's soul happens when the father is absent physically or emotionally and the young boy becomes the solution for meeting mother's intimacy needs. Rather than giving to the child and blessing his growing separateness and independence, she keeps him bound to her as a source of nurture and pleasure. She is skilled at extinguishing the child's anger through brainwashing comments, seductive moodiness (producing guilt in him for not meeting her needs), punishing his protests, and, in the worst case scenario, sadistically torturing the child for lack of cooperation.

As a result of having his inner-being invaded by a larger-than-life mother, the child's individuality is emotionally engulfed. He develops no ability to be separate as he grows physically. His enmeshment leads to extreme internal vulnerability to intrusive women. Later in life, because of his disabled will, this adult male is easily engulfed by others who are seductive, needy, and sexual. Often a man will not know why he is so weak and gives in to the come-on of a woman other than his wife. During the interaction, he is helpless before her mysterious power to lure him across his marital boundaries into a sinful sexual interaction.

The addict that repeats this pattern has not yet discovered that he was engulfed and that his internal boundaries are severely damaged, or nonexistent. Some addicts go through life having affair after affair and not understanding why. They may experience periods of success in avoiding entanglement, but eventually someone with the "right" emotional make-up comes along and they fall again.

In order to escape this condition, a person must finish the task of emotionally separating from mother. **Individuating** involves 1) seeing the truth of what has happened (often the Lord must reveal the truth), 2) feeling and expressing the hidden rage (this will give power to separate), 3) grieving the loss of the symbiotic closeness, and 4) allowing himself to feel and release the pain of loneliness, as well as the terror of being engulfed. Jesus can then come in to fill the emptiness, and can establish internal boundaries where they are weak or nonexistent.

Where an engulfing mother was especially manipulative (guilt-generating), harsh, or draining, the emotional effect will be such that it feels like she is living inside the addict. She has not only engulfed his will, but also his identity. Invasion of the personality that is this thorough often results in gender identity confusion and homosexuality. During healing prayer, the addict may literally cough up or scream as this "internalized bad mother" comes out.

Engulfment by mother overwhelms the strength of masculinity in a man, leaving him with a generalized sense of powerlessness through which his initiative is paralyzed. His ability to act on the truth will remain weakened unless he enters into the healing of the Lord.

Emotional Incest

In extreme cases, mothers can be emotionally incestuous with sons. Emotional incest occurs when mother's love-needs engulf the child, as has been described. This may or may not involve sexual intimations; it may remain "merely" emotional, but is so damaging as to warrant the term "incest." She may make inappropriate comments about the young boy's developing body, or reveal too much of her naked body to him. She may say something like; "If only you were older I'd marry you myself." She may hug the child too long or press his head into her breasts in a sexual way.

Emotional incest can be as devastating as physical sexual abuse and is especially common for mothers who do not have a good relationship with their husbands. Sometimes a son, who never completed the separation and individuation stage, will stay in this type of relationship with the mother. In some circles this is called the "Good Boy Syndrome." Many homosexual men were "good boys." They did everything good for Mom. Frequently, a young man will get so sick of the "Good Boy" syndrome that at some point, instead of individuating, he will rebel against mother. Having been so sickeningly good, he will become the exact opposite. This, however, is not a separation, because he is feeling compelled to rebel against the "good boy," and cannot simply choose to become what he wants. He may be just as bound to his mother as before, but it takes a more negative form now. But it may be at least a step away from having an identity that fused to his mother.

In a healthy family, the father is present emotionally and helps a son individuates from his mother. If the father is absent, or unable to perform this fatherly duty, the son finds himself in a place of needing to alienate himself completely from his mother. He becomes so sick of the clinging mom that, instead of gradually becoming separate, he ruptures his relationship with her. He moves from being enmeshed to: "I HATE YOU!" So he never really separates in a healthy manner.

This unhealthy residue of the mother-son relationship is often projected onto other women. Men, who have had a very manipulative, controlling mom may project their feelings onto all women, unless they have resolved those issues. When such issues have not been resolved, there is a tendency to write off the opposite-sex entirely.

The Absent or Rejecting Mother

Some children simply did not get the nurture that they should have from mother. The result is a sense of emptiness, loneliness, and sometimes dread that can be very painful. When this is the case for the addict, the deprivation of nurture may be projected outside of himself – all women become a symbol of mother's failure to nurture. One of the aspects of an addict's restlessness is trying to connect to that nurture by connecting again and again to women sexually, in an attempt to fill the emptiness. This need to find the lost nurture of Mom is also one of the roots of a homosexual orientation for women. Because women tend to be more relational and less sexual in relationships, this addiction may also show up as an emotional dependency with other woman.

When the addict's lack of nurture is severe, there may be what is called a sense of non-being. This may be experienced as a powerful drive and source of restlessness. If adult women become the identified symbol of that missing nurture, then the need to connect to women in a sexually addictive pattern can become a powerful force.

Absentee moms are one source of rejection for the sexual addict. It is likely that most sexual addicts have experienced some form of early rejection from their mothers. It may have been direct rejection which is what Fred experienced:

> I remember how my mom doted on my sister. She would dress her up in frills and treat her like a princess. But she wouldn't give me the time of day. She would send me out to play and literally not let me back in the house for hours. I remember feeling that she didn't like me and didn't want me around. And when I was inside, my sister had lots of power to get me in trouble. All she had to do was scream and I'd be sent to the corner with a harsh tone and no investigation of the truth. After a while I just stopped trying to get my mom's love.

Rejection was often indirect. A mother's actions may have been a series of small breaks in trust, which the emotionally vulnerable child picked up and carried in his heart. Young boys often misinterpret their mothers' actions, suspecting that they are somehow responsible for them. It is not uncommon to find hidden beliefs within a grown man's heart that approximate messages such as, "I can never succeed at making a woman happy." Or perhaps, "Women see me as an irritant. I am worthless in their eyes." Examples of indirect actions that foster strongholds of rejection follow:

- A constantly angry, cupboard-slamming Mom

- A depressed, unresponsive, low energy Mom

- An alcoholic, mood swinging, unpredictable Mom

- A mom who repeatedly verbally bashes men in general and her husband whom the child loves. Since the child is male, he feels (and may be treated so as to ascertain) that he is bad and unacceptable also

The addict who feels a deep sense of rejection by his mother will be afraid of intimacy in his adult relationships. This sets him up for sexually addictive activities. Because the knowledge of his deep-seated rejection is outside of his awareness, he will instinctively avoid committed relationships with women, but not know exactly why.

Revenge

Sexually addictive patterns carry an element of hatred and revenge towards women. By having gratuitous sex with a woman, a man subtly denies her worth. By using her as an object that serves only his carnal, sensual needs, he disdains her emotional and spiritual value. Thus, he pays her back for the sense of worthlessness about his own being that he attributes to relationship with woman. Some men enjoy intense feelings of prowess as they use their charm to elicit a woman's emotional response, crafting every sentence to increase her sense of trust, and then leaving her flatly after the sexual conquest is accomplished. Consciously or unconsciously, he acts out revenge for the pain that he has suffered in relationship with women of the past. This is called **misogyny**, which is the fear, disdain or hatred of women. It is often unconscious, and so a person is initially unaware of it within himself.

A strategy of misogyny is not hard to understand. If the addict hates all women, he does not have to become vulnerable to them. Of all the creatures on the earth, she has the greatest power to meet his deepest needs. But she also has the greatest power to shame and reject him. The addict's generalized hatred of women provides a fortress that keeps him at a safe distance from the vulnerability of his neediness. At a very deep level, the addict senses and hates his need for the affirmation of women. Hating women is a projection that eases the pain of his own shame. Some men go to the extent of becoming a physical or emotional bully in opposite sex relationships. In his contempt, he exerts a "lordship" and control that prevents his companion from abandoning him. But he also keeps her at an arm's length emotionally because he never becomes truly vulnerable to her.

The concept of staying emotionally safe and acting out revenge are two sides of the same coin. In attempting to assess his motives in sexual addiction, the addict must look at how the two concepts are related in his own relational style with women. Healing misogynistic patterns involves the healing of the heart. It requires forgiveness of primary, developmental figures, along with repentance and renunciation of hatred for women, which in part may have been a strategy to keep from having to risk again in relationships.

Conclusion

Gordon Dalby sums up the dilemma of the mother wound when he writes:

> Certainly, the first woman a male ever loves is his mother, and that love relationship is based upon the most elementary physical dependence. Any man who fails to recognize and accept this given fact of his life risks projecting that dependence and its associated fears onto the woman (or women) that he loves later as an adult. [4]

A man cannot help but transfer the emotional elements of his relationship with mother onto other women. With the aid of Jesus and other safe people, he must face wounds incurred in early relationship with mother so that he can begin to risk true intimacy in present-day, committed relationships.

Notes
Personal

References

1. Frank Lake, *Clinical Theology*, pp. 143-144. Darton, Longman and Todd, copyright 1966.

2. Gordon Dalbey, *Healing the Masculine Soul* (Waco: Word Books Publishers, 1988) 45.

3. Frank Lake, *Clinical Theology* (London: Darton, Longman & Todd Ltd., 1966) 372.

4. Gordon Dalbey, *Healing the Masculine Soul* (Waco: Word Books Publisher, 1988) 36.

HOMEWORK

Homework

1. "Being" is a core sense of being loved that is connected to one's ability to peacefully exist without having to earn acceptability. It is the ability to trust that one is not in danger of losing love or significance, even if he is doing nothing to "earn" that significance. Considering this idea, how do you view your own "being"? Where does your acceptability come from? Do you have to "earn" your significance?

2. Read the testimony of the woman given on page 138 that deals with mother/infant bonding. Write your own truthful testimony.

3. Moral development is centered in agape love. Write your own definition/understanding of agape love. How does this understanding of agape love relate to your own moral development?

Healing the Father Wound

Chapter Sixteen

The fathers eat sour grapes, and the children's teeth are set on edge. As surely as I live, declares the Sovereign Lord, you will no longer quote this proverb in Israel.
(Ezekiel 18:2-3)

The Father Wound

A father has a unique ability to "name" his children, establishing both their value and identity as individuals. He communicates their value through his emotional and spiritual connection with them. He expresses that connection through attention, conversation, and play. When he is doing his job, he not only points out the uniqueness of their gifts, calling, and personality, but he also affirms them with his personal interest in their welfare. When this connection is missing, a child's psychological and spiritual development will flounder.

This culture is particularly noteworthy for fathers who are absent physically and emotionally. The sort of love that a father gives is uniquely masculine, giving shape, form and definition to a child. When a child lacks masculine input, he may lack form in his personality and life. Thus, the wound that results from a father's absence (physical and/or emotional) yields an inability to set and keep boundaries, and a distinct lack of self-control. Also, the child will not have seen modeled the kind of love that protects, provides for, and champions the family's or God's purposes.

When a man has not had a strong, decisive and disciplining father, he will often lack the emotional strength and structure within his personality to resist temptation and act upon the truth. His soul may be blob-like, like a body without a skeleton, unable to retain form for long.

Similarly, a daughter may lack inner strength in her love relationships when her father has been absent or emotionally skewed. Often the need for masculine affirmation becomes sexualized. In her sexual exploits, she is really looking for her father's love and affirmation.

Both the mother's and father's love are essential for a child to have a complete sense of being loved. Without the sense of well-being from mother, and the benevolent provision, protection and boundaries from the father, the erotic drive that emerges in adolescents will be raw and untamed. In this situation, erotic love becomes unwieldy and enslaving, rather than something that adds to the beauty of a committed monogamous relationship.

If a man or woman has been broken by poor fathering, the person will need to develop a relationship with God the Father in order to receive the affirmation and discipline that he or she needs. The process of receiving and internalizing this form of love can be sped up through the prayers of godly men who stand on behalf of

God. God uses others to call out and bless the uniqueness and masculine "form" of the one who has been wounded.

Research Regarding the Father's Role in Sexual Development

A father has a powerful place in the psychosocial development of his children. When he is present, loving, and active in the parenting role, both male and female children develop a more healthy heterosexual identity than when he is physically or emotionally absent.

A father's absence seems to have the most damaging impact upon male children. If he is missing before age five, tendencies towards dependence and passivity are likely to develop. If the father is absent between the ages of six and twelve, hyper-masculine behavior (that is, a false masculine or macho mask to hide a sense of deficiency) may result.

Hyper-masculine behavior arises in a child as he takes in what he sees in culturally driven rituals designed to establish masculinity. The fatherless son ("fatherless" here can refer to one who has not been fathered, which may have been the case even if the dad were physically present) may provoke fights as a display of his machismo. Overcoming the masculine power of others is a false way to feel confidence (albeit fleeting) in his own masculine identity. He may learn how to "hold his liquor" as a sign of being a real man. Or he may embrace the idea that "scoring" sexually with women is proof that he is adequate, potent, and manly. For some addicts, one component of repeated sexual sin is related to the attempt to gain an internal feeling of manhood. In some cases, he uses his sexual exploits to keep from feeling the pain of rejection caused by daddy's absence. In all these scenarios, the young boy compensates for the loss of his father by acting extremely masculine through adopting one or more of society's hyper-masculine roles.

Research indicates that, in general, that the daughters of absentee fathers are more likely to become overly responsive to males and display early inappropriate sexual behaviors. If, on the other hand, the father died early, his daughters tend to become inhibited in their relationship with men.

Two factors contributed by father strongly affect the sexual orientation and sexual boundaries of his children. The first is his psychological and emotional presence that imparts masculine love to a child. The second is the influence the father has on the gender-appropriate behavior of his children. The father has a high degree of influence on the identity and behavior of his children through his teaching and life example. If he models and teaches behaviors that are gender and sexually appropriate, his children will be much more likely to be well adjusted in their sexual behavior. Fathers have a unique place, symbolically, representing God the Father. If a father misrepresents the truth about God, his authority and influence can have damaging effects on his children.

Fathers Have Unique Power to Name Us

Train up a child in the way he should go, even when he is old he will not depart from it. (Proverbs 22:6)

Every son needs his father to tell him who he is. Every daughter needs her father to validate her femininity. In fact, a father has a unique ability to "name" his children, establishing both their value and identity as individuals. He communicates their value through his emotional and spiritual connection with them. He expresses that connection through attention, conversation, and play. When he is doing his job, he not only points out the uniqueness of their gifts, calling, and personality, but he also affirms them with his personal interest in their welfare. When this connection is missing, a child's psychological and spiritual development will flounder.

Consider the story of two brothers, Jacob and Esau, from Genesis chapters 25-27. Esau was his father's favorite. He appears to be a parable of hyper-masculinity with his hairy body, compulsion to hunt, and blatant disregard for relevant spiritual concerns, such as his birthright. As we know, he traded the latter to his brother for a cup of soup. On the other hand, as we view Jacob's life, he seems more effeminate. He was his mother's favorite and hung back at the tents with the women. Jacob was mother's "good boy." The conspiracy between Rebecca and Jacob to deceive Isaac into blessing Jacob, instead of Esau, is based in an emotional alliance where mother has turned son into a surrogate husband. If I am right in my conjecture, the house of Isaac was a substantially dysfunctional family.

Isaac's lack of emotional presence in the family was strikingly destructive. Esau, the rightful recipient of the birthright, was spiritually dull, shallow, and focused on earthly things. Yet he felt his father's blessing when he brought home a succulent antelope or wild pig. Later, he was devastated, after coming to his senses, with regard to his lost birthright. Jacob, on the other hand, felt an intense need to get his father's blessing, even though it was not rightfully his. He was desperate enough to deceive his father into getting it, despite the spiritual risks involved.

Jacob knew the value of a father's blessing, but used deception to get it. Similarly, his mother was aligned with him, instead of with her husband. She felt distant from Isaac emotionally and found a substitute relationship in Jacob. No doubt her lack of trust was engendered by Isaac's self-preserving, non-protective nature. That side of Isaac was revealed when he saved his own skin, while traveling in Egypt, by telling Pharaoh that Rebecca was his sister. Isaac was not able to stand in his calling as a man, husband, and leader. Through his fathering and headship, Isaac perpetuated the family traits of betrayal, insecurity, and deception, rather than protection, provision, and peace.

Biblical Pattern for Masculine Nurture

Fathers, do not provoke your children to anger, but bring them up in the discipline and instruction of the Lord. (Ephesians 6:4)

It is clear in scripture that God has appointed fathers to the responsibility of bringing up their children, by both the Word of God and loving actions which flesh-out the truths of the Gospel. He is the parent responsible for establishing the pattern of the child's obedience in the family. His role is not to terrorize the child or subdue him through the use of excessive force. That only stirs up anger in the child, who will then perpetuate the anger in his relationships.

Bringing up the child in the discipline and instruction of the Lord means that the father's parenting will bear some distinguishing characteristics:

1) It is a continuous job. As long as the child is a dependent, the father is to be responsible for providing for the child, providing every opportunity for him to grow up well, secure in his or her identity. This happens both through instruction and through the father's consistent lifestyle in accordance with what he has taught. He treats the child as separate from mother, and thus helps establish his offspring in their own identities apart from mother.

2) It is a loving job. In Greek, the words "to bring up" literally mean to "nourish tenderly." Nourishment implies an emotional and physical connection, care for wounds, and an obvious desire on the father's part to secure the best that he can for the child. It is also about empowering the child to stand. He nurtures the "fighter" in his children – that ability to stand and press through life's challenges.

3) It is a congruent job. By congruent, I mean the father's walk matches his talk. There must be a harmony between the father's teaching of God's truth and his actions for them to produce psychological and emotional wholeness in the child. If the father's speech and actions are congruent, the child will be able to make a much smoother transition from man as father, to God as Father.

Facing the Father Wound

The High-Admonition / Low-Nurture father

One of the most common family-of-origin patterns for addictive personalities is the high-demand-for-performance with low-nurture environment. Children from these environments must constantly face the giant hurdles of parental expectation that litter the track of their development, but find little or no support from parents in getting over them. In such an environment, the coping strategy is often to find ways to circumvent them instead.

Gordon Dalby shares in his book, *Father and Son*, an example of how this internal rebellion to authority might develop in response to such an environment. A father commands his son, who is outside playing, "Come in right now for dinner." The boy may not feel free to yell back, "I don't want to come inside, I'm having too much fun playing." Instead, the boy learns to procrastinate. He may say, "Yes sir. I'll be right there." Yet, ten minutes later, the boy is still outside playing. This delaying and goofing around become the weapon a child uses to safely have his own desires met against his father's demands. This behavioral pattern takes root in the child's psyche. As an adult, he will give himself parent-like directions that sound like the voice of his father. "Do this, don't do that." "You shouldn't be feeling that!" "Don't look here, don't touch there." Since the pattern of inner rebellion is already established, the adult now feels an inability to act on what he should do. The hurdles seem too high. It is much easier to turn to the objects of his addiction to kill the guilt of his inability to do what is right and the pain of his rebellion.

When we look at Jesus as a role model, we see great submission to His Father in Heaven. We see that even He struggled to obey in the Garden of Gethsemane. But His response was not a blind act of giving in. It was a process of relationship with the Father - talking with him honestly and openly. We, too, can and should learn to be honest with ourselves and God regarding our inner patterns of avoiding responsibility.

When a Father Fails to Relate to a Son or Daughter Emotionally

Most young children have not yet learned to deny their emotions and can be seen making heart felt responses to life. Often these emotional responses are shut down by the father through direct communication that indicates that emotions are not welcome out in the open. A father may unintentionally do this by encouraging a child to be brave about a problem, or by making a statement such as, "big girls/boys don't cry." By merely ignoring their emotions, or leaving them invalidated, he also gives the message that they are not important. The confused child then tries to please his father by repressing or suppressing his feelings.

Perhaps the most subtle way that a father shuts down his children is by failing to relate to them at an emotional level. He communicates by his lack of emotion that they should refrain from being emotional also, or perhaps that emotions aren't necessary. Children learn much by observation of their fathers' behavior.

When a child shuts down, he is no longer able to receive upbuilding input from adults. He ceases to grow into the full potential of one made in the image of God. This leaves children with a profound sense of emptiness and the inability to connect to others. This inability to connect emotionally, in turn, leaves them vulnerable to false ways of connecting. One of these is promiscuous sexuality.

When a Father is Absent (Physically or Emotionally)

A father may be physically or emotionally absent from the home. Sometimes he makes an obvious decision to leave the family, as in divorce, or by running from his responsibility for provision, protection, and parenting. This produces a deep wound. A child will often take responsibility for the father's abandonment, thinking that somehow he drove the father off. He may think painful thoughts such as, "I must not have behaved well enough to make my dad love me." "What did I do wrong to make him go away?" "How can I change to make him come back?" This type of child will not only make the wrong conclusions about himself, but will also begin to believe at a deeper level that all men are untrustworthy.

Chronic feelings of abandonment point to an issue of broken trust. If trust was broken by an absent, abandoning father, there may be a generalized belief in the heart that all men are untrustworthy and will eventually leave the relationship.

Passivity in a father is a subtle form of abandonment. It can be more disturbing to a child than if he weren't there at all. He is there, physically present, and yet not reaching out emotionally, despite the child's clear need for attention, affirmation and interaction. Additionally, if a father is passive, it probably means that his wife, his counterpart, is the dominant force in the emotional and decision making aspects of the family. A father may be a good provider and still be passive. Research indicates that when the mother is dominant in family relationships, there is a high probability, on behalf of the children, that there will be anger or hatred toward the opposite sex, in both male and female children. This increases the possibility of unhealthy sexual relating.

The Security of Being Second

Father functions to give form to his children's emerging lives. When he doesn't, the child is not adequately de-centralized; he fails to learn self-control and a healthy regard for authority. Masculine presence is necessary to growing beyond a selfish, "need-based" orientation toward life. The lack of fathering keeps us stuck in childish ways of seeing and behaving. Where healthy masculinity is absent from the family, the ability to act upon the truth by setting boundaries, embracing self-discipline, and submitting to authority is substantially weakened in the children of that family.

When a Father Manifests Various Forms of Rage

Both physical and verbal abuse are manifestations of rage which victimize a child. Both are forms of power and control. When wielded by an ungodly father, they produce a powerlessness, shame, and worthlessness in the child that hinders true intimate relationship. When powerlessness is established in the heart of a child towards his father, the child experiences a helplessness to act upon the truth, and a heightened sense of inner rebellion.

The victim of verbal or physical abuse often does not develop a true sense of self; consequently, he will look to others, expecting them to define him. Often, attempts at this definition will come through sexuality as a source of affirmation.

The Wounds of the Unfaithful Father

A father who models "womanizing," or the attitude that women are only sexual objects, infects the natural desire of his son and promotes distorted ways of acting out. A son, looking for his father's approval, may take on his sexually broken attitudes with the hopes of pleasing him. Many sons emulate the promiscuous behavior of their fathers, thinking that somehow, through it, they will become men.

Affairs which become obvious to children in adulterous families promote deep feelings of betrayal and mistrust regarding covenant relationships. Ironically, this lack of trust prevents true intimacy and trust when the grown child later marries. Often he may be predisposed to recreate the pattern of infidelity in his own marriage. Children of families that have covert or overt affairs feel a deep sense of abandonment. They will often live a secret life of fantasy in which they try to find secure, connected relationships. Frequently, these fantasies become true-life affairs.

Wounds of the Shaming or Perfectionistic Father

The perfectionistic father is closely related to the high demand/low nurture father. Perfectionism breeds a performance-orientation and an inability to receive grace from God or others. Children of perfectionists tend to feel that they will never be able to measure up. In the shamed child, messages such as "I am a worthless person and will never amount to anything," or, "I am a failure," or "If I just try harder I'll be accepted," run continuously at a subconscious level of the heart. These life-scripts propel the child of the perfectionist to relentlessly try harder. God is not allowed into the battle because the perfectionist wrongly assumes that He will reject and condemn the sinful failures.

Distortions in the Image of Our Heavenly Father

Sandra D. Wilson has identified five of the most common distortions of God that come out of addictive families.[1] It is not surprising to find that they are related to the wounds that come through fathers to their children. The following subtitles are taken from Wilson's work.

1) The Cruel and Capricious God

This image of God is formed in families where the attitude mostly resembled a concentration camp in its expectations. Imagine Fred's family, where the environment combined extreme emotional neglect with harsh and cruel treatment. The fruit in his adult life is to experience scripture reading with terror, and the painful expectation of being annihilated by God if he did not meet His standards. The fatherhood of God still does not sound comforting to Fred, but rather is associated with the cruel and abusive treatment that was received in the family of origin. Fred's belief, "Men always hurt me," was long ago transformed into "God will always hurt me." It is very difficult for a Christian with this view of God to develop a deepening relationship with Him. In Fred's case, to give up control and become vulnerable is extremely frightening. He is sure that closeness to God means pain.

2) The Demanding/Unforgiving God

The demanding/unforgiving God is a few shades less frightening than the cruel and capricious God. One may earn His approval, but only through hard work and doing good Christian deeds. This view of God comes through perfectionistic demands from a father, on the one hand, or the neglected child, on the other hand. In both cases the emotional set-up results in striving to earn the love of the father. Robert, for example, performed the "hero", or responsible role, in his family of origin and transferred his strategy of *being good* to earn parent's approval to *being good* to earn God's approval. Bob is a very good Christian with the wrong motivation. Subconsciously, he is performing for a demanding God for whom he cannot do enough.

3) The Selective and Unfair God

The selective and unfair God loves others, but does not love the one who holds this view of God. The child in this scenario carried his sense of being "different-and-not-as-good-as" over into their relationship with the heavenly Father. He feels like a second class citizen of the Kingdom as well as in church, and tends to see how others are blessed and how he is not. When an addict holds this view of God, he gives mental assent to the scriptures that indicate all have fallen short of God's glory and all have received the same measure of grace, but in the heart still believes that God discriminates by treating His other children better.

4) The Distant and Unavailable God

The distant and unavailable God is not cruel, demanding, unforgiving, selective, or punitive; He is just unavailable. This view of God often results when dad was not in the home due to death or early abandonment. It can also result from his emotional absence or passivity. This view of God may include the belief that God loves His people, but that He does not interact with His children in a personal way.

5) The Kind, but Confused God

In this distorted version of God's image, God the father is loving, but ineffective in solving problems of the world or the individual. In this scenario, the child has transferred the observations of a father, ineffective in dealing with family chaos, to a heavenly deity who cannot intervene effectively in the lives of his children.

More Distortions

The Unpredictable - Moody God

If a man's father has been moody, unpredictable or has broken many promises, his children may see God in the same light. They will not trust God to come through in situations where trust is needed. Thus, they will be impaired in their faith and in fully entering into relationship with him.

The Sexually Perverse God

In this view of God, the heart is sure that He will somehow be sexual if the worshipper becomes intimate with him. When this person feels close to God, he also feels sexual energy. This reality is shameful, confusing, and seems obviously distorted, but yet remains. This distortion can be the result of a father's or relative's incest, either physically or emotionally.

To receive healing, the molested person must come to a deep realization that his incest was lust, and not love. He must come to see the vast difference between the two. As he faces the truth, he can truly forgive and process the accompanying grief about being deprived of real love. This process helps diffuse the "love is always sexual" belief system and will also help separate the image of father from the image of God.

The Most Essential Healing Tasks

The importance of dealing with our father wound cannot be overstated. As we begin to see the sources of pain that are related to our fathering, we can start to gain objectivity about some of the reasons we are motivated to do what we do. Since the images of our fathers affect our images concerning God, our relationship with the Lord can change for the better as old wounds are resolved.

The elements of a person's relationship with God that are affected by our past relationship with our fathers are:

1) The ability to be intimate with Him (hearing His voice)

2) The ability to receive His love and forgiveness

3) The ability to trust Him and believe His promises

4) Perceiving His Word accurately and with balance

5) Extending love and forgiveness to others (As we clear our heart of faulty images of father, we can begin to receive God the Father's love more easily. As we realize that He forgives and accepts us, we will be able to love and forgive others more easily)

All of these areas will hinder the healing of our sexual addiction if we ignore them. Therefore, we must allow God to guide us into healing with respect to our earthly fathers.

Learning To Let Go

We need to face the reality that our earthly fathers were not perfect and have failed us in many ways. We need to let them off the hook (stop demanding that they pay for their mistakes) and let love enter our lives as we receive it from God. The process of forgiveness is essential. Separating ourselves from the damage that occurred in relationship to our earthly fathers often means dealing with heart-level decisions to not let men in, or to block out the masculine presence from one's life altogether. These are among the inner vows that must be broken, which were discussed previously in chapter eleven.

By repenting of and breaking such vows, we will begin to see the good of the masculinity that was imparted to us. In a sense, we find what has been unavailable within. In addition, we will gain an openness to receiving the masculine strength of God, who dearly wants to impart all good things to us.

Before we can reconcile with our fathers, we must identify what has been broken. Sometimes this is the hardest step of all. In trying to be good Christians, many of us learned the art of denying how others have hurt us, especially our family members. This is how we survived. Jim, for example, became so focused on how he had sinned sexually, that he fail to recognize and identify how others sinned against him. In order to avoid the pain of acknowledging their failings, he overlooked their offenses and explained away their behavior by believing that they did the best they could. On the one hand, Jim's assessment may be true. It seems to be merely a merciful assessment. But on the other hand, it does nothing to acknowledge the wounds within which continue to cause fear in relationship with God and others.

The bottom line is that our fathers were imperfect in their care for us and, at times, may have been very hurtful. We need to ask God to help us identify the hurts in our lives so that we can let go of them and continue the healing process.

Remember the Process of Healing

When we think of dealing with all of the character flaws of our fathers, our tendency is to want to forgive them in one generic prayer, and have all the hurts done away with. The fact is, healing occurs over time and is a process of learning to acknowledge hurt, loss, and disappointment. Then we will be able to accept our fathers and realize that the same grace that allows us to love ourselves with all of our shortcomings allows us to love them.

Part of the process of healing is obtaining from God a vision of what redeemed masculinity truly is. Most of us have had poor role models and need to gain new meaning for the old symbols of "man" and "father." We cannot do this outside of God's guidance. We must look to Him as our Source of knowledge and experience.

Seeing God as our Father

We all have a need for a fulfilling relationship with a father who cares for, nurtures and empowers us. God can meet this need when we are willing to accept our role as His children. What follows are some essential, revealed truths worthy of our meditation. As we ponder them in prayer, they can help us develop the attitudes and mindsets that will unveil the reality of Who He is as our Father:

Accept God's Discipline as a Gift, Knowing His Actions are Love

And you have forgotten the exhortation which addresses you as sons? My son, do not regard lightly the discipline of the Lord, nor faint when you are reproved by Him. For the Lord disciplines him whom He loves, and chastises every son whom His receives. It is for discipline that you have to endure. God is treating you as sons; for what son is there whom his father does not discipline? If you are left without discipline, in which all have participated, then you are illegitimate children and not sons. (Hebrews 12:5-8)

Receive Adoption as Your Inheritance

For you have not received a spirit of slavery leading to fear again, but you have received a spirit of adoption as sons by which we cry out, 'Abba! Father!' The Spirit Himself bears witness with our spirit that we are children of God, and if children, heirs also, heirs of God and fellow heirs with Christ, if indeed we suffer with Him in order that we may also be glorified. (Romans 8:15-18)

But when the fullness of the time came, God sent forth His son, born of a woman, born under the Law, in order that He might redeem those who were under the Law, that we might receive the adoption as sons. And because you are a son, God has sent forth the Spirit of His Son into our hearts, crying 'Abba! Father!' (Galations 4:4-6)

References

[1] Sandra D. Wilson, *Counseling Adult Children of Alcoholics* (Dallas, Word Publishing, 1989) 95-102.

HOMEWORK

Homework

1. Describe your father's style of relating to you. Be specific about how he related to you emotionally. Was he consistent? Do you consider him abusive?

2. List any of the symptoms of a wounding father relationship that you identified within the material in this section.

3. Did you relate to any of the distortions of God that were mentioned in the material? Describe them and attempt to connect them to your earthly father.

4. Go over the "most essential healing tasks" on page 151. List those that are relevant to you. Write about how they might be related to our relationship with your earthy father.

Facing Sexual Abuse

Childhood sexual abuse has a devastating affect on the sexuality of the emerging adult victim. If the wounds of sexual abuse are not healed, they will continue to drive the life of the addict, making it difficult to master certain compulsions.

Chapter Seventeen

No one is to approach any close relative to have sexual relations. I am the Lord.
(Leviticus 18:6)

General Definition of Abuse

Childhood abuse can be defined as: any application of personal power exerted upon a child which is destructive and which hinders his or her ability to thrive as God intends. Abusive acts (and omissions) come in various forms: physical , emotional, spiritual, omissions and, most significant for the subject of sexual addiction, sexual.[1]

Abuse seriously hinders the development of a person. It crosses over boundaries of love and respect and seriously cripples one's ability to give and receive love. Most forms of abuse are surrounded by the secrecy of the "no talk" rule of dysfunctional families, and so the scars that are left go untreated. As such, they fester with shame, self-hatred, guilt, spiritual oppression, and a variety of internal compensations, which may be acted out in sexual addiction.

Even though the subject of this chapter is sexual abuse, it is important to note that many of the feelings described in *Feelings Common to Victims* (later in this chapter) apply to other types of abuse. Abuse of any type is destructive and will cause pain in a person. Sexually addictive activities may be the anesthesia of choice used to keep these feelings at bay.

Sexual Abuse

Sexual abuse is one of the most devastating forms of abuse because it penetrates into the very essence of a person's gender. It can be defined as: *any act of sexual power (overt or covert) that is exerted upon a child under eighteen years old.* Sexual abuse is not usually violent, as in rape. More often the perpetrator is kind and charming towards his young victims, using their need for love and affection to seduce them into sexual acts.

Those who abuse come in all sizes, genders, and ages. One's abuser might be a father, a pastor, a relative, a sixty-eight year old grandmotherly neighbor, or a group of kids on the playground. The abuser may be years older or near the same age.

Acts of sexual abuse involve the pain of betrayal and the shame of being used and degraded by lust. Following the abuse, self-doubts about who was responsible for the act may torment the victim. He is often confused because he experienced physical pleasure during the abuse; his body was merely responding in accordance with its design. Yet to have enjoyed something that was degrading causes many people to feel extreme conflict over the pleasure they have felt. Sadly, most conclude that at some level they were responsible for the encounter. One lady said, "I guess I was just too sexual for the grown men around me." Many abusers encourage such ideas as a part of their seduction. Some threaten the victim so as to insure that he or she will not tell. As a result, confusion and guilt make a home in victim's heart.

Following the event these painful, conflicting feelings contribute to fear about reporting the abuse to someone who could help. As a result, the victim of sexual abuse often opts for secrecy and minimizes the abuse, hiding it away in his or her heart. The abused person may remember the events but compensate for them by making excuses for the abuser such as; "I know he had a hard childhood himself," or, "At least it was the man down the street and not my dad."

As time passes, the event (or series of events) is suppressed by the victim. It becomes a cold, hard lump in the core of his being. Clarity is soon lost; the psyche may obscure the painful memories, hiding them behind memories of events that are more pleasant to remember.

Long Term Effects of Sexual Abuse

All abuse is damaging, especially sexual abuse. This is true no matter how minimal the acts of abuse seem to have been. The extent of the damage done to a person depends upon several factors.

- The effects are more severe if the circumstances that surrounded the abuse disrupted the ability of the child to enjoy the protection and nurture of the parents. Parental abuse always produces more severe damage because, as the perpetrators, the parents cannot be sought for refuge; by abusing the child, they simultaneously abandoned him, leaving him without a refuge.

- If the child hides the abuse for many years, the pattern of avoiding intimacy may become strongly established and more difficult to heal.

- The sensitivity and disposition of the child affects how he handles the abuse

- Younger children seem to internalize abuse into their developing core in a deeper way.

Shame

Shame is one of the major byproducts of that abuse. It is the voice which warns the person not to become known. Shame includes the set of negative beliefs and feelings about one's self. The person feels flawed and defective, and therefore dreads that he will be seen for what he feels he is – grossly defective. His sense of dignity was stolen through the sexual abuse, and so he now believes that he is not worthy of normal love. To overcome shame it is important to understand the different feelings, thoughts and attitudes that keep it alive.

Feelings Common to Victims

As stated before, the victim has been subject to the overbearing power of another. This power to abuse is based in the authority of the abuser; the abuser took advantage of the victim's love and dependency needs (especially in the parent/child relationship). This misuse of this power results in a crippled will and a damaged ability to function in relationships. Some other common feelings are:

Powerlessness: Powerlessness is feeling helpless, paralyzed, and overwhelmed by another person who has wielded some form of personal power over another person against his will. Powerlessness disables the will so that a person cannot escape a dangerous situation. The disabling may continue on in similar situations in the future.

During a time of prayer, for a man we will call Bill, a memory surfaced of a time when he was eighteen and sitting alone in the public Jacuzzi at the apartment complex where he lived. An unfamiliar man entered the Jacuzzi and eventually began to molest him. At the onset of the stranger's sexual advances Bill was overcome with an immobilizing fear. Even though he was physically strong enough to stop his abuser, Bill was emotionally paralyzed by his sense of powerlessness. When I asked him if he remembered that feeling from another time in his life, he easily connected it to the fear that would grip him when his father would pull out a belt to physically beat him. Bill was a sexual addict.

Bill did not have a clear awareness of the sense of powerlessness that would sometimes overtake him. He had split-off his own sense of powerlessness. He, like many abuse victims, had developed a "good/bad split" as described below by Dan Allender in his book *The Wounded Heart*:

> A sexually abused person often forfeits the experience of pain by a process of splitting, denial, and loss of memory. Splitting involves a process of segmenting memories and feelings into separable categories of good or bad. The categorization of the self as all good or all bad is then intensified by the construction of a huge barricade between the two. It is not possible for the person to see errant motives in her 'good self' or legitimate desire or even honorable intention in her 'bad self.' The two are separated by an iron curtain: on one side exists all the lust, vengeance, hate and hunger of the soul; and on the other, all the love, forgiveness, and warmth. If feelings from the dark side are experienced, they must be either denied or embraced in an orgy of compulsion. The binge eater hates herself, but periodically 'allows' for a break in her 'good self' routine by a few minutes of debauchery. [2]

This scenario describes the inner dynamics of the Christian sexual addict's double life. It also explains how Bill could be involved in sexual usury one moment and become incapacitated by sexual advances the next. Bill's powerlessness stripped him of the freedom to choose. Like his abuser, many addicts prey upon the powerlessness of their victims. If they are also abuse survivors, it is very possible that they use sexually intrusive acts to overcome their own sense of powerlessness and fear of becoming vulnerable. To successfully escape painful feelings, he must deaden his heart through acts of false intimacy.

> The sexually abused man often puts his trust in his own strength after he has been violated. He develops a mind-set of invulnerability to compensate for the frightening time when he felt extremely powerless. A number of my male abuse clients were long-distance runners, avid weight lifters, and macho risk takers. They often expressed the same attitude of control and invulnerability by refusing to feel any emotion that reflected weakness or to feel intimate (other than sexually) with any person. The message was clear: 'I've been violated once, and I will never feel that powerless again in the presence of another person.' [3]

Facing the fear of powerlessness is necessary for the addict. For healing to occur he must enter into the reality that he is powerless over sin. He must have the courage to believe that vulnerability with God will result in being empowered by His grace and love. The heart has great difficulty believing that the very thing that brought destruction holds the possibility for healing. He must overcome the real, subconscious fear that powerlessness before God will result in re-victimization as it did with his abuser.

Worthlessness/Depersonalization: Worthlessness is a feeling of loss of value as a person. When a person is treated like an object, used for pleasure, or for the venting of aggression by another, he will experience a loss of his sense of value as God's creation.

Fear: Fear results from having been snatched out of a context of love and security. When a person is not treated lovingly, he will begin to distrust those who have the power to not love him; he may also be anxious about coming into contact with people who can offer him love.

Abandonment/Betrayal: The feeling of abandonment is intimately connected to betrayal. A person feels abandoned when someone to whom he has given his heart turns from him, or withdraws love. Abandonment issues often generalize onto other relationships.

One devastating symptom of betrayal is hypervigilance towards future acts of betrayal. A person who has suffered the betrayal of abuse experiences a loss of hope that future intimacy will be safe and life-giving. The abuse victim's sense of betrayal carries with it a distorted and suspicious stance towards new relationships. Consciously or subconsciously he avoids being fooled again.

The one who is betrayed by abuse often concludes that he could have avoided abandonment if he had been less needy. So the abuse victim guards against his own inner need, concluding that it would be better to live a detached life with a deadened heart rather than be humiliated again.

Anger/Contempt: Anger is the psyche's response to an emergency. It readies the body and mind to fight or to flee. Anger is an appropriate response in a threatening situation. However, when a person has been traumatized by sexual abuse, anger may become a character trait. It may be a way of keeping people away, scaring others so that they won't come close. It can become a shield against intimacy. Anger can be as small as irritation and as big as rage and murder. Anger normally results when a person's dignity has been injured and love needs have been blocked.

Contempt is "disparaging or haughty disdain, or scorn." It goes beyond anger, condemning the perceived source of personal injury. **The abuse victim has two common types of contempt:**

1)   He has self-contempt based upon his own view of himself.

> The most devastating aspect of the self-hatred that comes from having been abused is the contempt towards one's need for satisfying human relationship – a longing to be valued and enjoyed. Many victims blame that need for having encouraged the sexual abuse. The problem with hating and pushing away this part of oneself is that God created us for relationship. The need to be valued, appreciated, and loved, and to love others in return, is intrinsic to our created purpose. To hate that central need is to be at odds with the most important parts of oneself.

2)   The abuse survivor also has contempt for others who might get too close to uncovering his longing to be loved. This kind of contempt is used as a shield:

> The sexually abused person often carries contempt as an antidote to the bite of pleasure. The first stirring to aliveness or passion in contact with another feels like venom that may take both parties into a destructive spiral of lust or revenge.[4]

By using contempt, the abuse survivor can deaden his sense of shame. He rides the power of his anger which aids in his illusion of control when he is acting out. Contempt may result in many different styles of relating; the rage-aholic, the perfectionist, the mood caster, the withdrawing one, etc. Whatever the style of relating to the world, the objective is to stay in control — to achieve a false intimacy without risking vulnerability. But control is a double-edged sword. What keeps people out also keeps God out. Contempt hinders the work of God because it refuses to believe in His love and refuses to risk again with the One who can bring deep healing.

Dirtiness: Dirtiness is a variation on shame, in which the person feels defiled (usually through a sexual act), unworthy, and unacceptable before a holy, clean God. His feeling of dirtiness may be intertwined with a false, guilt-ridden awareness that his need for love and attention was a contributor to involvement in inappropriate sexual activity, such as incest.

During the process of healing, abuse survivors must come to grips with the reality that they were violated by the perversion of another. Putting the responsibility for the violation back in the perpetrator's hands and leaving it there is one of the important tasks of healing. Beyond that only the blood of Jesus can restore them to a renewal of innocence.

Perversion: Perversion is not any particular feeling, but is a generalized sense of shame that comes from having abnormal sexual urges. The scripture sets clear boundaries for what is normal and, thus, defines perverse sexual feelings indirectly. Beyond what has already been described in other places in this chapter, the dynamics of perverse feelings follow.

Perverse desires are often the result of seeking to relieve generalized sexual urges through involvement with a "safe" (non-threatening) participant. For example, involvement with animals may provide sexual stimulation without the threat of rejection. Peeking into windows at another's nakedness may provide a false sense of closeness without entering into the risk of relationship.

Perversion may also result from the sexualization of an unmet developmental need. The homosexual neurosis is an example of an attempt to take-in the masculine traits of other men in order to complete one's personal sense of deficiency.

Guilt: Guilt is a sense of remorse coming from doing something that is in conflict with one's conscience and belief system. With normal guilt, righting the wrong and/or receiving forgiveness will bring resolution. But neurotic guilt is closely linked to shame and self-hatred, and will not be healed until its roots are discovered. In healing guilt, those receiving prayer will need to crucify the ways in which they act out self-atonement. That is, they will need to see, acknowledge and repent of the ways they try to undo their sense of badness through good works. They must be helped to turn to the blood of Jesus for their justification.

Incest

Sexual abuse is not always physical. Parents can be incestuous with their children by using sexual words and attitudes that cause nearly the same emotional damage to the child. "Abuse is measured not by the act itself, but by the destruction it leaves. It's very easy for adults to minimize their own childhood experiences of abuse by saying, 'Oh, it wasn't that bad.'" [5]

Incest is sexual abuse that occurs within the family structure of blood, or marriage relationships. This includes the nuclear family, stepfamily, cousins, aunts and uncles, and grandparents.

Parent/child incest

In general, mother/son incest has has been treated more lightly in research literature than father-daughter incest. Until recently, it has been thought to be less traumatic because it is:

1) often less physical,

2) often less forceful, and more relational and persuasive, and

3) cultural factors reinforce the attitude that a boy should have enjoyed his sexual abuse.

If the boy abused by his mother didn't enjoy the events of the abuse, he may fear that he is homosexual, and become obsessed with trying to prove that he is not through repeatedly acting out with women.

> Ninety-five percent of the [mother-son] cases involve absent fathers with weak, dependent mothers. Forward suggests that the mothers are seeking substitutes for their spouses. In these families, the son becomes both a replacement for, and rival of, the father. As such, the son experiences a wide range of damaging emotions (guilt, desire, love and hate) that result in identity problems later in life. Many of the boys eventually become homosexuals; some become rapists and murderers. Others suffer from sexual dysfunctions such as impotence. [6]

As you might suspect from this quote, the incestuous mother is likely to be emotionally engulfing, and will tend to scare her victim's heterosexual desire into hiding, rather than fire it up.

Studies on boys who were sexually abused indicate than the trauma tends to be internalized and then manifests in self-destructive activities such as overeating, self-mutilation, suicide and drug addiction. Other symptoms include hyperactivity, recurring fears, fits of crying and recurring nightmares.

If the sexual abuse was perpetrated by a father or some other man, psychosexual confusion often results. Many male survivors abused by other men fear homosexuality or, conversely, become homosexual in their orientation. Others over-compensate for their gender insecurity.

One man, who had been molested by a man, married a dominant "mother figure" who was ten years his senior. Later he recalled needing her to take care of the part of him that still felt like a small boy. During the marriage he acted out a hyper-addictive pattern by demanding sex five or six times a day. The encounters were shallow and brief. His wife seldom felt satisfied. Whenever she became responsive in the sexual relationship, he became impotent. During her ensuing pregnancy his wife had no desire for sex. This brought up intense feelings of rejection in the husband as well as serious questions about the adequacy of his manhood. It was during this time that he began to molest his eight-year-old stepdaughter. The cycle was complete (Paraphrased from: Sexual Abuse, Adele Mayer, Pg. 61-62)[8].

Female sexual abuse and incest victims experience a range of symptoms. Some pass through multiple marriages, all-the-while suffering from various forms of sexual dysfunction. Others become lesbians. Some become sexually anorexic, a term coined by Patrick Carnes, which describes a condition wherein the person's "hunger" for sex vanishes, thereby removing them from the risk of being re-wounded. Like the anorexic who starves herself from food, the sexually-abused sexual anorexic may starve himself or herself from sexuality, because it has been so hurtful in the past.

Some female incest victims become sexually addictive, evidencing promiscuity and indiscriminate sexual activity. They are looking for father figures in the men with whom they have intimate relationships. But many times their partners of choice express their dominance in abusive ways. The addict may abuse her children in alcoholic rages, demand that she participate in degrading sex acts, take advantage of her dependency, or coldly snub her relational needs on a regular basis.

In both women and men who are incest survivors, there can be a time bomb effect in which life is relatively symptom-free until their thirties or forties, when the pain of abuse starts to surface and their emotional lives seem to spiral out of control.

Emotional Consequences of Sexual Abuse

In one study, research figures indicate that 39% of 160 *addicted* men and 63% of 24 *addicted* women reported being sexually abused in their family background. This is in contrast to a population of nonaddicted adults where 8% of the men and 20% of the women reported sexual abuse. Of men who committed incest as part of their addiction, 55% were childhood victims of incest.[9] Some specialists believe that these figures actually represent under-reporting of sexual abuse, and that the percentages are actually greater for sexually abused addicts. Whether or not under-reporting is a reality, we can see that sexual abuse contributes to sexually addictive patterns.

There are a variety of feelings that contribute to the addict's acting out sexually. The dirtiness that an abuse victim often feels can lead to a self-fulfilling prophecy; the addict thinks in his heart, "I am perverted and worthless. The abuse I received was my fault because I'm too needy. I'm bad, I deserve to be stuck in this mire." He then acts out as a way to punish himself for the past and as a way to confirm sense of badness (which may be unconscious).

Probably the single most destructive outcome for one who has been sexually abused is the belief that "sex *is* love," which has become deeply embedded into the personality. The abuse victim can rarely, if ever, separate sexual desire from intimacy. A child is prematurely eroticized by incest, and from then on, experiences a confusing array of feelings that connect abusive sexuality to needs for blessing and affirmation as a person.

One woman described the arrival of intense, unwanted sexual feelings whenever she began to feel intimacy in her friendships with men. Many times these men were already married, or were men who were trying to help her in the context of ministry. To her horror, she would often feel sexual feelings when God seemed close to her. During prayer she realized that these feelings were a means of avoiding the pain and fear surrounding her sexual abuse. She recalled how she would focus on the sexual feelings during the actual abuse, rather than the emotional pain. In feeling sexual she could avoid pain. Now, many years later, this detour had become a permanent route. To receive healing, she needed to choose to turn from indulging the sexual feelings, and to face the emptiness and fear of abandonment that lay beneath them.

A very high percentage of prostitutes report being sexually abused by their fathers or another male relative. Receiving money in return for sexual acts represents a solution for the feelings of powerlessness that they have as victims. Unfortunately, along with this distorted means of control, there is a resignation to the life role of being spoiled goods.

At times, a victim's rage about his abuse may become fused with erotic pleasure. The person may therefore act out sexually with others in an abusive way.

Abused to Abuser

Statistics state that fifty to eighty percent of sexual offenders were themselves sexually abused as children. Those who have been abused and become perpetrators include men and women.

Some research suggests that the "abused becoming abuser" phenomena is the result of the abuse victim identifying with the abuser in an attempt to master the unresolved trauma. When this scenario is acted out, the first victim of sexual abuse repeatedly re-enacts his or her own abuse in an unconscious attempt to overcome feelings of powerlessness, by gaining control over the next generation victim. The victimizer thereby temporarily regains power and control through his sin.

Often pedophiles display fixation on an unresolved sexual conflict by molesting children that are the same age as they were when they experienced their own sexual trauma. The sex offender, seeking to avoid the wounded child within, projects his unresolved feelings onto a real child outside of himself, and then overpowers that child. This strategy is a variation of identifying with the power of his own abuser.

Another scenario is possible for the pedophile or incestuous parent. As a result of taking on adult responsibility too early in life, a person may experience a loss of childhood – the destruction of the part of them that never got to be childlike. This wound is then transformed at adolescence into a sexualized longing to be connected to children, who symbolized the lost "internal child." The adult, in his brokenness, tries to reclaim his childlike characteristics and complete himself through sexual intimacy with children.

Probably the most common reason for a perpetrator to engage in seduction of children is simply that they are easier to abuse than adults. Most children are relatively innocent and inexperienced at discerning evil in others, especially if they have an exaggerated need to be loved. They innocently partake of sexual activities because they trust the adult when he assures the child that sex is okay. Thus, they are easy targets. Frequently the sexual abuser is charming and warm towards them and even seems to possess special gifts in relating to children. Both fathers and mothers have been known to use their children in situations where intimacy with their spouse is difficult and hurtful. Expressing their need for sexual intimacy with their children is easier than working through their frightening, adult relationship.

Steps to Pursue Healing

1) Be willing to feel anger and rage over what you have undergone. You may feel angry with the perpetrator, or with God. Don't chase the anger away prematurely by a false sort of forgiving. Real, healing forgiveness (which will be discussed in another chapter) is done after you have been willing to experience the anger, and perhaps during it. You may need to enter into dialogue with God over why He let you be subjected to evil. This may take time. Like David and the other psalmists, be very open with the Lord about what you feel, but try not to believe your diseased feelings. David was very frank with God, while always keeping in mind what God was really like, even though he didn't often feel it, and even though his circumstances seemed to say otherwise. He was able to hold in tension his feelings and the revealed truth about God, without denying either one because of the other. We need to do the same. Don't pretend your heart is fine and that you don't need to face the pain and anger within. God knows what feelings are there already – He already sees them – so you might as well face them! Regularly ask the Lord for the courage to face your heart, the grace to do so, and for His truth to become a deeper part of you than the pain has been.

2) Make the choice to become honest with your feelings and beliefs about intimate relationships. By facing your heart, the beliefs and feelings that may long have been hidden, you will be entering into the pain of having been abused. That suffering will be redemptive, not destructive, if you suffer at the Cross. There Jesus died to take sin and its effects from you. It can be either an opportunity to become bitter, or to enter into deeper communion with Jesus. What comes up from the hidden depths of your heart won't be pretty — but the more you face it, the more you'll be able to trust in the cross of Christ to justify you, instead of your own good deeds or thoughts.

3) Ask God to help you to grieve the many losses that are involved in abuse. What you have lost can never be regained; because this thought seems overwhelming, many people flee their grief. But we can only recover as we grieve the loss that cannot be regained. You cannot have another childhood. However, if we are willing to face the reality of what we've lost, we encounter Jesus in the very places within us that the pain once occupied.

4) Take responsibility for your sinful reactions to the sin against you. It is true that those reactions were survival responses, and quite necessary at the time. However, they have now become barriers to relationship. Only you can repent of them.

5) Continue to develop a relationship with God that centers your need for love and approval in Him. You can only love others (even those who abused you) if you first have received the assurance of His love for you in the deep place of your heart.

6) In the next chapter, we will explore the essential key of forgiveness. This is crucial in the healing of sexual abuse.

Conclusion

Childhood sexual abuse has a devastating affect on the sexuality of the emerging adult victim. If the wounds of sexual abuse are not healed, they will continue to drive the life of the addict, making it difficult to master certain compulsions.

If the reader is aware of early sexual encounters, he should be treated with true concern. The one who has suffered this kind of trauma needs to know that God is eager to heal. God is faithful to do His part as the addict allows Him into the pain of his abuse.

References

[1] Andrew Comiskey, *Living Waters*, chapter 8: "Broken Boundaries, Invaded Heart." Published by Desert Stream Ministries, copyright 1996.

[2] Dr. Dan B. Allender, *The Wounded Heart* (Colorado Springs: NavPress, 1990) 120-121.

[3] Dr. Dan B. Allender, *The Wounded Heart* (Colorado Springs: NavPress, 1990) 73-74.

[4] Dr. Dan B. Allender, *The Wounded Heart* (Colorado Springs: NavPress, 1990) 83.

[5] Shawn Corkery, "Cleansing Out Abuse," *Desert Stream Newsletter* Spring 1994.

[6] Adele Mayer, *Women Sex Offenders* (Holmes Beach:Learning Publications, Inc., 1992) 50.

[7] Adele Mayer, *Sexual Abuse* (Homes Beach:Learning Publications, Inc., 1985) 61-62.

[8] Patrick Carnes, *Contrary to Love* (Minneapolis:CompCare Publishers, 1989).

HOMEWORK

Homework

1. Look at the definition of abuse on page 155. Do you have any memory of sexual abuse in your history? Write out a description of that abuse and how you think it affected your sexuality.

2. Look at the general symptoms of wounding and resulting defensive detachment. In one column list the symptoms you have had in the past. In another column list the symptoms you still have. List any specific times that you remember making lasting decisions for safety in relationships. Are you ready to break those vows of detachment? Write about why or why not.

3. There are nine feelings described in "Feelings Common to Victims." Make a list of those feelings you have and what you believe the root of those feelings is.

Forgiving and Making Amends

Chapter Eighteen

So, if you are offering your gift at the altar and there remember that your brother has something against you, leave your gift there before the altar and go; first be reconciled to your brother, and then come and offer your gift. (Matthew 5:23-24)

This scripture admonishes us to be reconciled to others as a part of our worship of God. If we worship the Lord while in the midst of unrestrained strife with others, our worship lacks integrity. God considers those who bear His image as representatives of Himself. This is most clearly illustrated by Jesus' comments regarding our good works to others:

Truly I say to you, to the extent that you did not do it to one of the least of these, you did not do it to me. (Matt. 25:45b)

If we are at odds with our brother, then we are at odds with God. Therefore, He wants us to be reconciled to others. Whatever we do to another, we do to Him. This includes our good works as well as our sins. When we sin against another, we are sinning against that person as well as against the Lord. Forgiving others and seeking their forgiveness, therefore, are critical matters for our spiritual lives.

In this chapter, we will look at the process of being reconciled to others. This process involves both forgiving those we have not yet forgiven, and inviting those we have hurt to forgive us. We must take responsibility for reconciliation so that we will not be hindered in relation to God.

Why Restoration?

You shall not hate your brother in your heart, but you shall reason with your neighbor, least you bear sin because of him. You shall not take vengeance or bear any grudge against the sons of your own people, but you shall love you neighbors as yourself. (Lev 19:17-18)

When we hate our brother in our hearts, we bear sin because of that hatred. Sin separates us both from God and our brother. Grudges and acts of vengeance are sins of not loving others. However, we do the will of God when we close that separation through our efforts to reconcile.

The flow of God's grace is hindered if we do not continually give grace to others. What we sow, we also shall reap (see 2 Cor 9:6). With the measure that we measure out to others, it will also be measured back to us. Worked out practically, this means that if we hold others in debt, God will require a debt of us also. We pay this debt in a prison of self-doubt and torment. Our failure to release others via forgiveness forces us to pay, until we decide to forgive.

We Need to be Loosed

Truly I say to you, whatever you shall bind on earth shall be bound in heaven; and whatever you loose on earth shall be loosed in heaven. (Matthew 18:18)

This scripture occurs in the context of Jesus' teaching on forgiveness. In Matthew 18, Jesus teaches about the parable of the unforgiving servant. Verse 18 has to do with the power of forgiveness to free others, and the power of unforgiveness to bind them.

It is my belief that we are bound to those we've not forgiven, both spiritually and emotionally. We forsake, or deflect, the blessings of God if we continue to walk in sin; our sin acts like a barrier to the grace that would otherwise be ours. Whether it is the sin of our bitterness towards another, or whether we've inspired bitterness in others' hearts by our actions, we fail to partake of the life of God fully. In 1 Peter 3:7, Peter writes to husbands, saying:

Husbands, in the same way be considerate as you live with your wives, and treat them with respect... ***so that nothing will hinder your prayers.***

In other words, if they sin against their wives (or, generally, if they sin against others) they choke off the spiritual power that would otherwise be theirs.

Isaiah expresses God's heart on these issues in the following passage:

Where will you be stricken again, as you continue in your rebellion? The whole head is sick, and the whole heart is faint. From the sole of the foot even to the head there is nothing sound in it, only bruises, welts, and raw wounds, not pressed out or bandaged, nor softened with oil...When you come to appear before me, who requires of you this trampling of my courts? Bring your worthless offerings no longer, incense (prayer) is an abomination to me, ...So when you spread out your hands in prayer, I will hide my eyes from you, yes, even though you multiply prayers, I will not listen. Your hands are covered with blood. Wash yourselves, make yourselves clean. (Isaiah 1:5-6, 12-13, 15-16a)

God has given us the responsibility to forgive others, and to ask forgiveness for our sins. This is true, whether it involves our knowing that someone has found fault with us (Matthew 5:23-24), or our awareness that we have found fault with someone else (Matthew 18:15-17). The binding can go either way. The flow of God's grace is hindered if we do not continually give grace to others. What we sow, we also shall reap (see 2 Cor 9:6). With the measure that we measure out to others, it will also be measured back to us. Worked out practically, this means that if we hold others in debt, God will require a debt of us also. We pay this debt in a prison of self-doubt and torment. Our failure to release others via forgiveness forces us to pay, until we decide to forgive.

Spiritually, God has given us the authority to release others from the effects of sin.

If you forgive the sin of any, their sins have been forgiven them; if you retain the sins of any, they have been retained. (John 20:23)

God has given us authority that is related to our will, and to our willingness to forgive sins. When we release others from what they "owe" us, they experience emotional freedom. I have often worked with people who have forgave their families. Many times, the family members have had no way of knowing that this has occurred, but will call that same day or week, and will be astonishingly renewed and friendly and reconciled. By choosing to break the spiritual cords that bind us to them, we set them free. But more importantly, when we forgive them, we set ourselves free.

Unforgiveness binds people to each other emotionally. This is one of the reasons that God wants us to initiate reconciliation with others. For example, you could be still angry with one of your parents for hurting you throughout your childhood. Your unforgiveness binds you to them in four areas:

1) What you think they owe you

2) What you fantasize about their future blessing of you, and/or their future punishment for hurting you

3) How you have ordered your life based on their actions (vows of the heart about protecting yourself in relationships)

4) What you have believed about yourself because of what their actions implied about you (your belief system and identity)

Each of these four areas of bondage affects a person's ability to be in ongoing relationship with your parents in a loving way. The third and fourth areas are usually generalized to relationships with friends or coworkers or authority figures, in which we may re-live our relationships with parents again and again.

Generalized beliefs about how others will act toward us in relationships are what the scripture calls judgements (see Matt 7:21). A judgement becomes a lens that colors our ability to see people clearly. It will hinder our freedom of movement in relationships. The process of forgiving others involves repenting of specific historical judgements that we made about the ones we are forgiving. We may also need to ask for prayer to break any hold that these judgements have over our hearts.

Being emotionally bound through unforgiveness is a form of idolatry and an enormous source of an addict's emotional pain and relational dysfunction. It is the reason why he does not do well with intimacy, and why he turns to finding pleasure for himself through self-serving sexual acts. Because he is bound by his hidden beliefs about relationships, he is fearful about being honest and risking intimacy. In order to be loosed, he must forgive others and thereby stop depending on them to give him significance. Then the eyes of his heart can turn freely to God in worship and allow Him to restore the integrity of his earthly relationships. True freedom comes when the addict forgives those who were involved in establishing the negative strongholds of his heart. This often means working with significant relationships like mother, father, perpetuators of sexual abuse, or significant opposite sex relationships.

Unforgiveness binds us to others. Consequently, we cannot receive from Jesus all that He wants to give us. When one forgives another, he sets himself free to worship God more completely. When he is willing to be reconciled to another and initiates that process, he gives opportunity for them to be set free, too.

What Helps Us to Forgive

Many of us have tried to forgive but have found it very difficult to let go of the emotional demands that we have placed upon those we've not yet forgiven. Our hearts have stubbornly demanded the payment of emotional debts we have ascribed to others.

It is often important and helpful to recall that significant others are just human beings. They, like us, are wounded and they may have done the best they could for us. Knowing this can help us to extend grace to others. But we need to be on guard that that is not our only basis for forgiveness. It may be the case that they didn't do their best to bless us, or may have even embraced evil. Discounting our wounds by understanding the limitations of others can also be a barrier of denial over the deep pain of our hearts. Giving mental assent to forgiveness can be a way of avoiding the deeper, unresolved pain and conflicts about being intimately connected to others.

In both the parable of the unforgiving servant in Matthew 18, and the story of Mary's anointing of Jesus at Simon the Pharisee's house (Luke 7:36-50), the fundamental point is that each of us has been forgiven a great debt with regards to our own personal sin. I speak of sin here as more than the wrong things that we have done; it is the infinite chasm exists between man and God apart from the blood of Jesus. Nothing could overcome it or pay for it except the death of Jesus on the cross. Understanding the magnitude of the personal debt which has been canceled by the work of Jesus will provoke gratitude towards God in the heart of the believer. When we personally experience this great mercy, we realize that we are hypocrites to be exacting in the payment of others' debts to us.

In the story of Luke 7, Jesus knows the disgust in Simon's heart over the fact that a prostitute is showing her gratitude to Him by anointing, kissing, and wiping His feet. She made a dramatic, public display of her gratitude, having realized by the Holy Spirit that Jesus was the Son of God and the Forgiver of her sins. Mary's sense of her worth was not centered in the estimation of other people; her value was derived from God.

Jesus uses a parable-quiz to try to get Simon to understand what Mary's enthusiasm is all about. He asks the question, *"When two men owe the same person money, one five hundred denarii and one fifty denarii, and that man forgives them both; which loves him more?"* Simon answers correctly, *"The one to whom the most is forgiven."* Jesus then points out that Mary is like one who has forgiven a great debt. Thus, Jesus says of Mary, *"For this reason I say to you, her sins, which are many, have been forgiven, for she loved much; but he who is forgiven little, loves little"* (Luke 7:24-47).

Upon first reading this saying it might appear as if Jesus is implying that Mary's sins have been forgiven because she worked at loving much. But this cannot be true because we know from scripture that a man's works earn him nothing. Rather, Mary's actions were a result of her faith, knowledge, and gratitude that she had been forgiven already. She, like Paul, had become the bondservant of Christ. Her gratitude and love for Jesus was more than religion. Simon had religion. Her faith involved a deep work in Mary's heart, fueled by thankfulness over the Lord's great mercy to her.

"He who is forgiven little, loves little," means that we are only able to love to the extent that we have grasped the magnitude of Christ's mercy to us in His work on the Cross, where He died for our sins. We love and forgive because Jesus first loved us. We will become more forgiving the more we realize how generous and merciful God has been to us. We cannot move into the process of becoming reconciled to others apart from the Lord. We must be worshippers of God in order to forgive. It is only by the mercy of God, and our gratitude for it, that we can forgive as much and as deeply as we need to.

When we are unforgiving we are like the unforgiving servant in Jesus' parable. He did not realize that his debt (sin) to his master (God) had been forgiven. After the Master had forgiven him a great debt, he demanded payment of a very small debt from someone who owed him money. When that man could not pay, the unforgiving servant had him thrown into prison (a picture of unforgiveness – the debtor is bound). The parable of the unforgiving servant is an explanation of why we do not forgive – we do not realize in our hearts that our sins (our great debt to God) have been forgiven. Many of us deny that we are actually ourselves unforgiven, perhaps because we are out of touch with our hearts.

In the end, the unforgiving servant is thrown into prison to be tormented until he pays his debt (which can only be paid through the forgiveness of sins). Jesus concludes by saying that it will be like this for anyone who does not forgive from the heart. He is speaking of the emotional prison of bondage *to the person we will not forgive.*

Coming to the revelation of the great debt that God has forgiven each of us is crucial if we are to forgive from the heart. **It is something only revealed by the Holy Spirit. We need to pray and meditate to that end.**

How Can One Forgive?

When we forgive another, we set ourselves free from bondage to him or her. Furthermore, our relationships and perceptions of relationship are often healed when we choose to forgive.

Forgiving others starts with a decision. When we forgive, we release a person and his sin against us to Jesus. We speak out God's mercy upon them. As we release them from their sin, we release and entrust them to Jesus and His way for them. Through Jesus' mercy, we choose to cancel their debt of sin against us. We set them free and free ourselves at the same time.

To forgive is to release someone from a demand to pay what they owe. Sometimes they owe us for obvious damage done. And sometimes it is subtler. Some of us must face our our demand for their blessing and affirmation, as from a mother or father. Whatever the case, forgiveness involves a willingness to give up unrealistic expectations of the unforgiven. It will involve grieving the loss of those expectations, and looking to God as the true Source of those things we need.

Forgiveness is often an emotional process that continues on after the decision to forgive has been made. Grieving the loss of the debt owed indicates that true forgiveness is going on because it shows that the heart realizes and is reckoning with wounds that were inflicted. Grieving also indicates that the over-investment in a person (which has been taking up psychological "space" in the heart) is being given up. This makes space for God to take His rightful place at the center of our being. Making the decision to forgive offers an opportunity for the addict to trust God, believing that He will be there to fill the emptiness as the debt is cancelled.

The Lord is our Recompense

Choosing to forgive someone is often, if not always, impossible for us, apart from the Lord's strength. Part of the difficulty involved sometimes has to do with relinquishing what is rightfully ours — we are choosing to cancel real debts. Often, what we need to forgive involves canceling a debt over something that should never have been taken from us. What about what we've lost? What happens to what we were due? Paul tells the Romans:

Do not take revenge, my friends, but leave room for God's wrath, for it is written: 'It is Mine to avenge; ***I will repay,*** *' says the Lord. On the contrary, ...do not be overcome by evil, but overcome evil with good.* (Romans 12:19-21)

The Lord will allow people to reap the evil they have sown. But they are not the only ones who will be repaid. He will repay to us what has been lost. It may not be something that can be regained – like childhood. But it is within His power to repay us in a commensurate manner. We can choose to stand on this promise, and thereby help ourselves to forgive, empowered by the Word of God. By knowing that the Lord cares about our loss and intends to be our recompense, we may find forgiveness less difficult.

Taking Responsibility for Our Lives

Forgiving and making amends is an immensely important part of our healing. Through both, we take responsibility for our lives. In forgiveness we are saying, "I no longer look to others to be responsible for my outcome. With and under the Lord, I choose my destiny." In making amends we say, "I choose to face rejection for the higher cause of a good conscience before God, even if others do not receive me."

Reconciliation with others takes courage, good judgment, discernment, and timing. The addict should give himself permission to consult others before beginning the process of restitution with any given person. Working through steps 1 through 7 in a typical 12-step program is a good preparation to do this work.

You may want to consider these steps as well:

1. Own the truth that you can be a stumbling block to another; yes, even you can cause a little one to stumble! (Luke 17:1-3) Ask the Lord to reveal to you the one(s) you have wounded and have yet to be reconciled to.

2. Own responsibility for your sin, even if the other's sin entered in as well. In case the other wounded you, make sure you forgive him or her before you proceed on. The task of restitution doesn't involve confronting the other for his or her failures; rather, it demonstrates actively your sorrow over your sin.

3. Go in the true self, blessed and empowered by God's grace toward you, yet humbled by the truth that your sin has damaged another.

4. Confess to the other the precise nature of your sin, and express your regrets for hurting him or her with your sin. Ask the other's forgiveness.

    The response to your restitution will vary. Some will receive it heartily and will freely release you. Others will appear mystified by your efforts, as if they were unaware of any damage done. Know in these cases that God may use your initiative here to initiate His will for them at a later time. For others, it may bring up a new layer of pain and brokenness in what has been for both parties a painful and complex relationship. In those cases, know that God always uses your humble efforts to advance His healing purposes. Stay focused on Him if things threaten to become cloudy with the other's pain. You are obeying God in seeking restitution; you are not catering to the created, nor do you need an immediately positive response to validate your obedience.

    Seeking restitution provokes in us a deeper work of repentance unto the Holy One who desires that we place no stumbling block before another. It frees up our worship of Him, and frees us for a new measure of humility and sensitivity in our relationships. Through restitution, the cross of Christ covers us in areas where we may tend to hurt others. Grace is released for us and through us as a result of this vital practice.[1]

Restitution With Others

The homework for this chapter asks you to list the people with whom you feel it necessary to make amends. There are several categories of people that you may encounter. Each may require a different type of approach when you are making amends

Group 1

Almost all of us have people in our lives that know we have this struggle and who know that we need to change. Some of these people have been wounded by our actions and endured our foolishness when we denied our need for help. As we begin to acknowledge our sin, we will want to go to these people at once and admit that we now see the problem. It is better, however, to acknowledge generally that you want to be restored to them and that you are working on your health, rather than trying to get specific before you know specifically what you have done. Specific amends should be made at the time you deeply realize how you have hurt them. This may be an ongoing process.

Group Two

Sometimes disclosure can do more harm than good. For example, I once met a young man who was raised by a caring aunt after his parents had disowned him. When he graduated college, this same aunt gave him a significant amount of money. The young man, having been a sexual addict for the previous three years of his college experience, spent the graduation money on pornography, rather than on a gift that he could keep. In keeping with the norms of his double life, he did not tell his aunt. During my interaction with him, it became clear that he thought his intense guilt could be soothed by telling his aunt what he had done with the money. That would have needlessly wounded his aunt. His conscience would have been cleared at her expense. She had not yet been wounded in the transaction, and that didn't need to change.

As we seek to be reconciled with others, we must ask ourselves, God, and others for counsel when there is doubt about how much disclosure is appropriate for each situation. Some situations are between us and God only.

Group Three

Often there will be people or organizations in our lives whom we have wronged and to whom we need to go to for the purpose of making amends related to money, cheating, or other integrity issues.

For example, you may need to turn yourself into the IRS for tax evasion. You may need to repay people from whom you stole. You may need to ask forgiveness of people that you took advantage of sexually. You may also need to confess the truth to those you deceived.

Doing what is right is confronting ourselves with the truth about the One who loves us unconditionally. **If we know that the love of Jesus is unshakable, we will overflow with willingness to do what is right, even if it is costly.** Zacchaeus's conversion was evident to Jesus when he said, *"and if I have cheated anybody out of anything, I will pay back four times the amount"* (Luke 19:8).

I don't mean to suggest that if you have stolen from someone that you need to pay it back four fold, but there is something congruent and right about making restitution by executing justice. If we repent, we need to be willing to deal with the consequences, which may be difficult and painful. We may need prayer for courage and strength to do what we need to do.

When it comes to turning oneself in, prayer is critical – asking God for His wisdom and discernment, and listening carefully for His answer. We will likely need the input of trusted Christian friends to help us listen.

Warning to Wives

Do not force your husbands to make restitution. Only the Lord can cause a heart to be contrite and repentant. If a wife presses too hard she may cause her husband to pull back from his recovery because he feels like she is trying to control him.

Another warning to wives! Do not seek revenge. It is hard not to want your husband to pay for the pain he has caused you, but he has also caused himself much pain in his addiction without you having to add to it. Once he has confessed his sin to you, and has begun to move towards recovery and restoration, you need to allow the Lord to do His work in his life. Do not expect him to make up for the past years that have been filled with pain and suffering. Your husband can never make up for the years lost, but the Lord can if you allow Him to – and you allow Him to do so by choosing to forgive him. That's the beginning of loving your husband unconditionally, rather than in light of his sins.

In time, God will restore what the locusts have eaten away. Your part in the process will be to pray, trust God, and process your own pain as you forgive your husband for the past. Your pain is very real, and very important to God, and He does not ask you to forgive and to love at your own expense. Rather, it is for your good.

References

[10] Andrew Comiskey, *Acacia*, chapter 6. Published by Desert Stream Ministries.

HOMEWORK

Homework

Why do you look at the speck of sawdust in your brother's eye and pay no attention to the plank in your own eye? How can you say to your brother, 'Let me take the speck out of your eye,' when all the time there is a plank in your own eye? You hypocrite, first take the plank out of your own eye, and then you will see clearly to remove the speck from your brother's eye. (Matt. 7:3-5)

This scripture says a lot about the process of healing. When Jesus uses the word "hypocrite," he actually is implying that there is play-acting involved – like an actor who is on stage wearing a mask. When He talks about the log and speck, He is calling us to stop play-acting and deal with the issues that will enable us to see life clearly.

We often lie to ourselves, projecting our self-hatred onto others. Sometimes we are dishonest hypocrites and lack integrity. We don't do this knowingly, but nonetheless, we judge others with the judgement we hold against ourselves. We hold others in contempt for doing the same things that we do. Often we go to the extent of controlling others to ease our consciences and to keep from having to do the real activities of restoration.

In order to see clearly, we must remove the logs from our own eyes. A part of removing the log means being honest with how we have hurt others and being willing to make amends to them whenever possible. Instead of justifying ourselves, restoration begins when we own our hurtful behavior.

This homework is a preparation to do just that. It will help you to come out of the sin of self-flattery and denial which keeps you from knowing how your relational sins have affected others. The questions that follow are in preparation for taking off the mask of adequacy and self-righteousness that you still hold up (at times feebly) in an attempt to avoid the possibility of rejection when doing the right thing – restoration of relationships.

Please remember that the issues of the heart take time. The activities requested in this homework may take some time to work through. Do them as you are ready. But do not forsake them.

1. Make a list of all the people you have harmed and are willing to make amends with.

2. Make a list of all the people who have harmed you – answer the following questions about each of these people:

   a. What are their names and relationship to you?

   b. What did they do to you?

   c. How did you feel then, and how do you feel now (in your heart) about what they did?

Preparation for Forgiveness

3. For each of the people listed in question 2 answer the following questions:

   a. What do I think they owe me? (i.e. an apology, money, the parenting and nurturing I deserve.)

   b. Am I holding onto any fantasies that they will be something for me that they cannot be?

   c. Have I allowed them to "name" me through their actions by changing my beliefs about my self: i.e., I'm worthless, stupid, will never amount to anything.

   d. Did I make any changes in my life based on this hurt (decided not to risk, not to feel, to always be the clown), that have had permanent effect on my relational ability?

4. For each item under #3 that you want to be done with (by forgiving the person that hurt you), write out a statement of forgiveness for:

   a. The specific areas of hurt

   b. The release of what they owe you

   c. Giving up of fantasy concerning them

   d. Repentance of accompanying belief system (i.e. I will no longer allow you to proclaim me worthless)

As you do the next part of the homework use your own experience to give you empathy for what others must have felt when you harmed them.

5. For each person that you have harmed (refer to the categories in the chapter), answer the following questions:

    a. What is his/her name and relationship to you?

    b. What happened?

    c. What were the consequences of your actions?

    d. What are your current feelings about the event(s)?

    e. What do you think might happen if you attempt to make amends with him/her?

6. Write out your own statement of readiness to make amends to others as a part of your healing. Date and sign it.

7. As the issues of personal forgiveness and facing the possibility of rejection become settled for each person in your heart (when you are willing and ready), begin to make those amends.

Defining True Masculinity

Mature masculinity refuses to be reduced to raw sexual desire in relationships. Instead, maturity involves being aware of the woman's deeper, personal needs, tempering strength with tenderness to insure that her joy will be maximized. The mature man is thankful; he is fulfilled by providing for his wife in this way.

Chapter Nineteen

Be on your guard, stand firm in the faith; be men of courage; be strong. Do everything in love. 1 Corinthians 16:13-14

Biblical Mandates

We have given little attention to boundaries God has commanded us to observe with regards to our sexuality. For some addicts, the boundaries laid out in scripture may elicit feelings of condemnation and shame. Yet, despite how it may make us feel, the scripture still defines sin and calls us to a higher level of holiness as those who have been bought by the blood of Jesus.

A man who is mature in his masculinity conforms to the following standards for sexual purity (scriptures paraphrased):

A man shall not have sex with animals, people of the same sex, or any close relative. (Lev 18)

They shall not fulfill the deeds of the flesh: immorality, impurity, sensuality. (Gal 5;19)

These shall not inherit the kingdom of God: fornicators, adulterers, effeminates, homosexuals. (1 Cor 6:9)

Mature masculinity does not entertain lust in the heart:

You have heard that it was said, 'YOU SHALL NOT COMMIT ADULTERY,' but I say to you, that everyone who looks on a woman to lust for her has committed adultery with her already in his heart. (Matt 5:27-28)

God has clearly established the boundaries for our sexuality. As far as sexual behavior is concerned, we are to remain within the confines of committed, monogamous, heterosexual marriage. This is the primary moral guideline that God has established for preserving the family, where the values of His Kingdom are passed on. In a godly family, we find commitment, love, training, discipline, and protection. These are all part of an environment of love in which growing children can know they are loved while developing identities founded on the truth. Ideals exemplified by the godly family unit stand against moral anarchy. Biblical morality consists of boundaries that God has given us to help us. His commands allow us to remain on the path of life; they prevent us from falling off cliffs of sin unto our own destruction.

To the extent that a man's identity is not rooted in Kingdom relationships, he will be unable to stand morally. He will thus feel disqualified to represent the truth, and will be an ineffective ambassador of the truth.

On the other hand, one who lives by God's order acknowledges eternity. He knows that:

The (present) heavens will pass away with a roar; the elements will be destroyed by fire, and the earth and everything in it will be laid bare. (2 Peter 3:10b)

He sees with the eyes of his heart that, in just a short while, the mirage of the earthly kingdom will evaporate and only the Kingdom of God will remain. Truths such as these give him a new perspective on his daily activities. As he takes in the Word of life, he recognizes his position as a stranger, an alien in a foreign culture who must always seek refuge, refreshment, and cleansing in the outpost of the Church. Set in a hostile wilderness of worldly ideals, the Church is acknowledged to be the oasis through which he lives.

He is bound to, and filled by the scripture that outlines the values of the Kingdom. He sees in it the divine order, which upholds him as a man of God and a truthful ambassador.

Manhood According to the Bible

Sexual purity is part of the bigger picture. We are not called merely to avoid evil; God has made us to embrace and to enjoy good. Men are called to be the champions of God's Kingdom. The word "champion" refers to one who shows courage and valor in carrying out the tasks of the Kingdom. We are to be examples and representatives for God. In the same way that Jesus was called to be a physical and earthly representation of the Father (John 12:44-45, 14:8-10), men are called to embrace the same pattern. God calls those whom He puts in leadership to lead primarily by example and service. Jesus demonstrated a life of service. Speaking in a parable He said:

A blind man cannot guide a blind man, can he? Will they not both fall into a pit? A pupil is not above his teacher, but everyone, after he has been fully trained, will be like his teacher. (Luke 6: 39-40)

The Father calls men to represent Himself, expressing His love, wisdom, actions, and leadership. This truth applies broadly, but can be narrowed in its scope and applied to our relationship with women.

> At the heart of mature masculinity is a sense of benevolent responsibility to lead, provide for and protect women in ways appropriate to a man's different relationships.[1]

This definition may miss some aspects of mature masculinity, but the core traits will surely not be less stated here.

You may be thinking, "I don't feel this sense of responsibility towards women, yet I know I have the appetites of a man." We must not confuse **sexual drive** with **masculinity**, as the world often does. The fact is that raw sexual drive tends to use women and make them objects, rather than honor, provide for, and protect them. Yet how many locker room conversations revolve around the number of conquests a man has had, as though it were a measure of his virility and manliness. In reality, using this strategy as a way of feeling masculine is a cheap imitation of God's call to manhood. It is based on relational insecurity. It wields sexual power as a defense against living in the vulnerability and authority needed to sustain committed and caring relationships.

> He may feel strong and sexually competent and forceful and rational. But we would say to him that if he does not feel this sense of benevolent responsibility toward women to lead [not lead them astray], provide and protect [not use], his masculinity is immature. It is incomplete and perhaps distorted. Mature means that a man's sense of responsibility is in the process of growing out of its sinful distortions and limitations, and finding its true nature as a form of love, not a form of self assertion.[2]

True masculinity is tempered agape love, which sanctifies raw sexual drive. The man with godly character wants to honor women with regard to their sexuality, rather than use them for his purposes. Mature masculinity is not mastered by the threat of woman's difference. The energy of her sensuality, the power of her emotions, and her capacity to reject him give way, through healing, to the masculine desire to protect her.

Man's Sense of Responsibility

A man who is mature in Christ will feel at home in the company of men of God who have a collective sense of purpose and destiny, as those who champion the values and activities of the Kingdom. He rightfully needs his brothers. Without them, he is vulnerable to the isolation and delusion of his addiction. With them, he prepares for his calling to love woman aright.

This sense of call and responsibility will grow as he conquers self pity, mentors others, and provides physically for those he loves. Most importantly, his godly masculine identity is expressed in how he concerns himself with the protection of women, emotionally and sexually.

This sense of responsibility is a by-product of having an identity as a son of God. A person can be a son of God without that being his identity; instead, he may identify with fleshly expressions of sexuality, or with his own talents, with his job, or any number of things. Being a son of God, and feeling oneself to be defined primarily as a son of God, are two very different things.

If we are finding our identities as sons of God, we will feel responsible to protect women. God demonstrated His mind on this responsibility when He looked for Adam in the garden, after the Fall. Although Eve sinned first, it was Adam who was commissioned with the commands of God. In the scripture, God holds Adam accountable for their treason.

The mature man experiences benevolent provision towards women because he regards them as the daughters of God. To be sexually involved with women outside of the Lord's commands, no matter how willing they are, is to lead them astray. A man who is mature in his masculinity does not look down on woman condescendingly, or abuse his power through the use of self aggrandizing authoritarianism. Instead, he leads them as fellow heirs of Christ (Rom 8:17), whom he prizes and honors, treating them as extensions of his own body, (Eph 5:28-29), as he remembers the second great commandment of God – love your neighbor as yourself (Matt 7:12).

Leadership Qualities of Mature Masculinity

You know that the rulers of the Gentiles lord it over them, and their great men exercise authority over them. It is not so among you, but whoever wishes to become great among you shall be your servant.
(Matt 20:25-26)

Mature masculinity does not demand service, but sacrifices in order to serve others. With regard to sexuality, this means a man sees a prostitute as a lost and broken child of God. Rather than indulging himself in her service to satisfy his sexual needs, he builds a recovery house to help her take hold of God's best for her. Instead of ruminating upon a voluptuous porn-star through lust and fantasy, he teaches his own daughter about sexual virtue and chastity. He allows the Word of God to do its sanctifying work in his soul first, so that he can call her on into God's ways of grace (Ephesians 5:23, 25).

Jesus laid down His life for the purpose of the salvation, sanctification, righteousness, and holiness of His bride. So it is with the man who is mature in his masculinity. He leads by example.

The mature man does not sabotage the authority of Christ over the woman. Though he is head, he lets the Holy Spirit inform her conscience, and he respects her free will. Thus, he does not demand sex and he does not apply sexual pressure to his wife, or draw her into sexual acts that she is uncomfortable with. He has crucified his need for the air-brushed anatomy and the unrealistic expectations of a sexual fantasy world. He does not bring these expectations into the bedroom with his wife. Instead, he remembers that he is sleeping with one who is also the bride of Christ.

Humility

The mature man acknowledges that he is a sinner. Taking up leadership is a task that requires humility. When a man confesses his sin before others, he is humbling himself before God. He confesses his need for God and the work of the cross in his life.

> In each of our lives we have ample cause for contrition at our passivity or our domination. Some have neglected their wives and squandered their time in front of the TV, or putzing around the garage, or going away too often with the guys to hunt or fish or bowl. Others have been too possessive, harsh, domineering, and belittling, giving the impression through act and innuendo that wives are irresponsible or foolish.[3]

Men are called to lead in the way of relationship. This means taking the lead by confessing when we are wrong, and repenting when our wives bring the truth about our sin to our attention. This is especially true when it comes to confessing our sexual trespasses against our wives.

The General Pattern of Initiative

Man does not have to initiate in all things and need not be threatened if his wife takes part in initiation. He is not threatened by his wife initiating sexually. For, according to 1 Cor 7:4:

The wife's body does not belong to her alone but also to her husband. In the same way, the husband's body does not belong to him alone but also to his wife.

However, the general pattern will involve the husband's initiative towards the wife. Areas of initiation include sexual propriety, financial leadership (provision), family discipleship, discipline of the children, pursuing God – giving up those things that need to be abandoned for the good of the family.

A man initiates in the training of his children when it comes to sexual immorality. The mature man has bridled his own sexual desire and is not afraid to speak about it with his son. Thus, he passes on the strength of his moral courage and participates in breaking generational patterns of sexual addiction. He has done battle with demons of lust and, thus, protects and covers his sons and daughters until they are able to stand in their own faith and moral conviction.

A strong but tender pursuit of his spouse characterizes the sexuality of the man who is mature in his masculinity. There is a unique presence in masculinity that arises out of a blending of power and tenderness. He indicates strength through the firmness of his grasp, yet is delicate where appropriate. He is romantic because he understands the nature of a woman and demonstrates that with his compassionate words which build her up, rather than using words to manipulate and get what he wants. He makes love to his wife verbally, aside from being physically involved with her. Mature masculinity refuses to be reduced to raw sexual desire in relationships. Instead, maturity involves being aware of the woman's deeper, personal needs, tempering strength with tenderness to insure that her joy will be maximized. The mature man is thankful; he is fulfilled by providing for his wife in this way.

Sex is not a substitute for relationship. The truly masculine man does not confuse the sexual relationship with emotional intimacy. *Sexuality, therefore, takes second place to friendship and communion of the soul.* When things are otherwise, it is probably because one or both parties needs healing. Healing is, therefore, a part of the maturing process.

Conclusion

Mature masculinity honors, protects, leads, and provides for women. He leads spiritually, financially and sexually through the humble process of submitting to God and being the first to face sanctification through the death of the old man at the cross. God raises up truth-filled sons who together fulfill their destinies as holy and whole lovers of women.

References

[1]   John Piper and Wayne Grudem, ed., *Recovering Biblical Manhood and Womanhood* (Wheaton: Crossway Books, 1991) 35.

[2]   John Piper, *What's the Difference?* ( ) 13-14.

[3]   John Piper, *What's the Difference?* ( ) 23.

HOMEWORK

Homework

1. Comment on the following statements:

   • I use my sexuality to bolster my self-esteem.

   • I temper my sexuality to fulfill my mandate to lead and protect others.

2. Choose which statement fits you best and then talk about its ramifications for your sexual addiction.

   • I feel outside the community of Christian men. It is not a force in my recovery.

   • I feel connected to a group of Christian men who carry the vision to walk out godliness.

3. When I think about my own lust and how it defiles those who are potentially God's family I feel _____. Comment on why it is so easy to forget this reality.

4. In my heart I (check one)

   ___Use my emotional, physical, intellectual and creative power to get what I want.

   ___Use my emotional, physical, intellectual and creative power to serve others.

   How does his affect my ability to walk out godly masculinity as defined in this chapter's material?

Accessing the Power of The Cross

Chapter Twenty

We know that God's fidelity towards us, no matter how unfaithful we are, remains solid and unshakeable. His grace is assured. On the other hand, we have seen that it is we who choose to either take hold of the grace offered us or to refuse it. We choose either to be known by others in our sin, and thereby be liberated, or we choose to hide and die. We choose to build supports around us to help us follow the Lord, or we remain passive and stagnant.

Once you were alienated from God and were enemies in your minds because of your evil behavior. But now He has reconciled you by Christ's physical body through death to present you holy in His sight, without blemish and free from accusation. (Col. 1:21-22)

In obedience to the Father, and out of compassion for the people He made, Jesus suffered and died for us. Then, rising from the dead, He demonstrated that God not only understands great suffering, but that He is more powerful than that suffering. He is greater than any obstacle we can possibly face, even death. The Cross demonstrates the power of God's compassion, which is with us in our trials. He is no mere onlooker in our travail; rather, He is our passionate Father, Counselor, and Defender, ready to regularly intervene in our lives.

This closing chapter considers the meaning of the Cross for our lives, as we press on in our healing journeys. Unlike many of us, God does not mind process, and uses it powerfully to restore us. If we can grasp the significance of Jesus' life, death and resurrection, we will far more easily follow Him as He leads us on the narrow path of life.

The material that has been covered in the past nineteen chapters, however, is very relevant as we consider the cross. The insights, behavioral plans, and information are important things that can help inform our pursuit of God.

In learning new material, repetition is important. Over these past many lessons we have considered…

Spiritual Aspects of Addiction.

There are many reasons why people find themselves stuck in the quicksand of addiction. Basically, that quicksand is one of many dangers into which human beings stumble. Fallen and therefore spiritually blinded, we look to nearly everything except the living water, which Jesus offers, in order to slack our thirsts. God wants to fulfill our needs, directly and indirectly through other people with whom we have relationships. But He must be our central Source, if we are to derive any refreshment from Him or from the gifts He has given us. By tending to one's relationship with the

Lord, we can come into right relationship with other people, which is what God intends. Freedom from sexual addiction is certain if we will come to Him and make Him our foundation.

Sexual Addiction is False Intimacy.

God has revealed in the scripture that man and woman are made for intimacy – God says that He is not enough! He alone can satisfy us, but He does this, in part, through other people. Since He designed man and woman to complement and complete each other, we can be assured that He will help us find this. But the Fall brought catastrophe into our relationships. The addict is afraid of what healthy relationships entail: trust, vulnerability, and commitment. Instead, he prefers control through the illusion of false intimacy. The addict must choose either to continue pursuing false intimacy or to pursue true intimacy. To continue with the false means the pain of the addiction's consequences. To pursue true intimacy means he will have to endure the pain of redemptive suffering. But this suffering will be part of his restoration.

The Pain of Sexual Addiction.

But the pain caused by sexual addiction is not at all redemptive – there is nothing good about it. Addictions, which are ways of avoiding deeper, unresolved pain, create their own suffering. Addictive acting-out reinforces and exaggerates shame and guilt, and brings chaos into relationships. It divides the heart, and allows for increasing mental and behavioral bondage.

Intervention in the Addictive Cycle.

Understanding the patterns of our own behavior, as we have traveled through the addictive cycle, can help us as we try to pull the plug on our addictions. Beginning with a trigger, the addictive cycle is put in motion and ends with more shame and a resolution. The resolution is usually very believable to the addict, and yet only perpetuates denial over the severity of the problem. Because the cycle tends to be completed once it has begun, it is important to know what places, people, and things provoke the cycle. Rejection, stress and abandonment tend to be among them.

Planning Your Way of Escape.

No big surprise: the cycle has to stop! The addictive "machinery" is fueled by underlying pain. And yet the addiction's unspoken goal is to avoid the pain. But the pain cannot be felt or accessed unless the addiction first stops. Then the root issues become accessible, and can be healed. Obviously we need God's grace to get that far. But we can appropriate His grace by obeying Him: by living according to His guidance, by living a low-risk lifestyle, and by knowing our distorted thinking patterns. If we develop escape routes, plans we are ready to use and which we've rehearsed, we can take hold of the grace God gives to stop acting out.

Surrendering to God.

Addicts can deceive themselves into thinking they've surrendered to God when, in fact, they have not. To surrender to God means we give Him our wills, and do what He says. To do this, we need to face our fears of powerlessness and loss of control. We need to acknowledge that our version of "control" is a flop. We need to exchange our goals, agendas and plans for God's. If we seek Him for wisdom and discernment regularly, He will be sure to speak to us and direct us to walk in His ways.

Confession: Discovering the Cross in Community.

Human beings are social beings, made to be in meaningful relationships. Addicts lack these. Meaningful relationships allow lasting change to occur: we were wounded in relationships, and need to be in a relational context to receive all the healing He desires for us. God uses others to mediate His life to us. But we can't claim to be in rich fellowship with Jesus or others if we live in darkness. Real community requires that we be real. We need to confess, regularly, and with brutal honesty. If confession isn't at least a little painful, it

Chapter Twenty | 183

probably isn't helpful either. Confession is a radically powerful means by which we access the power of Jesus' cross. If we will die to the flesh, in the Christian community, and especially through confession, our addictions will come to an end.

Practicing the Presence of God.

Christ has promised us that He is with us until the end of the world; He is Emmanuel, God with us. He indwells us, and so we never will be alone. His love, power, and knowledge are available to us who believe. By developing the habit of calling to mind His presence with and within us, we abide in Him. We thereby receive the inflow of His love into our bodies, souls, and spirits. We can open the doors of our hearts to Him by seeking humility, since He forsakes the proud. Because He yearns to teach us, listening to Him will provide answers for many of our questions. On the other hand, sloth, unbelief, idolatry, and introspection block the power of His presence with us.

Seeking God Through Spiritual Disciplines.

What good, Bible-believing Christian would seek God through use of the spiritual disciplines? The one that wants to be set free from addiction! Although people sometimes understand and use them amiss, the disciplines are not ways of earning God's grace. Rather, they help us appropriate the grace that is freely and readily available to us. Through reading and meditating upon the Word, through praying and developing a prayer life, through fasting and other spiritual disciplines, we can gradually grow in Him. We can expand, becoming more able to receive and thrive on His abundance.

Understanding the Addictive System.

Understanding a sexual addiction involves understanding things that are not initially obvious to the addict. The pain underlying the addictive process is rooted in shame, and the things that caused the shame to be there in the first place. Accompanying the shame that taints the addict's sense of himself are contempt for self, distorted thinking, and contempt for others. By focusing on the healing of shame and the distortions that are associated with it, we focus on that which drives the addiction.

Allowing God to Remove Our Defects.

Painful, traumatic incidents in our early lives have affected the ways we perceive reality – our basic belief systems about ourselves and others. By seeing and repenting of false beliefs, and ungodly responses to old hurts, we can be restored. We can acknowledge inner vows, defensive detachment, mental fortresses (strongholds), and judgements. In turning from them, our hearts will newly be able to enjoy relationships with other people. Also important is the repentance and renunciation of self-hatred, which is exchanged at the cross for self-acceptance.

Embracing Loss as a Way of Gain.

Even though an addiction is a bad thing, it has helped us cope. When we give it up, we need to grieve the loss of it. We cannot fully relinquish our addictions unless we grieve the loss of the things that have comforted us in the past. Besides sorrow, the addict will need to allow himself to feel many things he has avoided feeling previously. The pain encountered will often be the result of painful memories. The addict will need to stand in the fiery furnace of affliction, feeling pain that had been buried alive. But, as he does this with the Lord, he will be saved. He will be delivered from the furnace as he is purified and empowered in Christ.

Family Origins of Addiction.

Addictions don't appear out of nowhere. They are usually related to childhood traumas, which may predispose him to addiction. Catalytic environments, as well as catalytic events, have often marked the addict's youth. These may include abandonment-related events, as well as sexual events. Our families, in general, greatly affected our character. By discerning family secrets that have shaped us, we can bring them into the open and to the Lord, who desires to free us. We can place the Cross, which ended sin, between us and the sin of past generations, and thereby get free of the effects of generational sin.

Spiritual Cleansing.

Besides generational sins, we also may need to seek Jesus so as to be set free from curses that have come upon us from parents or other ancestors. Parental curses can open a child up to darkness that remains until it is renounced. The behavior of our relatives, as well as our behavior, can allow a Christian to be demonically oppressed. Such oppressions, as well as occult involvement and one-flesh unions, are easily dealt with by Jesus. He has given us authority to break the manifold expressions of evil off of ourselves and others, so that we might more fully enjoy the beauty and loveliness that attends His presence.

Facing the Mother Wound.

A person's relationship with his mother is the prototype for all other relationships to come. Wounds which were inflicted upon us in relation to mother are very powerful; the results can be a profound emptiness and an inability to develop close relationships. A wounded heart is also unable to feel remorse over evil done. Issues of separation, individuation, and engulfment are often in need of being addressed. As the Lord heals these wounds, however, our view of self and other, especially the view of women, is restored, and we are enabled to relate more healthfully.

Healing the Father Wound.

Our relationships with our fathers have much to do with how we feel about ourselves as men or women. If the father did not bless our gender, we will likely suffer deep feelings of inadequacy. Furthermore, God is often seen as a huge, heavenly version of our earthly fathers. That means that we often see God poorly, and respond to Him as though He was the broken father of our childhood. By receiving healing in relation to father, our relationships with our Heavenly Father will improve; His goodness will become more lucid. Part of that healing comes as we listen to the Lord, and ponder the powerful words He speaks to us.

Facing Sexual Abuse.

Sexual abuse is terribly destructive. The scars left behind will distort a person's sexuality. However, if the person is willing to face the painful consequences of abuse with the Lord, (s)he will discover that the Father's love and compassion are more powerful than even the worst wounds. He is willing and able to heal the feelings of worthlessness, shame, powerlessness, fear and anger. The Lord wants to restore to His children a sense of security in His love, so that we deeply know that He is tending to our needs with all of His attention.

Forgiving and Making Amends.

Forgiveness is one of the most important things we can incorporate into our lives. By forgiveness, all the pain that has been addressed in previous chapters can find its ultimate end, at the cross. Forgiving others allows the power of Jesus' work on the cross to free us from spiritual and emotional bondage. By releasing bitterness and resentment to Christ, we are released from the effects of sins committed against us long ago.

Defining True Masculinity.

The sexual addict needs to learn and base his life upon the real meaning of masculinity, in contrast to the fallen views that have perpetuated the addictive process. By receiving the truth about what God meant for men and masculinity to be, we can integrate with that part of ourselves psychologically. This allows us to act in the strength of the masculine, without being enslaved to fallen, false masculine expressions of sexual compulsion. One aspect of the true masculine emerges as the correct view of woman is set into one's heart; men begin to feel protective towards women, rather than wanting to use them. Further integration with the masculine thereby occurs, as the true masculine, having been humbled, is able to lead without taking advantage of others.

Carrying the Cross Unto Life

Charles Spurgeon writes beautifully of the meaning of Christ's cross for us:

> Our Redeemer's glorious cry of 'It is finished,' was the death-knell of all the adversaries of His people, the breaking of 'the arrows of the bow, the shield, and the sword, and the battle.' Behold the hero of Golgotha using His cross as an anvil, and His woes as a hammer, dashing to shivers bundle after bundle of our sins, those poisoned 'arrows of the bow'; trampling on every indictment, and destroying every accusation...How the diabolical darts fly to fragments, and the infernal bucklers are broken like potters' vessels! ...Beloved, no sin of a believer can now be an arrow mortally to wound him, no condemnation can now be a sword to kill him, for the punishment of our sin was borne by Christ, a full atonement was made for all our iniquities by our blessed Substitute and Surety. Who now accuseth? Who now condemneth? Christ hath died, yea rather, hath risen again....Talk ye of all the wondrous works of the Lord, ye who make mention of His name, keep not silence, neither by day, nor when the sun goeth to his rest. Bless the Lord, O my soul. [1]

The beginning of sobriety is our surrender to God and the admission that we are powerless over sin. Holding onto this pivotal truth makes space for God in our hearts, to come into and to disarm our compulsions.

In order to implement our plan of action for avoiding relapse, we choose to actively hold the door open for Jesus to come in and fill us. In our surrender, and the accompanying behavioral plans to stop acting out sexually, a void is created where we begin to feel our hunger and emptiness. Detaching from our sexual objects makes space for God to come into our lives much more deeply and powerfully.

Frequently we experience God's response as lagging behind our decisions to stop acting out. We experience the space or emptiness, which had been covered-up by the addiction, as a void or a desert. The desert is the place of being torn from our false way of receiving comfort; it's where the heart learns to rely on God. In this sense, perhaps we can apply Hosea 6:1:

Come, let us return to the Lord. He has torn us to pieces but he will heal us; he has injured us but he will bind up our wounds.

When we cast down our idols, God promises to provide for us through His healing power. But we may first have to face the void. Waiting for God's provision can be an experience of God's cleansing fire. It is a place of suffering in the flesh as we resist sin.

> Any authentic struggle with attachment must involve deprivation. We have to go hungry and unsatisfied; we have to ache for something. It hurts. Withdrawal symptoms are real and, one way or another, they will be experienced. If we can both accept and expect this pain, we will be much better prepared to face struggles with specific attachments. [2]

Until we are in Heaven, we will experience temptations. Resisting temptation is essential to winning each relapse battle. When we experience temptation, we are experiencing the battle between the flesh and Spirit (Gal. 5:16-17). Scripture clearly states that if we can abide in Christ through the Holy Spirit's power, we will escape the power of the flesh to drive us back into our old patterns. So our goal must be to learn how to access the resurrection power released through the work of the cross.

Through the cross, Jesus won us access to the resurrection power of the Holy Spirit. The truth that God is our Source must remain firmly intact as we stand in the place of temptation. As we continuously purpose to cling to the cross, the reality of its power will descend from our heads into our hearts and more strongly tether our souls to Him.

The cross represents the death of our sin and the beginning of new life in Christ. If we are willing to cling to the cross in constant awareness, repentance takes on new meaning. Our walk becomes more than a series of unending confessions. Instead, looking to the Lord and clinging to His cross, we begin turning back towards God whenever and wherever we become aware that we are sliding back towards our idols.

The cross symbolizes the hope of God's provision for us. As we meditate on the provision that was made there by Jesus, the knowledge of the cross begins to sink from our head knowledge into the depths of our heart. Then we can begin to stand for longer periods in the fiery furnace of fleshly desire. As we cherish the cross in our hearts, it becomes a life-support, an anchor, which bridges our ravaged inner life to God. As we hold the cross in our hearts His presence is there also, giving us the strength to resist sin.

Once we have repented, the cross is the place of death for things that separate us from God. The cross accesses the power of God and is the door to resurrection. He becomes our Hope, our Rest, our Refuge amid the residual storms of our addiction.

There is a rhythm of Kingdom life that recovering addicts, indeed all Christians, must learn in order to access the resurrection life of Jesus. It is the beat of sanctification – the powerful sound of the cross: death and resurrection, death and resurrection, death and resurrection. This pulse allows the life of God and knowledge of Him to increase in us. Without it, Christ cannot be formed in us. But if we are willing to return to the cross over and over again, then we will begin to understand the meaning of Paul's statement:

I have been crucified with Christ and I no longer live, but Christ lives in me. The life I live in the body, I live by faith in the Son of God, who loved me and gave himself for me. I do not set aside the grace of God, for if righteousness could be gained through the law (my own efforts), Christ died for nothing. (Gal. 2:20-21)

The cross is the symbol of the finished work of Christ

We can call to mind the symbol of the cross in order to resist sin; gazing upon it with the eyes of our hearts, we can ask the Lord for the power that was made accessible at the cross to be poured out upon us, and see Him do it. And we will discover that He is eager to empower us to "put off the old man." What follows is meant to enhance your meditation, regarding ways to apply the power of the cross to your life:

1. **It is an immovable altar to cling to in the storm of temptation.** Learning to gain access to the cross through our imagination can establish it as an anchor of hope around which we bind the wayward desires of our soul. Use the image of Christ on the cross to interrupt and constrain your sexual fantasies.

2. **It is a symbol of warfare and power.** Try placing the cross, in your imagination, between you and your object of lust. The cross can help put any idol in its true perspective.

3. **It is a place of safety, giving shelter from the attack of demonic harassment.** The cross is a place of shelter because it is the location of the shed blood of Jesus Christ. Once our sins and demonic access points are confessed, the blood of Jesus cleanses us of any legal right that the enemy might have to oppress us.

4. **It is a place of rest.** At the cross we can lay down our own strength as a potential way of escaping sin. Performance and striving can find an end at the cross along with our religious and pharisaical facade.

    For thus says the Lord God, the Holy One of Israel: 'In returning and rest you shall be saved; in quietness and confidence shall be your strength.' (Isaiah 30:15)

5. **The cross is an ending place for sin.** We, through God's grace, can lay our failures at the cross. It is a place where we can leave our sin, as well as the sin of others against us. The cross is the symbol that declares Jesus was made sin for us. Two thousand years ago He bore our sin and purchased our reconciliation to God. In truth, our personal sin helped hang Him there. We fulfill true righteousness and humility as we let him bear it.

    Surely He took up our infirmities and carried our sorrows...He was crushed for our iniquities; the punishment that brought us peace was upon him, and by His wounds we are healed...
    It was the Lord's will to crush him and cause Him to suffer, and though the Lord makes His life a guilt offering, He will see His offspring and prolong His days, and the will of the Lord will prosper in His hand. (Isaiah 53)

6. **The cross neutralizes all accusations against us.** At the cross we access the forgiveness of God! Through it our debt of sin is cancelled. True guilt and conviction are relieved there. At the cross we find a place of new beginnings. See Colossians 2:13-14.

7. **The cross represents the power of God to destroy sin.** The cross is the ending place for our cycles of sexual sin. It has the power to interrupt the force of our sensual rituals midstream, if we are willing to access its power.

8. **The cross is the door to the resurrection power of God.** If we are willing to embrace our weakness by admitting that we have no power over sin, we can begin to acknowledge the power of Christ working in us through the power of the Holy Spirit.

9. **The cross represents the most authoritative sacrifice.** The blood of Jesus is sufficient to cancel the covenant, curse, spell or demonic assignment of any other religion made through any other sacrifice or ritual.

If we are serious about overcoming our additions, we cannot escape the necessity of incorporating the cross of Christ into our lives as the focal point of God's power. It is a place of suffering, but it is also a place of mercy and grace. We need to take the cross into our hearts, as symbols of what Jesus has done for us, and as symbols of the fact that God's full provision and grace flow towards us because of Christ's merits, and not our own. Earnestly desire to know the revelation of the cross, and God will reward you with resurrection life.

Collaboration and the Cross

By of His death and resurrection, Jesus has opened the way to the Father for we who believe. Now, we cannot be cut off from the powerful compassion of the Eternal Father. Knowing the power of His love, Paul writes:

For I am persuaded that neither death nor life, nor angels nor principalities nor powers, nor things present nor things to come, nor height nor depth, nor any other created thing, shall be able to separate us from the love of God which is in Christ Jesus our Lord. (Romans 8:38-39)

Nothing can separate us from Christ's power, exercised in love on our behalf. No matter how many times we err or sin, His cross remains. He has put to death the power of sin, and we are free to appropriate that power as often as we like.

On the one hand, we know that God's fidelity towards us, no matter how unfaithful we are, remains solid and unshakeable. His grace is assured. On the other hand, we have seen that it is we who choose to either take hold of the grace offered us or to refuse it. We choose either to be known by others in our sin, and thereby be liberated, or we choose to hide and die. We choose to build supports around us to help us follow the Lord, or we remain passive and stagnant.

God's grace knows no bounds, and yet it does not cancel our responsibility. Nothing can. So we must choose to live in the tension of knowing that all power is available to us, yet we determine how much of it we shall receive. As always, the key to this mystery lies within the cross. Having suffered His cross to open all the treasures of Heaven to us, we now imitate the Lord and suffer the pain involved in obedience. We die daily to our sinful inclinations and to the allure of the enemy. And, choice by choice, as we die to darkness, we allow the power of Jesus' death and rising to surge into us. We carry our crosses and discover the power of His presence with us, remaking and transforming us.

Over time, we stand with Him in the newness of His risen life. Like Him, having been with Him in death, we leave the empty tomb behind us. Because of Christ's life in us, the grave, which should have been the end for us, fails to hold us. We show forth God's transforming power in the new hearts and minds He is creating within us. This is our inheritance. Here in part, and hereafter completely, Jesus has new life for us.

Behold, I make all things new....I will give of the fountain of the water of life freely to him who thirsts. He who overcomes shall inherit all things, and I will be His God and he shall be My son. (Revelation 21:5, 6-7)

References

1 Charles Spurgeon, *Morning and Evening* (Uhrichsville, OH: Barbour Publishing, 1998) June 11.

2 Gerald May, *Addiction and Grace* (San Francisco: Harper & Row, 1988) 179.

Appendix A

Levels of addiction

The table on the following page is adapted from *Contrary to Love*, by Patrick Carnes.

Levels of addiction

	Level One	**Level Two**	**Level Three**
Behavior	• Masturbation (discharge) • Heterosexual affairs (adultery) • Homosexuality • Fornication • Bestiality • Non-specified sexual sensuality • Pornography • Massage parlors • Hyper-sexuality in marriage	• Exhibitionism • Voyeurism • Indecent phone calls • Indecent liberties • Prostitution	• Incest and child molestation • Rape
God's View of Addiction	Lev 15: Unclean Lev 20:10 Lev 20:13 Detestable act 1 Cor 5 Leaven Ex 22:16, 17 Lev 20:15-16 Blood guilty	Not specified	Lev 10:11,12,17 Lev 20:21
Sanctions Against (Old Testament)	• Sacrifice and cleansing • Death • Separation from body	Not specified in detail, but exposing the nakedness of self or another is considered a sin.	Death Cut-off Die childless
Legal Consequence And Risks	Some are illegal but ineffectively and randomly enforces. Low priority legal enforcement yields little risk for the addict.	• Behaviors are regarded as a problem. • Risk is involved since offenders are actively prosecuted.	• Extreme legal consequences. • Creates high risk situations for the addict.
Victim	These behaviors are perceived as victimless, however, exploitation is a common form of victimization.	There is always a victim.	There is always a victim.
Cultural and Media View	Public opinion varies. Some of these behaviors have become political issues, some are sanctioned as positive (i.e. womanizing, affairs, there is competing negative hero image of glamorous decadence.) For some there is ambivalence or dislike.	The addict is perceived as pathetic and sick but harmless. Often these behaviors are subject of jokes that dismiss the pain of the addict. None are acceptable to the public, except possible the exhibitionist at the nudist beach.	Public is outraged but willing to become desensitized through media treatment. Perpetrators are seen by many as sub-human and beyond help.

Appendix B

Appendix B

Aversion Meditation

An oracle is within my heart concerning the sinfulness of the wicked: there is no fear of God before his eyes. For in his own eyes he flatters himself too much to detect or hate his sin. (Psalm 36:1-2)

The following concepts are designed as meditations on the detrimental effects of sexual sin. The premise of aversion meditation is that truth about the spiritual, relational, or physical effects of sexual sin will help deter you from that sin. It is using the truth of the Word of God to combat our distorted thinking, which is the primary device used to deny the truth.

Aversion meditation is one way of obeying Paul's command to take all *"thoughts into captivity and making them obedient to Christ"* (2 Cor 10:5). It is one of the ways we liberate our minds. This liberation is crucial, as our imaginations have been held hostage in the enemy's stronghold of sexual fantasy.

Through aversion meditation, we are shocked out of spiritual slumber about the reality of sin. We move its destructive realities and consequences to the forefronts of our minds. The truth is embedded in our hearts and helps us to turn from evil. Through aversion meditation, we can begin to break free of our self-flattery, restore our seared conscience, and enter into the fear of the Lord.

Instructions

Meditation has to do with taking abstract truths and painting them in vivid colors on the canvas of the imagination. It takes into account realities on various planes of existence, including how our sin might be affecting other people, God, and ourselves.

For example, let's say that you are meditating on the reality that using a condom is really not "safe sex." You might support your imagination by gathering some facts such as:

• Condoms leak.

• Out of the thirty brands of condoms, the four most popular brands leak the worst.

　　3 in 10 leaked 10% of the time

　　1 in 10 leaked 25% of the time

• Condoms are allowed to leave the factory with pores 5 microns in diameter. The HIV virus is 1 micron in diameter.

- According to the latest study done by the University of Texas, condoms fail 31% of the time in preventing HIV disease. This means that if you have sex with three HIV positive partners using a condom, there is nearly a 100% probability that you will be exposed to the AIDS virus.

- These statistics could be worsened by the fact that poor storage or shipping can significantly damage latex. Latex is damaged by excessive heat.

- Infectious herpes and genital warts can be spread in spite of wearing a condom.

- There is no condom for the heart.

(Statistics taken from: "Wait! Think For Yourselves!" - A pamphlet distributed by Choices/Teen Awareness Inc., P.O. Box 2124, Yorba Linda, CA 92686.)

While meditation is usually meant to be focused on Christ, aversive meditation is sometimes most effective for the beginner when it brings into crisp focus the scary consequences of sin. Although such a meditation is not centered on Christ, it is considering the truth of what He has revealed, and is valid.

The goal of aversion meditation is to let truth sink in. Stay with your meditation until you begin to feel impacted by the reality of sinful actions. Return to your meditation daily so that it becomes a part of your conscious life. If the truth begins to slip from view, return to your mediation again.

- Ask the Holy Spirit to deeply teach you the truth through your meditation.

- Use biblical as well as extra-biblical information to help embellish your meditation.

- Remind yourself of real life consequences that may be associated with your mental, physical, and emotional sexual activities (past, present, or future).

Start with whatever meditation has the most impact upon you. Continue with others as you feel they are appropriate.

Meditations

1. Your sexual sin is passed on to your children (Deut 5:7-10).

2. For a Christian, sexual acting-out joins Jesus to your sexual partners. This is true whether they are heterosexual, homosexual, some other animal or object, or someone in your fantasy (I Cor 6:15-18).

3. God is watching you in your sexual sin.

   The Holy Spirit lives in you (1 Cor 6:19-20).

   You have angels with you (Ps 91:11, Matt 18:10-11).

   What, after all, is that great cloud of witnesses (Heb 12:1)?

4. You might be killing yourself if you are acting-out with real people.

5. Sexual fantasy is really adultery if you're married, or fornication if you are not (Matt 5:27-29).

6. It is our personal sin that crucified Jesus (Zech 12:10). He spilled His blood for your sin. When you embrace sexual sin, you trample the blood that saves you, which is mocking what He has done for you.

7. Masturbation really amounts to a narcissistic worship of self; it is, as Leanne Payne sometimes says, practicing the presence of one's genitals instead of practicing the presence of Jesus.

    "Masturbation, physically, is a self-bent thing. Its focus is inward. It doesn't share. It doesn't know the verb 'to give.' It is a fire that feeds itself. Hence the picture. Life encircled by a ring of guilt." [1]

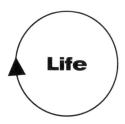

"[Masturbation is] a shell that inhibits freedom… A tremendous self-repulsion ensues. A physical loneliness. A lack of self acceptance." [2]

"For me the real evil of masturbation would be that it takes an (lawful) appetite ... and turns it back: sends the man back into the prison of himself, there to keep a harem of imaginary brides. And this harem, once admitted, works against his ever getting out and really uniting with a real woman. For the harem is always accessible, always subservient, calls for no sacrifices or adjustments, and can be endowed with erotic and psychological attractions which no real woman can rival.... no demand is made on his unselfishness, no mortification ever imposed on his vanity. In the end, they become merely the medium through which he increasingly adores himself.... And it is not only the faculty of love which is thus sterilized, forced back on itself, but also the faculty of the imagination. The true exercise of imagination, in my view, is (a) To help us to understand other people... Masturbation involves this abuse of imagination in erotic matters (which I think bad in itself) and thereby encourages a similar abuse of it in all spheres. After all, almost the main work of a life is to come out of ourselves, out of the little, dark prison we are all born in. Masturbation is to be avoided as all things are to be avoided which retard this process. [3]

8. As you are getting high on orgasm, the Great Harlot is getting high on you (Rev 17:1-6).

9. Every time you act out, you sear your conscience and deaden your heart (Eph 4:17-19).

10. God has promised that your sin will find you out (Luke 12:2-3).

11. Participating in regular sexual activity outside of God's boundaries is equivalent to Baal worship in its practice of worship and drive towards reproduction, procreation, and fertility (II Kings 23:7, Ezek 16:15 ff.; Ezek 16 is an allegory with many pertinent references).

12. Your meditation here…

Appendix C

Steps for Confessing Sin

The apostle John encouraged his readers to confess their sins to God: *"If we confess our sins, He is faithful and just and will forgive us our sins, and will purify us from all unrighteousness"* (1 John 1:9).

Forgiveness was purchased two thousand years ago when Christ died on the cross (2 Cor 12:13; Eph 4:32; Col 2:13; Heb 10:17). Therefore, when an individual confesses sin, the forgiveness Christ purchased on the cross is received and made subjectively real through the ministry of the Holy Spirit.

While confession is always made directly to the Lord, the New Testament indicates that, sometimes, we are to enter His Presence to confess with other believers, so they can minister His mercy. James states, *"Therefore confess your sins to each other and pray for each other so that you may be healed. The prayer of a righteous man is powerful and effective"* (Jas 5:16).

The following steps are suggested elements in the confession of sin, particularly in the context of community. Moving through these specific steps very often brings more freedom from guilt and demonic oppression than would otherwise occur. Confessing sin to another person provides a context in which the power of shame is broken, as the individual tangibly receives forgiveness and blessing from the body of Christ.

Oil and water are helpful in ministering forgiveness to others, as tangible symbols of the real yet invisible work of the Holy Spirit. Both elements appear in scripture as symbols of the Holy Spirit's ministry (e.g. Mk 6:13; Jas 5:14; Jn 4:14, 7:37-39). These palpable symbols often help access the individual's heart, so that the person receives God's forgiveness both intellectually and emotionally. It is possible that these symbols may remind the person of what they experienced as "dead religion," and so they should be used with discretion.

Step 1: Forsaking Denial

The one receiving ministry must first come out of the darkness; that is, he must realize that his sins are neither small nor insignificant. This is done by asking the Lord to reveal the depth of the damage done through the sinful acts. We ask Him to show us where we've permitted hindrances to exist in our relationships with God, others, and self.

By listening to God on his behalf, those praying may help bring to light specific ways in which the sin is damaging the individual. In complex situations, those praying will want to write down the various sins, as each one is revealed.

Step 2: Confessing Sin

Confession means that the individual speaks out the specifics of his/her sin in the context of community. Confession involves three things: (1) Naming the sin specifically to God, and acknowledging that it is sin and not merely unhelpful behavior. (2) Thank Him that He has already provided forgiveness for that sin at the cross. (3) Repent; choose to draw on God's power and to cease from sin. In other words, knowing that His grace is greater than our problems, we choose to forsake sinful behavior, believing in faith that He will empower us to obey Him.

In general, the more specific the confession, the more powerful the release. It is helpful to have the individual focus the eyes of his heart, as he confesses, on Christ or the cross, the ending place for sin.

During confession the individual can be encouraged to release feelings of guilt, shame, and sorrow to flow out of his heart unto the Crucified One. For some, it may be helpful to add a physical dimension to the prayer by actually thrusting the sin or pain onto the cross.

As the sin is confessed, we bind it away and onto Jesus. This is the true ministry of binding and loosing. We bind away sin and loose forgiveness (see Matt 16:19, and Matt 18:18).

Step 3: Declaring Forgiveness

The Christian receiving the confession, as part of his priestly office, then states that the confession has been heard before men and God and proclaims to the individual that the shed blood of Jesus has canceled the sin. For good references, see I John 1:7 and 9.

An essential truth is then spoken: "You are forgiven in Jesus' name, by the power of the blood of the Lamb, shed for you." Christ gave His disciples the authority to declare forgiveness in His name, and by His power (John 20:23). Note that the one praying is not forgiving the sin; only God can forgive sin. He is simply declaring the scriptural truth that the forgiveness Christ made possible through His sacrifice two thousand years ago applies to this sin.

Hearing forgiveness spoken out can be very powerful for an individual. For the first time, many are actually able to deeply receive forgiveness from God, and thereafter able to feel forgiven, through the prayers of another believer.

Step 4: Breaking the Hold of Sin Over a Person

Pray to break the hold of the sin over the individual. We should pray as led by the Holy Spirit. For example, prayer may be needed to break a vow or a judgement; or, one might pray against habitual thought patterns, to break generational sins, or for spiritual cleansing. The latter may require that we command any darkness or demonic presence to depart from the individual.

Step 5: Cleansing with Water

If it is appropriate, those praying now use water as a symbol of cleansing. They sprinkle water liberally over the individual, in order to demonstrate the power of Christ to absolve sin, and also to cleanse us from its defiling effects. Using water may help the individual's heart (rather than the mind only) accept, by faith, cleansing from a guilty conscience, as his body is symbolically washed with pure water (Heb. 10:22).

Step 6: Blessing the Real Self

Anoint the individual with oil and bless his true self (the self coming out of hiding) to solidify his union with the Lord. The oil here signifies the abiding presence of the Holy Spirit. In addition, the whole group now encourages the individual to arise in newness of life, and to take his rightful place as a child of the Most

High God. This encouragement comes as those praying bless the courage, strength, and humility that it takes to become known in the body of Christ. The group represents the body of Christ, welcoming the individual into restored relationship with the church. As a result, the self coming out of hiding becomes more centered in God. The Lord's love moves to the center of the person's heart as the source of comfort and life.

This is adapted from *Living Waters: Pursuing Sexual and Relational Wholeness in Christ*, chapter 4, by Andrew Comiskey, Copyright 1996, by Desert Stream Ministries. Used by permission.

Notes

Personal

Appendix D

Renouncing Baal

In seeking to be set free of addictive sexual behaviors, it is important to look at the principle evil spirits that rule over sexual worship and sexual perversion — Baal and Ashteroth. Understanding the spiritual origins of sexual chaos is important if we are to have a true perspective on sexual addiction. We are not to be under any dominion that is not God's, if we want to get free of our struggle.

Much of the information in this teaching is from *The Healing Presence*, chapter fourteen: "Renouncing false gods and appropriating the Holy," by Leanne Payne,[4] as well as the Living Waters Guidebook, chapter 5.

Baal in the Old Testament

Baal is the god of sexual idolatry and perversion. Baal was the supreme god worshiped in Canaan and other pagan nations of the Old Testament. He is mentioned over sixty times in the Bible and was the primary reason God did not allow His people to mingle with the pagan cultures. Instead, God commanded that His people to completely destroy those cultures, leaving none of the spoil intact.

The name Baal means "lord, possessor." There were many Baals and the form of worship varied from place to place. Because the name Baal connotes husband, God's people at times called Yahweh, who is the true "Master" and "Husband" to Israel, by the name of Baal. This, of course, led to confusion and overlap in worship practices in the Israelite culture. Baal was the male sun god, and was worshiped in pagan cultures on the tops of high mountains in order to catch a view of the rising and setting sun.

Ashteroth was Baal's female counterpart. She was the wife of Baal and the "queen of heaven," (Jer 7:18, 44:17). She embodied the feminine qualities of life, symbolized by the moon. Idols to her were set up in the temples and worshiped through diverse and perverted sexual sacrifices. As we know, there were times when Israel also worshiped Ashteroth through the disobedience of her wayward kings (Judges 2:13, 10:16, etc.). Her priests were eunuchs in woman's clothing, indicating her emasculating power. It is the demonic power behind Ashteroth that causes men to bow to pornography. When men devote themselves to the sensual power of others, they abdicate the good of their true masculinity.

Temple worship of Ashteroth involved women prostitutes given for the use of male worshippers. Worship consisted of lustful orgies carried out in elevated temples and in gardens.

Essentially, the worship of Baal and Ashteroth is what is happening implicitly in the worship of the creature over the Creator. Worship of created things, such as the sun or moon, has historically ended in the worship of man's procreative faculties – the genitals.

You also took the fine jewelry I gave you, the jewelry made of my gold and silver, and you made for yourself male idols and engaged in prostitution with them. And you took your embroidered clothes to put on them, and you offered my oil and incense before them. Also the food I provided for you – the fine flour, olive oil and honey I gave you to eat – you offered as fragrant incense before them. That is what happened, declares the Sovereign Lord. And you took your sons and daughters whom you bore to me and sacrificed them as food to the idols. Was your prostitution not enough? You slaughtered my children and sacrificed them to the idols. (Ezekiel 16:17-21)

The spirits of Baal and Ashteroth prey on those who hold or act upon the belief that all that is important about man revolves around his genitals. The core of Baal and Ashteroth worship is phallicism – the worship of the male sexual organ. Phallicism exalts the male generative power and is a perverted view of what masculinity is all about. This is why the idols for this religion were totems in the image of the phallus, Ashteroth poles, as well as smaller sexual images that are often unearthed at excavation sights of these ancient civilizations.

We can see how man's or woman's undue emphasis or insecurity about the size and shape of his or her sexual organs is the emotional core of various forms of modern Baal-worship. When sexuality is closely linked to adequacy, then it may become a form of worship.

As it progresses, the worship of Baal evolves to sexual sacrifice, as Baal and begins demanding human lives. This is the other face of Baal worship – child sacrifice to Molech, as is seen in abortion. The two combined are a picture of modern day Satanism.

The evil spirits of Baal and Ashteroth dovetail together to empower sexual addiction. As a man begins to buy into the ideals of virility, physical strength, and sexuality as a source for his sexual identity – worshipping himself and the use of his genitals – his thinking is darkened to the truth of what masculinity in Jesus is all about. He is primed to buy into the activity of yielding his faculties again and again to the sensuality involved in the worship of Ashteroth – the worship of a false feminine sensuality. The ideals of Baal give him the illusion of control, while the power of Ashteroth holds him in bondage to images of idealized women.

Demons attend this type of worship and gain access to and power over the human personality, causing increased bondage to sexual perversion.

The Fruit of Creature Worship

For although they knew God, they neither glorified Him as God nor gave thanks to Him, but their thinking became futile and their foolish hearts were darkened. Although they claimed to be wise, they became fools and exchanged the glory of the immortal God for images made to look like mortal man and birds and animals and reptiles.

Therefore God gave them over in the sinful desires of their hearts to sexual impurity for the degrading of their bodies with one another. They exchanged the truth of God for a lie, and worshiped and served created things rather than the Creator – who is forever praised. Amen.

Because of this, God gave them over to shameful lusts. Even their women exchanged natural relations for unnatural ones. In the same way the men also abandoned natural relations with women and were inflamed with lust for one another. Men committed indecent acts with other men, and received in themselves the due penalty for their perversion.

Furthermore, since they did not think it worthwhile to retain the knowledge of God, He gave them over to a depraved mind, to do what ought not to be done. (Romans 1:21-28)

We can see that once man begins to take his eyes off God who transcends creation, he begins to worship and bow down to created things. Eventually, the focus will turn to sensuality and sexual perversion. Worse yet, as a man is filled with unrighteousness and wickedness, God gives him over to a depraved mind so that he no longer understands the truth. He loses his ability to perceive that which honors himself and others.

Even though a man (or woman) may think, "I'm just oversexed", or may even understand that he has a sexual addiction problem, it is important to state here that sexual addiction is a form of worship and bowing down to the gods of sexual perversion.

We who partake in sexual addiction must come out of this kind of darkness. The first step is to renounce resolutely the principalities that oversee sexual worship. God can then come in and begin His work of freedom in our minds and bodies.

But among you there must not be even a hint of sexual immorality, or of any kind of impurity, or of greed, because these are improper for God's holy people. Nor should there be obscenity, foolish talk or coarse joking, which are out of place, but rather thanksgiving. For of this you can be sure: no immoral, impure or greedy person – such a man is an idolater – has any inheritance in the kingdom of Christ and of God. (Ephesians 5:3-5)

Both John the Baptist and Jesus had a basic message of repentance. *As Christians, we must settle the sin question if we want to be delivered from it.*

Our job is to die to sin before we face death in our body. There is no chance to reconcile sin after death. Then it will be too late. One makes a decision in this life regarding sin. He must die to the old man, the one bent toward evil, toward the satisfaction of the flesh.

We've talked in previous lessons about the generational strongholds that often move down through family lines. In the life of the sexual addict, there is a great probability that one of these strongholds involves the worship of Baal and Ashteroth. Though not an obvious worship, these strongholds involve a *bowing down* to the idols of sexual pleasure and sexual perversion.

In such cases, we must renounce the idolatrous strongholds by name. Even if we have not been involved personally with these idols, we must renounce them for our families, thereby stopping the legacy of our ancestors.

God's Plan in Dealing with Baal

God's plan for dealing with Baal is pictured in the following scripture, in which Elijah faces off with the priests of Baal and says:

How long will you waver between two opinions? If the Lord is God, follow him; but if Baal is God, follow him. (1 Kings 18:21)

In this story the people did not answer. Let us not be cast in the same mold. We need to take a strong stand for God and must be sure it is Him that we want to serve.

I will call on the name of the Lord, and the God who answers by fire, He is God. (1 Kings 18:24.)

We need to ask for the fire of God in our lives so that Baal can be put to death.

Notes
Personal

Appendix E

Appendix E

Understanding Shame

Spiritual roots in the garden

We see in the story of the Fall the origin of man's innate tendency to hide. Shortly after their treason, Adam and Eve fashioned fig leaves for themselves and covered their nakedness.

The effect of the Fall was a disabling, archetypal shame, which has everything to do with sin entering into the human situation. This is why, when God came looking, Adam was missing. He was hiding. God asked Adam why he and Eve had been hiding. Adam's answer is telling, as to all peoples' survival strategies:

I heard you in the garden, and I was afraid because I was naked; so I hid. (Genesis 3:10)

Adam was afraid of his nakedness, emotionally and otherwise, before God and others. Knowing that his very being had been contaminated by sin, Adam's fear was centered in the possibility of being rejected by God, whom Larry Crabb refers to as the "Ultimate Person." Now fallen, man seeks after safety by hiding the truth of who he really is. Instead, he fashions many varied social and psychological fig leaves. In so doing, he avoids the vulnerability of exposing the true state of his heart (the wounded, fearful self who is unable to trust others). He thus avoids the possibility of being rejected by others.

After physically hiding from God, Adam blamed his condition on Eve. This was the first recorded act of rationalization, and the first time we see man use distorted thinking to hide from the pain of acknowledging his faults.

As Adam shifted the blame to Eve, he pushed down his conscience, refusing to acknowledge its voice. Rather than be responsible and contrite, he blames Eve and, implicitly, God as well: *"The woman You put here with me - she gave me some fruit."* Here we see man defending against his painful feelings of unacceptability by splitting-off a part of himself. This separation from self is what cements shame into place, until the relationship with oneself is healed.

In trying to escape the feelings of remorse, guilt, and responsibility for his own treason, Adam wounded his beloved wife, treating her with contempt, as a mere liability. Sin gave birth to separation in all of man's relationships: separation from God, from one another, and most significantly for this topic, separation from himself.

Shame — Separation from self

Shame, which has to do with man's separation from himself, gives rise to man's problems with intimacy.

The core characteristic of shame is the disowning of self, which demands to be covered up. Shame calls for secrecy and darkness. One who experiences shame has an adversarial relationship with himself. He separates from himself to survive because the true and wounded self is felt to be too bad and unacceptable. It is, therefore, disowned and pushed away into darkness. Shame is, in essence, self-hatred.

Shame is humility gone wrong

Humility is an accurate assessment of ourselves. It helps us to recognize our true state as those who sin and need a Savior. Those who are humble realize that they are finite (limited). We need the realization of our finiteness as a constant reminder that we are not God. The humble man will not try to overcome his shame-based sinful patterns without God, because he knows that his strength is not enough. Serious problems result when a person does not know his limits.

Shame may masquerade as humility, but is a complete counterfeit. It is a belief in one's worthlessness, a sense of being beyond healing. When left unhealed, a variety of symptoms remain. On one end of the continuum is a perfectionist striving to perform for God and others in order to be accepted. Completely out of touch with his damaged heart, the person's pride serves as a defense against seeing the heart's true condition. At the other end of the continuum is an overt refusal to receive love, as well as a failure to accept and forgive oneself. Unlike humility, shame does not say, "I am limited and must look to God." Instead, it declares, "I am flawed and defective as a human being. God cannot love me." It is neither a correct nor a healthy view of reality. At the core of the person's identity is a sense of having failed as a human being. The shamed heart cries out for love, but cannot receive it.

Because the addict has never wanted to feel the pain of his shame, he has learned to hide it from himself. Since he is alienated from himself, he must live in a false self - a survival self with all its delusions and addictive acting out. He cannot, therefore, get to the true source of what is driving his unwanted behavior. His style of relating to others is designed to cover up the pain of the underlying shame-based personality. Rather than being the root problem, the addiction issues out of roots of shame.

Shame, as well as the addict's faulty belief system, prevent the reality of his true identity in Christ from sinking into his heart. Through the unchangeable work of the cross, God established positional identities for those with a new identity in Him. One of these truths is our justification in Christ, which means that God imputes Christ's perfect righteousness to us. As Christians, we are declared righteous and clean. This truth should greatly increase our sense of value and acceptability before others. The fact of this positional truth has not been integrated by many into the heart's belief system and identity. If shame is not healed, a man or woman cannot let his/her true self be exposed so as to be renewed in the image of God. The addict, then, must choose exposure of his shamed self, if he wants to be healed. This may be a difficult process because he has become an expert at keeping himself hidden.

The experience of feeling shame

The scriptures declare that *"pride goes before a fall"* (Prov 16:28), and *"God resists the proud"* (James 4:6). As far as the addict is concerned, pride does not necessarily manifest as an excessively high opinion of himself. His denial of the magnitude of his problem prevents him from seeing himself accurately. This inaccurate assessment is his shame-based, impaired thinking. It obscures the true condition of his heart.

Pride keeps a believer from seeing his need for God. Therefore, God cannot restore his wounded self.

An oracle is within my heart concerning the sinfulness of the wicked: there is no fear of God before his eyes. For in his own eyes he flatters himself too much to detect or hate his sin. (Ps 36:1-2)

Pride is self-flattery that embodies denial of one's true feelings and promotes separation from self. Pride is a shield against feeling shame.

Shame is felt when the shield of pride is broken, resulting in a sudden confrontation with the true feelings of hatred towards oneself. Such a breakthrough is usually catalyzed by some social failing that cannot be rationalized or denied. For the addict, this breaking-through usually happens after orgasm, when he faces the reality that he has acted out again. The resulting experience of feeling shame is self-loathing, full of remorse and despair about his failures. At its worst, statements such as, "I am a no good, hateful wretch with horrible, irreconcilable faults," will play relentlessly for hours after an incident.

His sense of his own "badness" reveals the faulty attitudes, judgments, beliefs, and painful feelings he holds in his heart towards himself.

> It is like internal bleeding. Exposure to oneself lies at the heart, [of feeling] toxic shame. A shame-based person will guard against exposing his inner self to others, but more significantly, he will guard against exposing himself. [5]

The shame experienced by the addict resulting from his addictive cycle is different from the core shame developed in his family of origin. The shame which results from acting out has been coined "meta-shame," by John Bradshaw, author of *Healing the Shame That Binds You*:

> The meta-shame is a displacement of affect, a transforming of the shame about self into the shame about 'acting out' and experiencing life-damaging consequences. This meta-shame intensifies the shame-based identity.... 'I'm no good; there is something wrong with me' plays like a broken record. The more it plays, the more one solidifies one's false belief system. [6]

What Bradshaw calls meta-shame is not the real issue in healing shame, although it does fuel the activities of the false self. Meta-shame (shame about an imperfect false self) will be dealt with as the underlying belief system of the addict is confronted by the truth of the gospel.

Shame is not the same as guilt (which can be healthy or unhealthy). Healthy guilt is the regulator for our conscience. It is felt, to our benefit, when we act in ways contrary to our values. True guilt and conviction are eased by repentance and a corresponding change of behavior.

In contrast, the relentless ache of shame is the bleeding-through of a painful set of beliefs about the badness and unworthiness of a person. No amount of repentance makes it go away. When the addict feels shame, it is the experience of exposure to his split-off self, which has not yet been renewed in the image of God.

Multicolored fig leaves – The fruit of shame

Adam and Eve tried to cover their shame with fig leaves. Rather than the origins of modesty, theirs was an act that symbolized man's tendency to construct elaborate coverings for his shame.

Mark 11 records an unusual story in which Jesus acts out a parable involving a fig tree. After reaching beneath the leaves for fruit and finding none, Jesus cursed the fig tree to die. At first glance, His actions seem hard to understand. But, when we realize that a fig tree's leaves indicate the time of its fruit bearing, we can see that this tree was, in a sense, a hypocrite. It was giving the appearance of fruit bearing, but was not really bearing fruit.

When Jesus cursed the tree to its roots he was not having a temper tantrum, but rather was using the tree as a parable. He was gesturing to God's disapproval about what Adam and Eve were doing in the Garden. God did not want them providing coverings for their own diseased roots, which could bear no fruit. So He provided animal skins, likely from an animal sacrifice, and covered them with it (see Genesis 3:21). This sacrifice was a type and foreshadowing of the coming sacrifice of Jesus.

God wants us to lay down the fig leaves of our own making — our prideful false selves — and receive the covering of the blood of Jesus. This will require our exposure. As John the Baptist said, referring to the Kingdom:

The ax is already laid at the root of the trees; every tree therefore that does not bear good fruit is cut down and thrown into the fire. (Luke 3:9)

After Jesus cursed the fig tree, the scripture says that the disciples saw that it died from the roots up. In the same way, God wants to deal with our shame, which is at the root of our dysfunctional survival strategies. When this happens, the false self can die and the true self can be resurrected in the likeness of Jesus, bearing fruit produced by the Holy Spirit.

Some coverings don't look so fruitful; sexual addiction is one of them. The addict's whole way of operating – the Dr. Jekyll and Mr. Hyde personality, the cycles of sexual sin, the distorted thinking, and so on – only serve to cover up the damage and pain of the underlying shame about self. Addictive activity provides a momentary euphoric high that must be repeated time and time again to avoid coming into contact with the true and shamed self.

Shame yields grandiosity

Grandiosity is another manifestation of the addictive fig leaf that is frequently present with the sexual addict. Grandiosity is a survival strategy that can appear self-enlarged, or wormlike and helpless.

Each exaggerates: one is more than human; the other is less than human. It's important to see that the less-than-human, the hopeless one, is also grandiose. Hopelessness says that nothing and no one could help me. I'm the sickest of the sick...I'm the best/worst there ever was. [7]

Both sides of grandiosity refuse to accept the work of Christ. Both are strategies that avoid facing the truth. The worm, the martyr, and the person trapped in self-pity are all different faces of grandiosity, wherein the person does not want to give up the sense of feeling special derived from living in a pitiful identity.

Shame yields narcissism

Narcissism is a form of grandiosity that frequently plagues the sexual addict. Narcissism involves extreme self-involvement. The narcissist's identity revolves around what his environmental feedback implies about him. He may be a super achiever, a bodybuilder, one lost in the vanity of wearing only the right clothes, preoccupied with what others think of his sexual organs, or consumed with the acquisition of wealth. All interactions with others serve as ways to cause them to worship his image. He has little true empathy for those outside of himself because he is so focused on how they can reflect his greatness, sexual prowess, acceptability, or desirability. Beneath this facade there is both envy and rage linked to his emptiness. The core of this narcissism is deep-seated shame.

There are many ways that narcissism expresses itself in the sexual acting out of the addict:

- The exhibitionist believes the exposure of his genitals excites and attracts others.

- The womanizer thinks sex is something that he is particularly good at, and that it is his gift to the world.

- The flirtatious woman feels affirmed when she elicits sexual arousal.

- The date-rapist believes that the woman he pressures into sex meant "yes" when she was saying "no."

- The super-spiritual addict pridefully believes he is healed after he hasn't acted out for short periods of time.

The sexual addict, who has built a "good Christian" fig leaf to cover his narcissism, may try to keep his sexual boundaries intact as he becomes emotionally intimate with someone else. But frequently, over time, with emotional exposure and resulting lowered barriers to the inner self, core fears of rejection will begin to surface. To survive, the addict's narcissistic covering ("sexuality gives me value") must emerge as a defense against the possibility of experiencing intense feelings of shame. As the pattern progresses his need to use his sexuality as proof of acceptance will kick in, and will dominate powerfully over the knowledge that love regards others first. Suddenly the addict ceases to be concerned with relating out of mutual giving and respect. As the addict loses empathy for the other, he ensures that the interaction builds up his image and affirms his sexual desirability. By acting on the distorted and grandiose thoughts associated with his beliefs about his sexuality, the addict can "win." In other words, he must be sexual to avoid his shame.

Origins of crippling shame

It is enough to say here that shame enters the heart early in the developmental stages of a child's life, frequently because of abandonment, abuse, and shaming actions of parents.

The child bears the charged emotional milieu of the family home. Perhaps Mom or Dad used to rage out of control, used guilt to modify behavior, expressed direct doubt or condemnation towards the child, or perpetrated direct sexual, verbal, or physical abuse.

Just as often, the shaming process happened indirectly as parents, in denial of their own shame, imparted strong feelings of fear, anger, grief, or anxiety. When these feelings were not explained, the child had no choice but to internalize and carry them. Thus, the child subtly began to take in these feelings and store them as his own.

Dysfunctional parents use denial to avoid their own feelings of shame. To successfully avoid their own sense of "badness," they must act as if they are perfect or "shameless," by projecting their inner reality onto situations outside of themselves. In this projection, the child becomes the source of bad feelings and is blamed for the feeling state of the parent. The nonverbal message to the child amounts to, "If you would just stop doing whatever you are doing, I would not be so out of control." Even though this message is not given directly, the child must conclude that he is the problem. He must come to this conclusion because his parents are not helping him decode the situation by owning their own feelings. Slowly, a core identity of worthlessness is built and reinforced within the child. He begins to believe that if he could just get better, Mommy or Daddy wouldn't be so upset. So he tries harder (perfectionism) or develops some other survival strategy to make his pain go away.

At some point, the shamed self becomes too painful to live with and the false self begins to form and harden into place. This false self has many faces: the addict, the perfectionist, the dominant and controlling one, the worm, the shy one, the clown, the scapegoat. All of them are cover-ups for shame.

Most shame develops in the early stages of a child's personality formation. Because of this, the split-off self is the child-like part of a person. Often a person with shame will experience an inability to attach to others, or to experience intimacy with others in relationships. The place in his heart that should be able to trust others and be vulnerable in relationships has been hated and sequestered away.

Healing Shame

Jesus said, 'I tell you the truth, unless you change and become like little children, you will never enter the kingdom of heaven. Therefore, whoever welcomes a little child like this in my name welcomes me' (Matt. 18:3-5).

For the addict, changing and becoming like a child must be preceded by reconnecting with the part of him or her that can be child-like. He or she must integrate with that split-off part. Healing shame is accomplished through loving the child-like part of oneself, accepting its weaknesses and wounds, and reintegrating with it (or receiving it) into the personality. The addict must welcome this child part with the help of Jesus.

This reconciliation is a process that starts with discovering and experiencing negative emotions towards self first, then tracing them to the deeper attitudes and beliefs that embody self-hatred. Next comes confession to the Lord, repentance of sinful attitudes towards self and, sometimes, the building of relationship with the lost part, leading to healing.

Healing shame is almost always accompanied by healing of traumatic memories (from which issue diseased attitudes), and forgiveness of perpetrators - usually parents. Through this process, the faulty belief system is healed.

Healing shame is very important to the spiritual life of the believer because it is connected to his ability to enter into the fullness of the Kingdom. Speaking about our inheritance as children of God, Jesus exclaimed:

I praise you, Father, Lord of heaven and earth, because you have hidden these things from the wise and learned and revealed them to little children. (Luke 10:21)

What things are hidden from those who cannot access the childlike parts of themselves? The fact that their name is written in heaven. Jesus, here, refers to a man's adoption into the family of God - the experiential knowledge that he is loved by the Father. He then goes on to say regarding the father:

No one knows who the Son is except the Father, and who the Father is except the Son, and anyone to whom the Son wills to reveal Him. (Luke 10:22)

Jesus reveals the Father through the part of man that holds the child-like qualities. It is through this part of himself that the addict can receive the love of the Father's adoption. Receiving God's love in the depths of his heart can displace the lies fostered by years of shame-based parenting, or by significant events of abuse. The Father's love dismantles the driving power of trying to avoid the feelings of shame. Our call is to press into His love, by embracing the healing process, and letting Jesus walk with us into our most wounded places.

As shame is healed, addiction withers and is replaced by inner peace, love, and the ability to risk and connect in relationships.

Homework

1. Describe how you avoid your true feelings (how you avoid being in contact with your wounded self). For example:

   I shift the focus off of my personal responsibility by blaming my problems on other people.

   I use anger to keep others at a distance when they try to speak truth to me about my responsibility in relationship.

   I keep myself so busy that my feelings about myself can't surface.

   I rationalize to keep my mind off of how I feel about who I am.

   I use scripture in a manipulative way to justify what I am doing.

   Write others below:

2. The following chart is a worksheet. Use the three columns to write out information that applies specifically to you. In the first column write out your shame-oriented thinking. These are the self-defeating or self-degrading thoughts that oppose the truth of God's word. In the second column write out a truth from the scripture that will counter your negative thinking. Use the "Who I am In Christ" sheet that is provided at the end of the homework. In the third column write truth, in you own words, that will counter your shame-oriented thinking. Speak this to yourself when you catch yourself thinking negative thoughts towards yourself. We will call this activity of speaking the truth to yourself, "Internal Communications." What follows is an example a partially filled out worksheet. Read what's been written already and then write out your own shame-based attitudes. Then, in prayer, ask God for the healthy attitudes to replace them and for the healing Scriptures:

My Shame Based Attitude	My New, Positive and Realistic Replacement Attitude	The Word of God
I am not very gifted.	I am open to the gifts I have and, as I walk with God, He will reveal other gifts that I don't yet know about.	*I am a partaker of the divine nature* ~ 1 Pet 1:4. *I am complete in Him* ~ Col 2:10.
I am stupid.	I have sufficient mental resources to fulfill the role God has for me in the world.	*I have the mind of Christ* ~ 1 Cor 2:6, Phil 2:5. *The Spirit will teach me all things* ~ Jn 16:13.
I am not perfect and I should be.	I don't have to be perfect; no one but Jesus is or can be, anyway, so I don't need to be perfect, nor should I even try to be.	*In Christ I have everlasting life and won't be condemned* ~ John 6:47. *God resists the proud and gives grace to the humble* ~ Jas 4:6.
I am a failure.	I can and should have limitations. If I am trying not to have limitations, I'm trying to be perfect, which is idolatrous since only God is perfect.	*I am accepted in the Beloved* ~ Eph 1:6. *I can do all things through Christ who strengthens me* ~ Phil 4:13.
I don't know how to love.	As I am encouraged and see and believe the good in myself, I can learn to encourage and believe in others.	*I can receive comfort from God and then comfort others with that same comfort* ~ 2 Cor 1:3-5.
If people really knew me they wouldn't like me.	My uniqueness does not always have to parallel the uniqueness of others.	*I am the apple of my heavenly Father's eye* ~ Ps 17:8, Deut 32:10.
I am too needy.	I am not too needy. I have legitimate needs and I can find safe people to meet them.	*I have become complete in Him* ~ Col 2:10. *I have access to the Father through the Holy Spirit* ~ Heb 4:18.
I am a fake.	I am learning to be real.	*I am being changed into His likeness* ~ 2 Cor 3:16, Phil 1:6.

3. Take some time to write out a statement that embodies your decision to value the part of you that you push away. Avoid describing your special abilities and gifts, accomplishments, and physical attributes. Use Psalm 139 as a resource.

Appendix F

Appendix F

The Process of Forgiveness and Reconciliation:
Women Who Are Married to Sexual Addicts

by Sonja Stark

Sexual addiction ranges on a continuum, from low levels of involvement to high ones. At its lowest level (level one), sexual addiction may involve things such as fantasy life, struggle with pornography, Internet, or compulsive masturbation. Level two addictions involve things such as affairs, prostitution, exhibitionism, or voyeurism. At the highest level (three), sexual addiction involves matters such as rape, incest, and molestation. Over time, sexual activity becomes increasingly more compulsive, with a greater risk to the addict and his own health.

When considering the situation of a woman married to a sexual addict, we must consider the level of his addiction. Furthermore, we must discern the extent of the sinful behavior.

When we talk about adultery, it is important to distinguish between the following ways of acting out: 1) one-night stand; 2) entangled affair; or 3) sexual addiction. There is almost no emotional involvement in situations 1 and 3. To the contrary, the entangled affair has an intense emotional involvement. An affair involving intense emotional power is going to be much more difficult for a wife to deal with than one that is brief and superficial.

The purpose of this paper is to explain the process of forgiveness the spouse has to work through in the small group (SALT). The stages in that process, which may not progress in this order, are: I. Feeling the hurt, II. Guilt, III. Victim mentality, IV. Anger, V. Grieving, VI. Discuss and extend forgiveness, VII. Acceptance and VIII. Reconciliation.

I. Feeling the Hurt

Feeling the hurt means coming out of denial. Often, the spouse is unable to perceive reality and was deceived for many years. It is very painful to face the truth. Maybe she caught him in an act of unfaithfulness, or perhaps he has confessed it to her. She might have been aware of some problems but didn't know that they were so deep, or that his acting out happened over a long period of time. She may have known about the addiction and thought it had ended, only to discover that, in fact, it progressed.

Feelings she has to process:
- Powerlessness over his sexual addiction. She can't fix him and change his behavior. She realizes that she needs help from outside.

- Numbing shock mixed with disbelief.

- Deep sense of betrayal.

- Confusion: Do I know this man? Is this really true or just a bad dream?

- Guilt and self-blame: It must be my fault!

- Rejection: As a woman and lover/partner.

- She feels defeated because she worked so hard on her marriage.

- Fear of abandonment, of being alone: Can I live without him, will he leave me?

- Isolation: Nobody understands what I am going through. Where can I go and pour out my heart?

- Fear of being judged and blamed by others.

- Jealousy: Who is this other woman?

- Abandonment: Friends and family abandon her because they don't know what to do or how to help her, or do not want to get involved.

- Obsession with his sexual behavior, suspicion, tries to control and manipulate the situation.

- Fear of being infected with STDs and/or HIV.

Common defense-mechanisms:

- She minimizes what happened: It was "only" one time.

- She excuses his behavior: Men have a stronger sex drive than women.

- She intellectualizes his behavior: She tries to explain what happened.

- She accepts the pain to maintain the relationship and moves on with life without actually recovering: She's merely masking the pain

II. Guilt

It is very important that the wife understands that the addict is responsible for his own sin. Certain situations or character deficits on her part might have contributed to his acting out, but she did not cause it. He chose to sin.

There also may be guilt about the fact that:

- Some of the women in the group had taken part in the sex addicts' activities in an attempt to hold the relationship together. They compromised their own moral standards by participating in inappropriate or unsafe sex.

- She views the affair as punishment – she was not a good enough spouse.

- She believes that she caused it by withholding sex in general from him, refusing a certain kind of sexual activity, or being emotionally unavailable.

- It is all her inadequacy: If she only were sexier, stronger, smarter.

III. Victim mentality

Many women have been victims in their childhood, so they accept the situation. They experience a sense of hopelessness and get depressed, feeling unable to do anything. Some become suicidal and do not know if they can trust anyone ever again. Some other common attributes of victim-like thinking are:

- Self-pity: "Nobody loves me. I thought I was special to him, and now I know that I am disposable. I feel like garbage."

- She repeats what happened to her all the time in her mind. She is constantly on the lookout for a sign that he is acting out again. She becomes chronically anxious and agitated.

- She withdraws and becomes isolated so that no one will find out what happened.

- She escapes from the pain, finding her comfort in different addictions: alcohol, TV, overeating.

Such women often think they are the only ones to whom such a thing has ever happened. To be in a support group where they are hearing many other similar stories helps them to meet other women who understand and who are going through similar processes.

The spouses in this support group may rationalize their own addictive behavior by means of subtle excuses. The pain often hinders them from seeing objectively. It is important that they realize that they have their own addictions, to things such as: sex, substances, people, and receiving poor treatment.

Leaving the victim identity

It is important that these women eventually leave behind the perception of themselves as victims; they need to learn to set boundaries in their relationships:

- Even if it seems that her husband's behavior caused these emotions, each woman is still ultimately responsible for the way she responds to him, God and others.

- She must have the willingness to risk the pain of abandonment to achieve recovery. For example, if the husband continues to act out and endanger her health, she will need to take measures to ensure her well-being. Or, if he struggles with pedophilia, she may need to report him.

- She needs to learn to consistently reject painful behaviors on the part of partner.

- She is unwilling to accept the role as victim.

IV. Anger

After coming out of denial, and as she starts to see that she is no longer a victim, serious anger may arise. Because the woman has most likely felt herself to be a victim her whole life, the realization that she can be otherwise will bring big changes. She may fill with anger, especially toward her husband. She might be tempted to pay him back – to run away or to have her own affair. But a geographical distance is not emotional distance. If she never works through this traumatic event she might end up getting married again to a sex addict, only to repeat the pattern. The anger she feels might empower her, which is good as long as she seeks to make wise decisions. She no longer wants to be the victim. She has the option to stay in the anger or to release it to God and receive help from trustworthy people and to move on. If she deals with her anger before God, He will help her to come to a calmer, more joyful place, wherein she will be able to retain her newfound strength. It will merely be without its bitter edge.

A woman who has experienced betrayal may be angry with many people and things, such as…

Church

- For not being there for her. For not having confronted him.

- For taking her husband's side and blaming her for his acting out.

God

- For not preventing sexual addiction from invading her life.

- She may feel as though she's been punished or abandoned by God.

The Other Woman

- How dare she seduce him, and take him away from her!

- What is it that the adulteress has that I do not?

Husband

- For lying to her. When someone gets caught cheating, his or her impulse is generally to lie.

- For minimizing the act: it only happened once.

- She may blame him for her own addictive relationship. She may be angry at herself for being so dependent upon him, and yet take the anger out on him, since he has provoked her.

- For breaking their marriage vows.

- For betraying her.

Herself

- She turns the anger inward. This deepens the sense of hopelessness.

- She is angry that she has been overly naive – that she trusted too blindly or that she ignored her suspicions about his infidelity.

- For not taking care of herself and her own needs, for being a victim.

V. Grieving

Women who experienced betrayal have to grieve many losses. It might be helpful for them to make a list.

Here are some areas of loss:

- Loss of trust in him, herself and the world.

- Loss of intimacy and integrity of their relationship.

- Loss of marriage (if she gets divorced).

- Loss of health in the case of STD, HIV or psychosomatic illnesses.

- Loss of friends – if he acted out with her girlfriends.

- Loss of her own dignity: his acting out humiliated her. She might feel ashamed that she had inappropriate or unsafe sex with him.

- Loss of reputation: they might have previously had significant social status, which may be jeopardized. People will find out.

- Loss of sex life. She might need to undergo a long time of abstinence before she can have sex with him again.

- Loss of an illusion over how good her marriage was, and that she was special to her partner.

- Loss of times spent with her children – because she was so preoccupied with issues related to her partner, she neglected them.

VI. Talk through what happened and extend forgiveness

For her to heal and forgive, she must be convinced that her partner grasps how deeply she has been violated. That is why she has to talk about what happened, and how it affected her on a most personal level — how it affected her marriage and family life.

She needs to explain the losses and let him experience some of what is going on inside her. This could be a first step towards reconciliation. She has the right to ask him questions, but she does not need to know all the details of what happened. This can feed rather than satisfy her obsession.

For her good, she can then forgive him for his sin, laying him and his addiction at the foot of the cross. She must let go of her right to get even and extend Jesus' mercy to him. Without forgiveness, she stays bound to his sin.

VII. Acceptance

Once the women in the group get to a place where they can start to forgive their husbands, they will be on their way towards acceptance of what happened. They can gradually arrive as they do the following:

- Come to an understanding that he is suffering from a spiritual and emotional illness, and that she can lovingly detach from that illness.

- Let go of the past.

- Accept the fact that it will be a long process (2 - 6 years).

- Let the hardships and problems become our teachers, and become grateful for the lessons they teach us.

VIII. Reconciliation

For many, a crossroads is reached over the issue of whether to separate, or divorce. The spouse holds the key. A major break happened in their relationship. The recovery process is linked with how the spouse responds.

Reconciliation can happen if the partner:
- Shows genuine repentance.

- Is willing to get tested for diseases, if he acted out with people. This demonstrates his respect for her feelings and his commitment to their relationship.

- Is willing to face the pain of his addiction and adultery.

- Is willing to commit to a lifetime of renewal. They need to make a priority of creating something new. He must be invested in starting their relationship over again.

- If the husband has sought and earned her trust through confession, repentance and restitution.

Forgiveness does not depend on his behavior; reconciliation does.

Many things are involved in the process of reconciliation:

- Learn to trust again by making yourself vulnerable again. Trust is an ingredient of believing, and to believe is to actively pursue the thing hoped for.

- Renew marriage vows and establish a new commitment to the marriage.

- Reconciliation is a two person process. Both have to be very honest and transparent with one another.

- Improve communication skills.

- Spend quality time together.

- Experience healthy sexuality.

- Begin to give and receive nurture from mate.

- Develop a greater appreciation for mate.

- Husband needs to be in accountability relationships, and/or support group, and/or therapy.

- Refuse to accuse him of old affairs – give up the act as a weapon in future conflicts.

- Continue to extend forgiveness.

Trust will be the main issue. It will take a long time to rebuild trust. The husband will have to work hard to prove over and over again that he is trustworthy. The marriage can be restored if *both* work hard, crying out for God's help.

Appendix G

Appendix G

For Wives: How Does Sexual Addiction Affect the Marriage?

There are certain common themes that exist in the lives of women married to sexual addicts. Some of them are:

Restoration of trust

Rebuilding the trust broken by a spouse's addiction is often the key issue for a wife. Having sinned, the husband has to "prove" that he is willing to change and is trustworthy. He can do little things to demonstrate this, such as calling when he will need to come home late. The husband needs his wife to tell him what he can do to help her trust him again. He then needs to agree to only those things he knows he can carry out. A common tendency for wives is to be too suspicious, to question him all the time, and not to give him a second chance. The wife needs encouragement to believe that her husband can change. It is important for the husband to realize that these "little things" (coming home on time from work; spending the evening with her, rather than being locked in a room in front of the computer) assure the wife of the sincerity of his desire to change, about which he has spoken. His words have been misleading in the past, so he needs to demonstrate trustworthiness through words and deeds.

Though more difficult for a Christian wife to admit, often she is angry with God for "putting her in such a marriage." Not only is her trust in her husband destroyed; she may also struggle in trusting God to restore her marriage. While God is never responsible for the sinful choices any of us make, His shoulders are big enough to bear the burden of our disappointments and grief. Only God can do the healing work in your husband. God is in control. God is calling you to surrender your husband to Him. Only God can heal your husband. He alone can restore your trust. Encourage your husband in his relationship with God, because the more he is able to receive from God, the more he will be restored and healed.

Marriage counseling

It is often helpful to be in marital counseling. A professional therapist can help bring insight to areas of brokenness in your marriage. In addition to counseling, it is also helpful for each of you to have your own support and accountability systems. Both partners need relationships with people who can hear your hearts. For each of you, it's critical that you have a place where you're each free to say whatever is on your heart or mind. It is equally important for the husband's accountability partner(s) to be someone you trust, and for your accountability partner to be someone he trusts. In this context your husband can confess his temptation and/or acting out. Both you and your husband need support.

Effects on marital sex life

It is important that you and your husband are able to talk openly about your sexual relationship. Wives of sexual addicts have often compromised their standards by participating in sexual activities with which they felt uncomfortable. Many wives have felt that the one way to keep their marriages intact was to give in to his sexual demands. Shame and the loss of dignity are often felt as a result of their sexual relationship with their husbands.

But it's not just the husband who brings past sexual relationships to the marriage bed. Depending upon your sexual history, you might need to see a counselor, or to participate in a healing group such as Living Waters for your own healing.

Some men act out their sexual addictions primarily within their marriages, always demanding sex. In such cases it is very helpful to have an agreed upon period of sexual sobriety (abstinence). Sexual addiction is about false intimacy, and both partners have to learn to be intimate in non-sexual ways. This is a good time to focus on emotional intimacy and non-sexual touch. It might be helpful to read books on how to grow better at communication, and how to foster emotional intimacy in a marriage.

Both you and your husband need to agree upon what constitutes a sexual fall. It is important for you to understand that your husband may not always be able to stay sexually sober. If your husband stops seeing prostitutes but still struggles in the area of masturbation or pornography, it is important to see this as an indication that he is growing. Sexual sobriety comes slowly for some. Freedom from long-standing struggles and acting out with people does not happen over night. It is especially important for you to have understanding and support as you choose to stay in a marriage where your husband is not always able to resist temptation. If your marriage has been very wounding and full of adultery, you might not be able to give your husband any grace in sexual matters. If so, you need to obtain the counsel of a therapist or pastor who can help you make decisions about what to do if and when your husband has a sexual fall.

Your husband might have periods where his sexual interest in you fluctuates. As he is facing his own brokenness, he might lose interest in sex or develop performance problems. He might not be used to "normal" sex, or for a time may only be aroused by specific sexual rituals that are not a part of your marital sexual relationship. If so, you will both need support and guidance in re-establishing your sexual relationship.

There might be other sexual problems as a consequence to his addiction. Feelings of betrayal and disgust might stop you from being able to be intimate with your husband. You need the time and freedom to receive God's healing for your hurts.

Although an understandable and common reaction, this can be troublesome for your husband. Your husband might perceive this as a punishment, and in his anger or hurt he may act out to escape the pain of rejection. Again, it is preferable to be in therapy, or to meet regularly with a pastor.

Sometimes a wife has to face the possibility of having been infected with sexually transmitted diseases (STD's) or HIV, and needs to get tested. If there is a likelihood that your husband has exposed you to a disease, it is wise to refrain from any sexual activity until the results of the test are known. This is a very shameful and humbling experience but often necessary for you to move on in your marriage. If you have been infected with a sexually transmitted disease or HIV, it is helpful to let trusted friends know who can give you the support you will need to face such a diagnosis.

Am I not sexy enough?

Your husband's acting out affects your feelings of self-worth and desirability. If he has acted out with other women, you might feel that they were more attractive to him than you were. It's important to remember that these relationships were a result of his brokenness and addiction. He was probably more concerned about having sex than he was about his sexual partner; addictive sex was the pull, not the other woman.

It will be harder for you to be restored in your self worth if your husband uses your lack of appeal as an excuse for his acting out. Blaming you for his struggles, and stating that you are not sexy or slim enough, is a way of shifting the blame from himself. It is a lie. Your husband is responsible for his sexual sin. His self-defending lies need to be confronted so that he can take responsibility for his own sin. For your own restoration, it will be important to mediate on scriptures that speak of the love your Heavenly Father has for you. As you receive the Lord's love for you, you are better able to resist the temptation to measure yourself by your husband's broken responses to you.

Homosexual tendencies

Some husbands act out sexually with other men. This may be a horrible reality for you. It will likely be helpful for you to read about homosexuality to get an understanding of his struggle. It is important for you to understand that his sexual addiction is the main problem and not his homosexual struggles. As he receives healing for the addiction, he can then begin to pursue healing for his homosexual struggles.[8]

Financial problems in marriage

This is also a common problem for marriage where the husband is a sexual addict. He might be irresponsible in financial areas, or may have lost his job because of his acting out. It is very important, for your own sake as well as for his welfare, that you stop preventing him from experiencing the consequences of his foolish behavior. If you have been co-dependent in the past you will need help to stop protecting him from his own failure. This is often difficult because his failures do affect you. It is hard to stand idly by while your car is being repossessed, or when your husband's boss want to know why is isn't at work for the third time this week. Part of his growing up involves facing all of the consequences of his actions. Love does not require you to prevent him from feeling pain; it requires you to do what is best for him, which means letting him feel unnecessary pain caused by unnecessary sin. You do this not to punish him, but to let him learn to stop sinning.

At the same time, you have the need to protect yourself and your children. In extreme cases of financial problems, you may need to separate yourself, financially, from your husband. Having your own checking account, and having the utilities in you name, for example, can ensure that your family with be able to be provided for financially. But his job and car need to be his responsibility, not yours.

How much do you need to know?

Many women have different views about this subject. Some wives don't want to know any details regarding her husband's addiction. Other wives feel the need to know every detail. There is not a universal wrong or right answer for this question. Each of you needs to be free to decide what you are comfortable knowing, considering such things prayerfully with the Lord, before you ask. But be prepared! It is better not to ask anything if you don't want to hear the answer. It may be too hard and somewhat unnecessary to hear all the details of his acting out. Information that is shared is not retrievable, and can burn images of your husband with other women/men into your mind.

Some women, whose husbands are sexual addicts, have an obsessive preoccupation with his addiction. This hinders you from looking at your own brokenness because all your emotional energy goes into his life. You need to determine why you want to know so much about his sexual past. Don't use his brokenness to deflect your own need for healing.

If you ask him questions, you cannot punish him for his honest answers. It is often better to listen without responding right away, although that can be difficult. Explain to your husband that you would like to have a time, after you have processed what he has told you, to share your feelings with him. You need to have the freedom to ask questions, but it is not helpful to ask questions all the time. The ability to trust him takes time, and will grow as you see that he is receiving more healing.

Do I stay with him or leave him?

This is a very difficult question for anyone to answer. Depending on how intensely your husband's addictions have affected the marriage, you may need some space from your husband. Any decision to separate is very serious and should be made under the supervision of a therapist or pastor. A support group does not have the authority or expertise to help a couple if they decide to separate or divorce.

If both of you desire healing for the marriage, and each of you takes responsibility for your individual brokenness and seeks healing, God can restore the marriage. An obstacle exists if your husband doesn't acknowledge his problem, minimizes it, or is unwilling to work on his addiction. In these situations it is helpful for the salt coordinator to intervene and to meet with both of you. If your husband is not willing to take responsibility for the damage his addiction has done to the marriage, you need to consider your options. Again, if you feel that separation or divorce is your only option, this option should be submitted to the authority of a pastor or the counsel of a professional therapist. A pastor or a therapist will be better able to help you sort through your emotional turmoil so you can make wise decisions. Times of emotional turmoil are awful times to make big decisions. A pastor or therapist can help you consider when and how to make hard decisions, and what the consequences might be.

In the case of child molestation, it is imperative that your children be in a living situation where they are not at risk. If there is sexual abuse occurring, it is unlikely your husband will be able to stay in the house, at least for a period of time. The issues related to your marriage are important; the safety of your children is more important. A family therapist, or your child's counselor, can help you determine what would be a viable living situation for your family.

Looking at your own needs

It is easy to focus only on your husband and his addiction. Some people mistakenly believe that his healing will "fix" all the problems in the marriage. But it is equally important for you to seek the Lord in the areas of your own brokenness. Co-dependency and denial are just two of the areas of sin to which many wives of sexual addicts are prone. It's usually easier to look at another's sin instead of our own. But wives have issues, too. Psychologists believe that one marries someone at the same level of emotional maturity as oneself. Your childhood may have been similar to his, for example. Perhaps you both come from dysfunctional families, and neither of you have learned to adequately express emotions. Or perhaps one of you has a strong need to be in control, and the other an equally strong need to be controlled. Your own family might have made you feel inadequate and unlovable, in ways similar to his broken response to you. Or perhaps you felt the need to marry a man who loved you and yet was emotionally distant, like your father may have been. Maybe you have your own addictions, ones you have not yet submitted to the Lord for healing. Not matter what your own sin is, or how you have been wounded by your husband's sin, it is God's desire to bring restoration and reconciliation to all areas of your life, both individually and in your marriage. Two of the most important ways you can contribute to the restoration of your marriage are by seeking your own healing, and by prayerfully supporting your husband's healing journey.

How much shall I tell my children?

Children need to be old enough to understand sexuality;this is usually by the time they reach their teenage years. If you want to talk to your children about the brokenness at hand, it might be best to do it together with your husband. How deeply your husband's addictions have affected your family life will help determine how much of his past they need to know. It might not be important for them to know what his brokenness is if he is a good, caring and loving father. Children might need someone with whom to work out their emotions about their dad's past.

In the case of divorce or separation, it is important for the children to know what is going on (to the degree that they are old enough to understand the problem). There might be situations where you don't feel comfortable having the children stay overnight with their father because you are afraid that the children will be exposed to broken sexuality. This may be an important issue to discern.

Hope for the Future

Just as the wounding of your husband's sexual addiction has gone deeply into you soul, so can the healing presence of Jesus. He will honor your desire to stay true to your marriage and to bring healing in the areas of hurt. Despair and betrayal can be replaced with new hope and trust in Him; He is the One who brings healing to damaged marriages. Though the process is often a long and difficult one, it is not a journey you should even think about taking alone. Friends, healing groups, your church are all part of what God uses to bring healing to your marriage. It is His desire to give you a healthy, whole marriage.

And the God of all grace, who called you to his eternal glory in Christ, after you have suffered a little while, will himself restore you and make you strong, firm and steadfast. To him be the power for ever and ever. Amen. (1 Peter 5:10-11)

Notes

Personal

References

[1] Leanne Payne, *The Broken Image* (Westchester: Crossway Books 1981) 89.

[2] Ibid., 90.

[3] Ibid., 91.

[4] *The Healing Presence*, by Leanne Payne. Published by Crossway Books, copyright 1989.

[5] John Bradshaw, *Healing The Shame That Binds You*, (Deerfield Beach: Health Communications Inc., 1988) 10.

[6] John Bradshaw, *Healing The Shame That Binds You*, (Deerfeild Beach: Health Communications Inc., 1988) 17.

[7] John Bradshaw, *Healing The Shame That Binds You* (Deerfield Beach: Health Communications Inc., 1988) 21.

[8] Helpful reading about homosexuality would include *Pursuing Sexual Wholeness*, by Andrew Comiskey (available through Desert Stream Ministries at 714/779.6899), *Setting Love in Order*, by Mario Bergner, as well as Leanne Payne's writings. (Books by Mario Bergner and Leanne Payne are available through Baker Books at 800/877.2665.)